LAND DEED GENEALOGY
of
DEKALB COUNTY
TENNESSEE

- 1868-1885 -

(Volume #2)

By: Thomas Partlow

Book Publishers

Southern Historical Press, Inc.
Greenville, South Carolina

This volume was reproduced
from a personal copy located in
the Publishers private library

Please direct all correspondence and book orders to:
www.southernhistoricalpress.com
or
SOUTHERN HISTORICAL PRESS, Inc.
1071 Park West Blvd.
Greenville, SC 29611

Southernhistoricalpress@gmail.com

ISBN #978-0-89308-832-3
Printed in the United Sattes of America

This Book

Is

Respectfully Dedicated

To

My Cousin

DOLORES JOHNSON

PREFACE

DeKalb County was created by an Act of the Tennessee Legislature in 1837 out of parts of White, Warren, Cannon, Wilson, and Jackson Counties. It was named in honor of Baron Johann DeKalb who accompanied Lafayette to America in 1777. He was appointed a Major General in the Continental Army. He was killed at the Battle of Camden in 1780.

These deeds cover the period from August 1869 to October 1885. They should be interest to those with families in the above named counties, as well as Smith County.

Thomas E. Partlow
Lebanon, Tennessee

TABLE OF CONTENTS

DEED BOOK K

J. W. Simpson to Elisha Loona 200 acres on the Caney Fork in what is called the Eagle Bend. 4 Mar 1861. Witness: W. M. Simpson. Recorded 2 Aug 1869. (Pp. 1-2)

Petition of S. W. McClellan, administrator of O. D. Williams, to sell the lands belonging to the estate of the said Desty for the purpose of paying debts. The widow, Arminta M. Williams, has received her dower. 2 Aug 1869. (Pp. 3-5)

Jackson Vantrees and wife Sophrona, formerly Sophrona Fight, one of the heirs of Henry Fite, to Joseph Clark their interest in in the dower of Martha Fite, widow of Henry Fite, which is located in the 13th District. 31 Jul 1869. (Pp. 5-7)

Giles Driver, Sr. to his son, Isah Driver, 125 acres in the 9th District. Bounded: William Lawrence Driver and Redick Driver's old line. 1 Sep 1856. (Pp. 7-8)

Giles Driver to his son, Paris Driver, 120 acres in the 9th District about one mile south of the town of Smithville. The condition is that the said Paris take care of me during my natural life. 16 Nov 1867. (Pp. 9-11)

S. M. Foster to William G. Foster the Morgan tract, formerly known as the Gay tract or Chimley tract consisting of one hundred acres. 23 Aug 1869. (Pp. 12-13)

Jasper Ruyle to M. A. Whaley one acre in the 2nd District. 24 Jun 1868. (Pp. 13-14)

Sheriff Charles Hill to . . . William H. Whaley a tract of land. 16 Jul 1866. (Pp. 15-17)

Wilson H. Bennett to L. B. Driver a quit claim deed to the tract of land on which I now live containing 60 acres. 17 Feb 1869. (Pp. 17-19)

James Hollinsworth to Josiah White 80 acres in the 2nd District. 21 Nov 1865. (Pp. 19-20)

Ealendor L. Baird to John D. Baird one and one half acres in the 1st District. 21 Aug 1859. (Pp. 21-22)

Alexandra Martin to my three grandchildren of my son, M. T. Martin deceased, to wit, Benita, Mattie, and M. T. Martin, the Pistole tract which I purchased of Stephenson C. Pistole in 1842. 31 Jul 1869. (Pp. 22-24)

W. H. Magness, trustee, to R. Cantrell 48 acres in the 7th District. 10 Sep 1859. (Pp. 24-26)

Alexandra Martin to my daughter, Missouria Hays, the home place, it being in the narrows of the Caney Fork River. 31 Jul 1869. (Pp. 26-28)

J. T. Trapp to R. W. McGinnis 23 acres in the 10th District. 18 Sep 1869. (Pp. 28-29)

J. H. Hendrixson to W. H. Hendrixson 55 acres in the 10th District on the waters of Indian Creek. 22 Sep 1869. (Pp. 29-31)

DEED BOOK K

Samuel S. Hooper to his son, Tennessee M. Hooper, 114 acres in the 9th District. 23 Aug 1869. (Pp. 31-32)

Peter Davis and wife Armintia to Sampson W. Williams 20 acres in the 1st District. 11 Aug 1869. (Pp. 33-34)

James B. McCormack to Allen Jones ine acres in Smith County on the Dry Branch. 10 Dec 1856. (Pp. 34-36)

Zachariah Kirkland to Samuel D. Camron 150 acres in the 8th District. 6 Aug 1860. (Pp. 36-37)

James Willis to Elizabeth Steel 11 acres in the 14th District. 11 Sep 1869. (Pp. 38-39)

John P. Tittsworth to Henry Adcock 60 acres in the 7th District. 15 Jun 1868. (Pp. 39-40)

William H. Garner and wife Hester to John F. Stacy ten acres in the 16th District. 22 Feb 1869. (Pp. 40-43)

Richard Lamberson to James C. Fisher a tract deed on a tract of land in the 21st District of Smith County. 28 Feb 1859. (Pp. 43-44)

L. B. Driver and Wilson H. Bennett to Sampson Chapman and Wiley Chapman 100 acres in the 2nd District, formerly the 11th District. 9 Sep 1869. (Pp. 45-46)

Sheriff to Martha B. Smith a tract of land in the 16th District. 4 Jan 1866. (Pp. 47-49)

Samuel D. Camerson to William H. Browin a tract of land on the Caney Fork River. 2 Oct 1869. (Pp. 49-51)

Elijah Yeargan to Phillip J. Pleger a tract of land in the town of Alexandria. 8 Oct 1868. (Pp. 52-53)

Phillip J. Pleger to George L. Hearn a tract of land in the town of Alexandria. 15 Oct 1869. (Pp. 53-55)

P. M. Wade and wife Nancy to Henry R. Coleman and John Harriman of Davidson County 400 acres in the 9th District. 19 Oct 1869. (Pp. 55-58)

Isaac Cantrell to Wiseman Green his interest in 100 acres. 24 Mar 1869. (Pp. 58-59)

Clerk & Master to L. B. Driver land belonging to Nancy Robinson deceased. 27 Oct 1869. (Pp. 59-61)

P. J. Magness, Jr. to Bethel Magness two tracts of land in the 5th District containing 50 acres. 1 Jan 1869. (Pp. 61-63)

H. C. Hardcastle to James N. Eaton 105 acres in the 17th District. 2 Nov 1869. (Pp. 63-64)

James L. Garrison and William R. Garrison to C. B. Wright their interest in a tract of land belonging to the estate of their father Benjamin Garrison. Witness: Whig Garrison. 11 Nov 1869. (Pp. 64-66)

DEED BOOK K

Samuel T. Mottley, surviving partner of Campbell & Mottley, to James Bozarth his interest in the land owned by William Bozarth and sold by the Sheriff. 30 Jun 1869. (Pp. 66-67)

Henry Garrison to O. B. Wright 140 acres in the 1st District. 13 Nov 1869. (P. 68)

Thomas S. Bennett to his daughter, P. F. Culwell, 50 acres in the 9th District, it being a part of my old home place on Fall Creek. 8 Nov 1869. (Pp. 69-70)

James Ingrum and wife Martha to James Murphy and John Murphy their interest in the Judith Hunt tract of land in the 4th District containing 85 acres. 6 Oct 1869. (Pp. 70-72)

Felty Culwell and wife P. F. to Joseph H. Dodd 50 acres. It being land that was transferred as a deed of gift by her father out of his old home place. 9 Nov 1869. (Pp. 73-75)

James H. Bozarth to Letty Carter 268 acres in the 8th District. 21 Oct 1869. (Pp. 75-77)

J. C. Canaday to John S. Harrison 112 acres in the 9th District. 23 Aug 1869. (Pp. 77-79)

Peter Cripps to T. W. Fitts three acres on Indian Creek in the 10th District. 23 Oct 1869. (Pp. 79-80)

I. J. Ford, Administrator of Thomas Tramell, filed in Chancery Court a bill against Isaac Johnson and wife Paralle Johnson, Sr., Frances C. Tramell, Thomas J. Tramell, William H. Tramell, Parallee E. Tramell, Jr., and Tennessee Tramell praying a decree to sell the lands belonging to the Estate of Thomas Tramell. Clerk & Master to Benjamin Davis 36 acres. 3 Nov 1869. (Pp. 80-82)

Estate of Thomas Tramell to Samuel Henley 59½ acres. 4 Nov 1869. (Pp. 82-84)

John B. Taylor to T. W. Fitts 75 acres in the 10th District. 11 Nov 1869. (Pp. 84-86)

Clerk & Master to John Merott certain lands attached against Joseph Johnson. 3 Nov 1869. (Pp. 86-89)

Clerk & Master to John C. Taylor a tract of land in the 10th District. The suit was filed in Chancery Court against F. R. Taylor, John C. Taylor, Ezekiel W. Taylor, Jr., Alexandria Neal and wife Mary, Pleasant Hendrixson and wife Anna, and Franklin Taylor as heirs of E. W. Taylor deceased. 23 Nov 1869. (Pp. 89-92)

A. E. Frazier and Tabitha Williams to Henry R. Coleman 200 acres in the 9th District. 6 Nov 1869. (Pp. 92-94)

Frances Turner to William and J. H. Blackburn a trust deed on 300 acres in the 2nd District. 22 Nov 1869. (Pp. 94-96)

W. C. Avant to Aaron Frazier 86 acres in the 4th District. 26 Nov 1869. (Pp. 97-99)

John Robinson, Sr. to Hiram C. Robinson of Jackson County 275 acres. 17 Jul 1866. (Pp. 99-101)

DEED BOOK K

Sarah Comer to L. B. Hale the land on which I now live in third District, it being the land on which I now live and containing 20 acres. Bounded: east by the dower of Celina Ann Hale north by the dower of Polly Ann Comer, widow of Jeremiah Comer. 23 Nov 1869. (Pp. 102-103)

Bartley L. James and wife Eliza J. James, formerly Eliza J. McGan their interest in a tract of land in the 1st District. Bounded: Frances Bomer, widow of Hezekiah Bomer. 3 Dec 1869. (Pp. 103-105)

E. M. Whaley to J. W. Bethell my interest in the dower of Sarah Bethell, widow of Tilman Bethell. Said interest was purchased by me from Chester Bethell. 9 Aug 1869. (Pp. 105-106)

James H. Bozarth to Abby Gambrell 103 acres in the 8th District. 29 Nov 1869. (Pp. 107-108)

Charles Hill to J. N. Eaton 100 acres in the 11th District. 5 Mar 1869. (Pp. 108-111)

Nicholas Smith to B. J. F. Turner four acres in the 15th District. 28 Jan 1869. (Pp. 111-112)

James H. Bozarth to Joseph Bozarth 125 acres in the 8th District. 6 Dec 1869. (Pp. 112-114)

Henry Frazer to Obediah Rich 30 acres in the 4th District. 6 Jul 1869. (Pp. 114-115)

Luara A. Cantrell to T. C. Cantrell and E. W. Cantrell my interest in the estate of my father Green Cantrell. 6 Dec 1869. (Pp. 116-117)

A. J. Bennett to William Robinson 33½ acres in the 13th District. 13 Dec 1869. (Pp. 117-118)

John C. Cannady to his wife, Marget A. Cannady, and four youngest daughters, to wit, Emeline C. Cannady, Philus I. Cannady, Amanda M. Cannady, and Mamie A. Cannady five acres. 4 Dec 1869. (Pp. 118-120)

J. L. Bond to Elizabeth Donnell 15 acres in the 9th District. 25 Nov 1869. (Pp. 120-122)

Tilitha Taylor, Elias Taylor, and Hannah Taylor to C. A. Cantrell 73 acres in the 6th District. 23 Nov 1869. (Pp. 122-123)

Dabnah M. League to Thomas C. Allen 300 acres in the 9th District. 23 Dec 1869. (Pp. 123-126)

James Robinson to John W. Gracy 300 acres in the 14th District. 26 Oct 1869. (Pp. 127-129)

Archabled Bain to William W. Foster 50 acres in the 9th District. 23 Dec 1869. (Pp. 129-131)

A. I. Bond to G. W. Cantrell 126 acres in the 11th District. 31 Dec 1869. (Pp. 131-133)

W. T. Haskins to Calaway Neal 110 acres in the 1st District.

27 Dec 1869. (Pp. 133-134)

Petition of the heirs of John Reynolds, to wit, Peter Reynolds, J. G. Reynolds, and others to sell the land of the said John Reynolds 227 acres. 5 Jan 1870. (Pp. 135-137)

W. F. Dowell to William A. Parker 16 acres in the 4th District. 11 Sep 1867. (Pp. 137-139)

Thomas Lawrence to James M. Malone six and one fourth acres in the 12th District. 15 Jan 1870. (Pp. 139-140)

John W. Price and W. S. Paty to R. C. Bone their interest in the Alexandria Steam Mill. 4 Feb 1869. (Pp. 140-142)

Alfred L. Hancock to James Hale 60 acres in the 3rd District. 15 Apr 1867. (Pp. 142-143)

Tilman Adcock to Benjamin Cantrell 16 acres in the 7th District. 25 Jan 1870. (Pp. 144-145)

Clerk & Master to B. C. Wilson 250 acres in the 5th District. 22 Jun 1866. (Pp. 146-149)

Tilman Adcock to N. T. Wall 28 acres in the 7th District. 28 Jan 1870. (Pp. 150-151)

William Foutch to R. S. Orten two acres on Helton's Creek in the 4th District. 3 Feb 1870. (Pp. 152-153)

Henry M. Fite to John H. Tramel a tract of land on Indian Creek in the 10th District. 7 Feb 1870. (Pp. 153-155)

William Frizzell to Isaac Lawson 27 acres in the 5th District. 1 Sep 1869. (Pp. 155-156)

Clerk & Master to Eli Vick the interests of Leonard F. Moore, Jacob E. Moore, Catherine Moore, Luke Neal, Matilda Neal, Jane Moore, William Lewis, Elizabeth Lewis, George Turner, Catherine Turner, Leonard Moore, Joseph Moore, Mary Moore, Isaac Mullinax, Elizabeth Whaley, William Whaley, E. M. Whaley, Tabitha Whaley, Tennessee Whaley, Isaac Whaley, M. C. Vick, W. D. Carris, Mary Carris, Lucinda Vick, Margaret Vick, Thomas Vick, Nancy Vick, Sarah Vick, William Vick, Eliza Vick, William F. Moore, Leonard F. Bratton, and Frances J. Bratton in a tract of land. 7 Feb 1870. (Pp. 157-159)

James Ingrum and J. M. Dunlap to Jesse Fowler their interest in the land that Martha Hunt bequeath to Judia Hendrixson. 31 Aug 1869. (Pp. 160-161)

Alford W. Walker to John M. Walker and James A. Walker 80 acres in the 1st District. 15 Feb 1870. (Pp. 161-163)

Mary Wright to William B. Kidwell a house and lot in the town of Alexandria. 1 Dec 1869. (Pp. 163-164)

Thomas Manson to William Tippit 80 acres in the 6th District. 13 May 1868. (Pp. 165-166)

Albert E. Frazer and Tabitha Williams, the only surviving children of John Frazer, to Jacob Atnip 50 acres in the 9th District. 26 Feb 1870. (Pp. 166-167)

William Hunt to James Ellis 80 acres in the 12th District. 15 Nov 1869. (Pp. 168-169)

Sheriff Charles Hill to William B. Farler 50 acres belonging to David Wooten. 9 Nov 1867. (Pp. 169-172)

S. W. McClain to Helen Schurer a lot in the town of Alexandria. Bounded: Lebanon & Sparta Road and the Masonic Academy. 1 Dec 1869. (Pp. 172-173)

Lanard Cantrell to William C. Cantrell 150 acres in the 6th District. 4 Mar 1870. (Pp. 173-175)

H. L. W. Capshaw to E. A. Green 54 acres in the 6th District. 29 Dec 1869. (Pp. 175-178)

G. W. F. Wale to D. P. Blankenship the lot in the 9th District on which the said Blankenship now lives. 28 Oct 1869. (Pp. 179-180)

Dabney M. League to J. W. Lafever of Putnam County a tract of land in the 8th District. 10 Mar 1870. (Pp. 180-181)

Robert E. Johnson, attorney in fact for Joseph Johnson for the purpose of selling lands, to James A. Alexandria two and one half acres in the 16th District. 11 Mar 1870. (Pp. 182-183)

Sheriff Charles Hill to T. L. Williams a tract of land belonging to W. A. Dunlap. 19 Mar 1870. (Pp. 183-186)

William A. Dunlap to James A. Nesmith one and one half acres in the 9th District near south east of Smithville. 25 Feb 1870. (Pp. 186-188)

James Oakley to John Corley 100 acres in the 12th District on Smith Fork. 13 Aug 1869. (Pp. 188-189)

James Simpson and Angeline Simpson to Waid Hickman 25 acres in the 15th District. 26 Feb 1869. (Pp. 190-191)

George Settle and wife Betsy H. to John C. Cannady ten acres in the 9th District on Pine Creek. 2 Apr 1861. (P. 192)

P. G. Magness, County Court Clerk, to T. B. Potter a tract of land belonging to the estate of T. B. Potter. 4 Mar 1870. (P. 193)

David Jones to R. B. West his interest in a town lot and house in the town of Alexandria, it being the place where the said West now lives. 1 Apr 1870. (Pp. 194-195)

R. C. Bone to Henry F. Bone a lot of ground belonging to the Alexandria Steam Mills. 31 Dec 1869. (Pp. 195-196)

Paris Driver to James L. Colvert a tract of land in the 9th District. 4 Apr 1870. (Pp. 196-197)

Isaac Turney and Jasper Rule to James Hale 44 acres in the 3rd District. 29 Jul 1868. (Pp. 197-198)

Giles Driver to my daughter Matilda Gray and her husband S. H. Gray nine and one half acres. 8 Apr 1870. (Pp. 198-199)

DEED BOOK K

S. D. Pearce and wife Kizia; James H. Faviat and wife Fenea Helen of Missouri appoint Monroe Cantrell of Warren County their power of attorney to collect from the estate of James Cantrell, the grandfather of the said James H. Faviat and Kizia Pearce. 17 Sep 1869. (Pp. 199-200)

Joseph Banks to Enoch Banks a tract of land in the 4th District. 14 Apr 1870. (Pp. 200-201)

Samuel T. Mottley to W. W. Patterson and S. F. Patterson a title bond. 2 Mar 1870. (Pp. 201-202)

County Court Clerk to Zelpha Roberts a tract of land belonging to the estate of Jane Johnson. 16 Apr 1870. (Pp. 202-203)

Paris Driver to Staley (Collard) a tract of land in the 9th District. 23 Apr 1870. (P. 204)

Isaiah Driver to William H. Magness a tract of land in the 9th District. 18 Feb 1870. (Pp. 204-205)

T. J. Williams, Administrator of Edward Robinson, to Lemuel Bayer a tract of land in the 9th District. 1 Mar 1870. (Pp. 205-206)

Joseph W. Heard to William H. Magness 126 acres in the 1st District. 19 Mar 1870. (Pp. 206-207)

Phillip J. Pledger and wife Susan A. to William G. Evins two town lots in the town of Liberty. Bounded: Methodist Church. 31 Mar 1870. (Pp. 207-208)

T. J. Williams and wife Elizabeth to Elijah Robinson 48 acres in the 2nd District. 28 Sep 1868. (Pp. 208-209)

S. Adcock to Mary and Jane Goodner 100 acres in the 4th District. 21 Dec 1869. (Pp. 209-210)

H. & B. Douglass to M. F. Doss a house and lot in the town of Alexandria. 20 Apr 1870. (Pp. 210-211)

Wingate T. Robinson to Elijah P. Robinson 60 acres. Witnesses: James Robinson and William Robinson. 2 May 1870. (Pp. 211-213)

John W. Campbell and wife Margrett A. to A. B. Hicks 24 acres in the 13th District. 22 Feb 1870. (Pp. 214-215)

John C. Bennett to William Robinson 25 acres in the 13th District. 4 Mar 1870. (Pp. 215-216)

Sheriff Henry Blackburn to William S. Hathaway a tract of land belonging to J. M. Dunlap. 25 May 1870. (Pp. 216-217)

Jacob P. Taylor to William H. Magness a tract of land in the 10th District and on the west side of Indian Creek containing 100 acres. 31 Oct 1865. (Pp. 217-218)

Johnson Adcock to James Allen a tract of land in the 7th District. 8 May 1870. (Pp. 218-219)

Burton Taylor and wife M. A. to Calvin C. Garrison one acre in the town of Alexandria. Bounded: Lebanon & Sparta Turnpike.

6 Jul 1869. (Pp. 219-220)

In consideration of an agreement between W. J. Isbell and William H. Magness, Sarah M. Isbell to the said Magness a tract of land in the 9th District. 12 Feb 1862. (Pp. 220-221)

Richard Tittsworth to James M. (Lee) 75 acres in the 16th District. 16 Aug 1856. (Pp. 221-222)

Isaac Adcock, Sr. to Jonathan D. Thweatt 131 acres in the 7th District. 10 Oct 1859. (Pp. 222-223)

County Court Clerk to John Bain a tract of land. 4 Mar 1870. (Pp. 223-224)

Jesse T. Hollis to Levi K. Taylor a tract of land belonging to the estate of E. W. Taylor. 4 Mar 1870. (Pp. 225-226)

Clerk & Master to Solomon Davis a tract of land belonging to the estate of T. C. Wroe. 20 May 1870. (Pp. 226-227)

Clerk & Master to Christopher Wright a tract of land belonging to the estate of Isaiah Bain. 20 May 1870. (Pp. 228-230)

Richard Tittsworth to Martha Elizabeth Cantrell a tract of land in the 5th District. 23 May 1870. (Pp. 230-231)

William C. Martin makes his declaration for a homestead. 23 May 1870. (P. 231)

Thomas K. Whaley, Isaac Whaley, W. H. Whaley, Seth M. Whaley, John D. Whaley, Matilda Burkett, James K. Burkett, and Lemuel B. Whaley to James Page the (Fish) Place in the 10th District. 8 Mar 1870. (Pp. 232-233)

James G. Fuston to David Colvert a tract of land in the 2nd District. 5 Dec 1869. (P. 234)

James G. Fuston to John W. Bethel four and one half acres. 17 Mar 1870. (Pp. 234-235)

John J. Calicott to Aaron Frazer a title bond. 26 May 1870. (Pp. 235-236)

William L. Hathaway to Eliza G. Garrison a house and lot. 23 May 1870. (Pp. 236-237)

Charles T. Burton and wife Sarah B., formerly Sarah B. League and daughter of (Riley) R. League to Edmond H. League, William R. League, and Dabney M. League all their interest in several lands. 28 May 1870. (Pp. 237-239)

J. J. Ford, Executor of Burgess Wilmuth, to H. C. Ford a house and lot in the town of Alexandria. Bounded: east by the Lebanon & Sparta Turnpike. 17 Dec 1869. (Pp. 239-240)

Noah Adkins to Blakely Allen 84 acres in the 6th District. 27 Aug 1865. (Pp. 240-241)

John Merritt to Samuel Fite 50 acres on Wolf Creek in the 16th District. 20 Oct 1869. (Pp. 241-242)

N. G. Alexander to Frances Kirby five and one half acres in the 5th District. 15 Mar 1869. (Pp. 242-243)

DEED BOOK K

William Penigar to Martha J. Adcock a tract of land on the Caney Fork in the Eagle Bend. 9 Jul 1868. (Pp. 243-244)

Elijah Foutch to Elijah Spence a tract of land on Helton's Creek. 7 Jun 1870. (Pp. 244-245)

M. A. Stark to J. B. Stark 182 acres in the 3rd District. 8 Jun 1870. (Pp. 245-246)

Charity Stark and M. A. Stark to J. B. Stark a tract of land in the 3rd District. 8 Jun 1870. (Pp. 246-247)

Lawrence Fite to Mrs. Janie Blackburn, wife of James H. Blackburn, the Martin place upon which the widow of George Turner now lives. 11 Jun 1870. (Pp. 248-249)

James H. Dodd to T. M. Hooper a tract of land on Fall Creek in the 9th District, it being a part of T. S. (Bennett's) farm by deed of gift by T. S. Bennett to J. H. Dodd by Filby Culwell and wife Frances Culwell to his daughter Frances Culwell. 20 Jun 1870. (Pp. 249-250)

J. H. Dodd to William Johnson a tract of land in the 9th District. 20 Jun 1870. (Pp. 250-251)

James R. Newsom and wife Harriett petition against William Neal, Amos Neal, William Preston and wife Jane, Joshua Neal, Samuel Neal, Nancy Neal, and Samuel Wauford, heirs of Allen Neal, to sell a tract of land. 22 Dec 1866. (Pp. 251-252)

S. H. Smith, attorney in fact for William H. Garner and wife Hester of Saline County, Illinois, to F. H. Smith and J. F. Staley 25 acres in the 16th District. 29 Jun 1870. (Pp. 252-253)

William Adamson to William H. Tramell a tract of land in the 10th District. 23 Apr 1870. (Pp. 253-254)

James H. Stark to William P. Smith a town lot in the town of Liberty in the 2nd District. Bounded: the church lot. 21 Jan 1869. (Pp. 254-255)

William R. Robinson and wife Armelia J. to J. D. Bone a tract of land in the 1st District. 29 Jun 1870. (Pp. 255-256)

Jeremiah Coggin to Polly Hale for life and then to go to her children a tract of land in the 15th District on the Caney Fork. 20 May 1870. (Pp. 256-257)

Alexander K. Durham and wife Louise C.; George W. Null and wife Nancy A.; Marian Pullum and wife Parilina; W. J. Winchester, and Joseph Winchester, heirs of Thursday Winchester, to William Winchester a tract of land in the 16th District. 16 Feb 1869. (Pp. 257-259)

Clerk & Master to Ellender Drake a tract of land. 11 Jul 1868. (Pp. 259-261)

James N. Bay to George Measles 48 acres in the 13th District. 2 Jul 1870. (P. 261)

James Turner to Isiah Brown one acre in the 1st District. 4 Jul 1870. (P. 262)

John B. Taylor to Doshie J. Taylor 11 acres in the 10th District. 16 Apr 1870. (P. 263)

E. M. Whaley to J. W. Bethel 13¼ acres in the 1st District. 17 Mar 1870. (P. 264)

John W. Bethel to J. N. Fite 13¼ acres in the 2nd District. 2 Jul 1870. (Pp. 264-265)

Aaron Cantrell to Jane Robinson 67½ acres in the 9th District. 14 Oct 1869. (Pp. 265-266)

Isaiah White and John J. White to Wright and Williams one acre. 5 Aug 1868. (Pp. 266-267)

Clerk & Master to Berryman Cantrell a tract of land on which Green Cantrell died seized and possessed. 4 Mar 1870. (Pp. 267-268)

Elijah Pettigo to Robert Lock 42 acres in the 8th District. 12 May 1870. (P. 269)

Joseph H. Blackburn and others to C. & G. Cooper a mortgage. 15 Jul 1870. (Pp. 270-271)

Jesse W. Scott to A. J. Yeargin a tract of land in the 13th District, it being one fifth part of said tract being the same bequeathed by Henry Bennett to Jane W. Bennett during her natural life and at her death to myself and other heirs of said Henry Bennett. 15 Apr 1870. (Pp. 271-272)

Henry J. Yeargin to Pamelia Yeargin a mortgage. 6 Jun 1870. (Pp. 272-273)

M. M. Brien, Jr. and E. Tubb, Executors of James Tubb, to M. A. Wood a tract of land in the 9th District. 4 Apr 1870. (Pp. 273-274)

Jane Cantrell and C. A. Cantrell to J. H. Parish nine acres in the 6th District. 13 Jul 1870. (Pp. 274-275)

John J. White to T. J. Williams and A. Wright 33 acres in the 2nd District. 28 Apr 1869. (Pp. 275-276)

Jacob Adams to Elizabeth Moore a title bond. 27 Jul 1870. (Pp. 276-277)

Sampson Yeargin to A. H. Robinson 55 acres in the 4th District. 11 Dec 1869. (Pp. 277-278)

Sampson Yeargin to Thomas Chapman 45 acres. 27 Jul 1870. (P. 279)

W. H. Baird to Isaac Ford Cotton a tract of land near the corporation of Alexandria. Said Baird is a resident of Barren County, Kentucky. 13 Aug 1870. (P. 280)

J. H. Dodd to Melissa J. Culwell a tract of land in the 9th District. 13 Jul 1870. (Pp. 280-281)

William Adamson to Sampson Yeargin 146 acres in the 4th District. 11 Dec 1869. (Pp. 281-282)

Thursday Winchester to W. D. Winchester 38 acres. 5 Aug

1870. (P. 283)

James Snow to the Elders of the Cumberland Presbyterian Church, Big Spring Congregation, a tract of land. 16 Aug 1870. (P. 284)

A. J. (Amonett) to Thomas Oakley 18 acres in the 17th District. 16 Aug 1870. (Pp. 284-285)

C. A. Cantrell to J. P. Humfre 73 acres on Turkey Branch of Sink Creek. 15 Aug 1870. (Pp. 285-286)

Ammon S. Davis to Alexander Martin a general warranty deed. 16 Aug 1870. (Pp. 286-288)

J. G. McIntire to Stanton Williams 50 acres in the 10th District. 28 Aug 1870. (P. 288)

T. J. Williams to Jesse T. Hollis 100 acres in the 12th District. 22 Aug 1870. (P. 289)

Charity Self and T. J. Bradford to W. F. Robinson a title bond. 6 Sep 1870. (P. 290)

Jesse T. Hollis to W. F. Robinson 110 acres in the 12th District. 5 Sep 1870. (P. 291)

Lemuel G. Batten to Thomas Shields 50 acres in the 9th District. 6 Sep 1870. (P. 292)

By descent from Joseph Turney, Emeline Turney, M. C. Dodd and wife Rebecca, George Turney, C. J. Turney, M. C. Turney, Mary Turney to W. L. Turney a tract of land in the 3rd District containing 135 acres. 28 Jul 1870. (Pp. 293-298)

Henry (Mandlebaum) died intestate in 1863. James M. Allen, Administrator, to Silas D. Blankenship a tract of land belonging to the estate. 4 Sep 1870. (Pp. 299-300)

A. L. Foster to J. S. Calicut a parcel of land in the town of Smithville, it being Lot No. 58. Bounded: south by the public square. 9 Sep 1870. (Pp. 300-301)

James E. Moore, S. D. Moore, J. A. Moore, W. M. Moore to Mary R. Purtle 107 acres in the 9th District. 15 Oct 1867. (Pp. 301-302)

James M. Vaughn to Aaron Cantrell 30 acres in the 9th District. Feb 1866. (Pp. 302-303)

Jane Robinson to Aaron Cantrell 67 acres in the 9th District. 9 Jul 1870. (Pp. 303-304)

John M. Love to Aaron Cantrell 125 acres in the 7th District. 4 Jul 1870. (Pp. 304-305)

Oval Pirkey and wife Sallie J. to S. W. McClellan a town lot in the town of Alexandria. Bounded: Lebanon & Sparta Turnpike. 7 Mar 1870. (P. 305)

H. & B. Douglas to S. W. McClellan a town lot in the town of Alexandria. Bounded: Alexandria Masonic Academy. 31 Mar

1870. (Pp. 306-307)

Jane Turney to William Truett 134 acres in the 3rd District. 7 Apr 1869. (Pp. 307-308)

Elijah Robinson and wife Nancy, formerly Nancy Givan, to William M. Fite their one third interest in the dower of Eliza Allen, it being her part of the land of her husband Robert J. Givan. 19 Oct 1868. (Pp. 308-309)

William B. Lawrence to Elizabeth Lawrence, wife of Joseph D. Lawrence, one half interest in a town lot in Alexandria. 8 Mar 1860. (P. 310)

Permelia Yeargin, H. W. Yeargin and wife Selina, Andrew J. Yeargin, Tabitha Yeargin, Sampson Yeargin and wife Rebecca, John F. Yeargin and wife Sarah, Charles (Yeargin), Isaac Cooper and wife Talitha to Henry J. Yeargin a tract of land. 6 Jun 1870. (Pp. 311-315)

John C. Cannady to Mary J. Fuston 12½ acres in the 12th District. 17 Oct 1858. (Pp. 315-316)

Joseph B. West to Thomas E. West two tracts of land in the 9th District. 16 Sep 1870. (Pp. 316-317)

Charles Hill to Asa Driver four acres. 25 Sep 1870. (Pp. 317-318)

John Simpson to William T. (Haskins) a trust deed. 26 Sep 1870. (P. 318)

Sheriff to John Barger a tract of land belonging to the heirs of Harrison Bain. 10 Feb 1866. (Pp. 319-320)

Clerk & Master to William H. Luckey a tract of land belonging to the estate of G. D. Luckey. 27 Oct 1869. (Pp. 320-322)

Isaac N. Fite and W. M. Fite to Samuel C. Duncan 50 acres in the 13th District. 4 Oct 1870. (Pp. 322-323)

Charity ( ), Sarah A. ( ), Elizabeth Ann Burkhorn to Perry Adcock a tract of land in the 7th District. 30 Mar 1867. (PP. 323-324)

William Adamson to John Colly 54 acres. 23 Apr 1870. (Pp. 324-325)

Harry P. Clark to Julina Walker, wife of Alexandria Walker, Sr., 50 acres in the 6th District. 22 Oct 1870. (Pp. 325-326)

J. M. Phillips to A. T. Phillips a tract of land. 31 Oct 1870. (P. 327)

Clerk & Master to William W. Malone a tract of land. 3 Nov 1870. (Pp. 327-329)

James A. Sinper of Warren County to J. C. Stipes 300 acres. 25 Oct 1870. (Pp. 329-330)

W. A. Dunlap and wife Harriet A. to Jesse B. Farler a tract of land in the 4th District, it being land formerly owned by John J. Garrison and wife Elizabeth. 2 Oct 1870. (P. 331)

DEED BOOK K

Reason S. Rowland to John H. Reynolds 68 acres in the 11th District. 12 Oct 1871. (P. 332)

J. M. Bailiff, by descent from Thomas Bailiff, to C. H. Bailiff a tract of land in the 1st District. 7 Aug 1870. (Pp. 332-333)

Tabitha Williams and Nancy Frazer to Albert E. Frazer a tract of land in the 9th District. 1 Oct 1869. (Pp. 333-335)

S. W. McClellan and wife H. C. to John Rollins 103½ acres. 11 Dec 1869. (Pp. 335-336)

W. F. Dowell to J. H. Hunt three fifth's of an acre on Dry Creek. 13 Oct 1870. (Pp. 336-337)

Barbry Miller to J. H. Dodd 120 acres. 13 Jan 1870. (Pp. 337-338)

Samuel Warford and wife Melissa H., formerly Melissa Hays, to John F. Yeargin 14 acres in the 2nd District. 13 Sep 1870. (Pp. 338-339)

John W. Botts to M. D. Doss a town lot in the town of Alexandria, it being land formerly owned by Mirah Botts. 9 Nov 1870. (Pp. 339-340)

Mary (Polly) Lockhart to William Goodman 155 acres in the 9th District. 22 Jan 1870. (Pp. 340-341)

Clerk & Master to William Sexton a tract of land. 14 Nov 1870. (Pp. 341-342)

County Court Clerk to Benjamin Vaughn a tract of land in which Safara Vaughn died seized and possessed of. 11 Nov 1870. (Pp. 343-344)

F. M. T. Hall to L. F. Moore a tract of land. 16 Feb 1870. (P. 346)

Joseph Mitchell to Frederick Starnes a tract of land on the Caney Fork in the 11th District. 14 Jun 1869. (P. 347)

William Goodman to Perry Stockton 40 acres in the 9th District. 12 Nov 1870. (P. 348)

William Goodman to Solomon Goodman 40 acres in the 9th District. 11 Nov 1871. (Pp. 348-349)

D. P. Blankenship to T. L. Sewell a tract of land on the road from Smithville to McMinnville. 22 Nov 1870. (Pp. 349-350)

A. K. Durham to Len Haney 127 acres in the 6th District. 25 May 1869. (Pp. 350-352)

Clerk & Master to Robert V. Wright a town lot in the town of Alexandria. 24 Nov 1870. (Pp. 352-354)

William A. Dunlap to Joseph Thomas and others a trust deed. 28 Nov 1870. (Pp. 355-356)

O. B. Staley to James K. Fisher a tract of land in the 6th District. 30 Nov 1870. (Pp. 356-357)

DEED BOOK K

Edward Sisk and wife Synthia to D. P. Blankenship a house and lot in the town of Smithville. Bounded: Penuel Academy lot. 3 Dec 1870. (Pp. 357-358)

John N. Rudd and wife Nancy to John William Weaver and Mary Jane Weaver one half acre in the town of Alexandria. 3 Oct 1870. (Pp. 358-359)

David Durham to Johnny Walker, the wife of Alexander Walker, and her three children, to wit, Frances Walker, Mary Walker, and Alexander Jordan Walker 40 acres in the 6th District. 17 Oct 1870. (P. 359)

James Bond to George W. Bond a title bond. 23 Oct 1870. (Pp. 360-361)

Pleasant Watts to his children, to wit, Rosanna Watts,Georgana Watts,Louisiana Watts,John Watts, Catherine Watts, and Isabella Watts for love and affection some livestock. 19 Dec 1870. (Pp. 361-362)

Manson M. Brien, Sr. to Jesse Petty seven tracts of land. 9 Nov 1870. (Pp. 362-365)

Etheldred Fish to Jane Turner and (Aragan) Mitchell a tract of land. 27 Dec 1870. (Pp. 366-367)

T. L. Sewell to Leroy Fuston two acres. 3 Jan 1871. (P. 367)

George W. Cantrell to J. P. Hunnassee 126 acres in the 10th District. 2 Jan 1871. (Pp. 368-369)

Clerk & Master to John Johnson a tract of land belonging to Joseph Johnson. 4 Nov 1869. (Pp. 369-370)

Joseph Mangrum to M. K. Smith a tract of land in the 9th District. 17 Aug 1869. (P. 371)

J. H. Dodd to James H. Dodd 93 acres in the 5th District. 1 Jan 1871. (P. 372)

Isiah Driver, Lawrence Driver and his wife Nancy to William G. Crawley a tract of land in the 9th District. 16 Feb 1870. (Pp 372-373)

Isiah Driver to William G. Crawley a tract of land in the 9th District. 16 Feb 1870. (Pp. 373-374)

William M. Bryant and wife Mary to William G. Crawley a tract of land in the 9th District. 24 Nov 1870. (Pp. 374-375)

William C. Cantrell to Alford Southern a tract of land. 19 Jan 1871. (Pp. 375-376)

Thomas L. Surrell to Cooper Milton one acre in the 9th District. 24 Jan 1871. (Pp. 376-377)

Henry Bain, Administrator of Andrew Bain, on 6 Apr 1868 filed suit against Elizabeth Bain, widow of said Andrew, and other heirs to divide a tract of land. 24 Jan 1871. (Pp. 377-378)

DEED BOOK K

Elijah Allen to William K. Phillips a tract of land in the 9th District. 25 Jan 1871. (Pp. 378-380)

William K. Phillips to Elijah Allen a tract of land in the 9th District. 23 Jan 1871. (P. 380)

Clerk & Master to John Blue three acres in the 1st District. 30 Jan 1871. (Pp. 381-382)

Sheriff James H. Blankenship to Jackson McDonnell a tract of land. 30 Jan 1871. (Pp. 382-383)

George A. Bing to John F. (Mason) 81 acres in the 9th District. 1 Feb 1871. (P. 384)

A. P. Adcock to Eleaner Adcock, my wife, and my children, to wit, John, (Anna), Christopher, Thomasson, Harriet, and Eleaner Adcock and my other children that may be born to me by my said wife a tract of land in the 7th District. 21 Oct 1870. (Pp. 385-386)

McAdoo Vannatta to John Vannatta 28 acres in the 1st District. 5 Mar 1860. (Pp. 386-387)

David Fisher to James K. Fisher 100 acres in the 6th District. 30 Jan 1871. (P. 387)

R. C. Hays and wife M. M. to G. R. Smith a lot in the town of Smithville. 24 Jan 1871. (P. 388)

Joshua J. Ford to Moses Fite 65 acres in the 3rd District. 3 May 1871. (P. 389)

E. H. Lassiter to T. L. Wood 66 acres. 10 Jan 1871. (P. 390)

H. W. Griffith to B. A. Adamson three fourth's of an acre in the 1st District. 4 Feb 1871. (P. 391)

B. A. Adamson to H. W. Griffith a tract of land in the 13th District. 4 Feb 1871. (Pp. 391-392)

John M. Walker to James H. Walker 80 acres. 6 Feb 1871. (Pp. 392-392)

John Washer to F. W. Holson 136 acres in the 11th District. 18 Jan 1871. (Pp. 393-395)

George Puckett to William G. Foster a tract of land in the 9th District. 11 Nov 1870. (Pp. 396-397)

R. B. West to Gipson R. West 50 acres in the 13th District. 17 Mar 1870. (P. 397)

Thomas B. Potter to Gipson R. West 50 acres in the 13th District. 16 Feb 1871. (P. 398)

Mary Harris to Fanny Sweeny and Rhoda Jane Sweeney three acres in the 9th District. 17 Jan 1871. (P. 399)

T. B. Askew, trustee, to G. H. Hardcastle a tract of land. 18 Feb 1871. (Pp. 399-400)

John Tittsworth to Elizabeth Penager a tract of land. 10 Jan 1870. (Pp. 400-401)

John N. Rudd and wife Nancy to John William Weaver one half acre in the town of Alexandria. 17 Feb 1871. (Pp. 401-402)

John Park, Sarah Park, Sr., and Sarah Park, Jr. to Nancy Harris and husband William 100 acres in the 9th District for taking care of me. 3 Feb 1871. (P. 402)

Wiett W. Shryer and wife Mary J. to L. J. Magness as trustee for Melissa A. Magness and two children a tract of land in the town of Smithville. 11 Feb 1871. (P. 403)

Malinda Redmon and Matilda Driver to E. H. Redmon a tract of land in the 5th District containing 147 acres. 15 Oct 1868. (Pp. 404-405)

William Etheridge, E. W. Taylor and wife Fatha to Andrew Allen 50 acres. 21 Feb 1871. (Pp. 405-406)

Clerk & Master to T. N. Christian a tract of land belonging to Henry Mandlebaum a tract of land. 3 Jan 1871. (Pp. 406-207)

William K. Phillips and wife Rebecca and Mary Lockhart to Elijah Allen a tract of land in the 9th District. 25 Jan 1871. (Pp. 408-409)

Joseph H. Mangrum to Jasper Fowler and wife Julia 50 acres in the 7th District. 27 Feb 1871. (Pp. 409-410)

Sammie Skerlock and wife Caroline, Mary Elizabeth Bain and husband John a tract of land in the 6th District. 25 Feb 1871. (Pp. 410-411)

Thomas Jefferson Cantrell to Berryman A. Cantrell my interest in the personal estate of my father Green Cantrell. 25 Feb 1871. (Pp. 411-412)

Moses Preston to G. H. Hardcastle 50 acres in the 17th District. 27 Apr 1868. (Pp. 412-413)

W. F. Dowell to F. C. White one acre in the 4th District. 27 Mar 1871. (P. 413)

Joseph H. Blackburn to A. J. Gilbert a tract of land. 6 Mar 1871. (P. 414)

William E. Foutch a tract of land. 4 Mar 1871. (P. 415)

H. C. Hardcastle to Thomas Oakley 18 acres in the 17th District. 6 Aug 1870. (P. 416)

Nicholas Smith and wife Penelope to James Oakley 47 acres in the 12th District. 14 Feb 1871. (Pp. 417-418)

Nathan Wall to Preston Turner and Henry Turner 25 acres in the 7th District. 5 Mar 1871. (Pp. 418-419)

Henry Rutland to his wife, Jane B., a tract of land in the town of Alexandria. 23 Feb 1871. (P. 419)

G. H. Hardcastle to Thomas Oakley 35 acres in the 17th District. 15 Feb 1871. (P. 420)

Sheriff to William Blackburn 100 acres. 23 Jun 1860. (Pp.

421-422)

S. B. Allen, H. McGuire and wife Mary A. to John Johnson a tract of land in the 9th District. 5 Mar 1871. (Pp. 422-423)

William F. Dowell to Harris Fowler one acre in the 4th District. 12 Oct 1871. (P. 423)

William G. Foster to Alexander C. Carnes a tract of land in the 9th District. 11 Mar 1871. (Pp. 424-425)

William C. Martin to W. P. Martin a tract of land on Sink Creek. 9 Mar 1871. (P. 425)

John B. A. W. Tubb, and Martha Grissom, formerly Tubb, heirs of John Tubb, to George Grissom a tract of land in the 17th District. 13 Mar 1871. (P. 426)

S. M. Fite to Andrew Carr a tract of land in the 16th District. 20 Oct 1869. (P. 427)

O. B. Wright and William H. Magness to William H. (Henley) 31 acres in the 3rd District. 2 Jan 1871. (Pp. 427-428)

Sheriff to P. S. Johnson a tract of land. 6 Mar 1871. (Pp. 428-430)

Sheriff to John Helmonteller a tract of 100 acres. 4 Mar 1871. (Pp. 430-431)

Hardin Cantrell to his son, W. C. Cantrell 150 acres in the 5th District. 23 Feb 1871. (Pp. 431-432)

Robert Cantrell to James Redmon 148 acres in the 9th District. 21 May 1859. (Pp. 432-433)

Hezekiah (Lock) to L. A. Lock 40 acres in the 16th District. 6 Mar 1871. (P. 433)

P. P. Johnson and wife Lucinda J. to David Worley a tract of land in the 9th District. 27 Mar 1871. (P. 434)

Thomas Lancaster to John Merritt 24 acres in the 14th District. 30 Mar 1871. (P. 435)

George W. Eastland to Marshall Thompson and Peg Goodman a tract of land. 11 Nov 1871. (P. 436)

Clerk & Master to John Vannatta a tract of land belonging to the estate of Wyate Jenkins. 22 Mar 1871. (Pp. 436-437)

Eliza Clark to I. N. Fite a tract of land. 18 Mar 1871. (Pp. 437-438)

Thomas D. Fite of Davidson County to Mary M. Williams, wife of Samuel Williams, during her life and then to her children. 11 Jan 1871. (Pp. 438-439)

Elizabeth Penager to Marshall Smith a tract of land in the 5th District. 20 Feb 1871. (Pp. 439-440)

John William Weaver and wife Mary Jane to Jonathan Griffith and Eliza J. Griffith a tract of land in the 1st District. 7 Feb 1871. (Pp. 440-441)

O. B. Wright and William H. Magness to John F. (Ray) 22 acres in the 1st District. 12 Apr 1871. (Pp. 441-442)

Henry R. Coleman to Jesse Price a tract of land in the 9th District. 10 Mar 1871. (Pp. 442-443)

J. J. Cantrell to his children, to wit, Perry G. Cantrell, Narcissus Cantrell, Constant, Martha, Mary E., Bauregard J., Eller B., Juan, Joraner, and Sopha S. Cantrell and the children that may hereafter be born a tract of land in the 6th District. 15 Apr 1871. (Pp. 443-444)

Richard Tittsworth to Isaac D. Tittsworth his interest in a tract of land in the 5th District. 10 Feb 1870. (Pp. 444-445)

Richard Tittsworth to John P. Tittsworth, his son, his interest in a tract of land on Pine Creek. Mentions the heirs of Frederick Tittsworth and the heirs of Thomas Tittsworth. 10 Feb 1870. (Pp. 445-446)

Bartley Warford to William E. Foutch a tract of land in the 17th District. 31 Jan 1871. (P. 447)

Clerk & Master to William Johnson a tract of land belonging to the estate of Henry Mendlebaum. 5 Dec 1870. (Pp. 447-449)

M. M. Brien and Eliel Tubb to William C. Gilbert a lot in the town of Smithville on the south side of the Public Square. 1 Oct 1869. (P. 449)

J. B. Gilbert and wife Elizabeth to A. C. Carnes a tract of land in the 9th District about one mile south of Smithville. 29 Apr 1871. (P. 450)

Spencer King to William C. Cantrell a tract of land. 23 Apr 1871. (P. 451)

William H. Young to Robert Nixon three acres. 20 Jul 1869. (Pp. 451-452)

Joseph Clark to John W. Bethel 24 acres in the 2nd District. 1 Jan 1869. (Pp. 452-453)

James G. Fuston to Bransford Evins one acre. 25 Dec 1869. (P. 453)

Blakeley Allen to Alexander Wallis 100 acres in the 6th District. 3 May 1871. (P. 454)

Burnett Yeargin to Jerome Goodner a tract of land in the 1st District. 3 May 1871. (Pp. 454-455)

Jerome Goodner to Charles Yeargin a lot in the town of Alexandria. 1 Apr 1871. (Pp. 455-456)

John F. Goodner and wife Sarah J., W. S. Cantrell, and Lillie A. Cantrell to Benjamin A. Cantrell their interest in the real estate of Mary Cantrell. 3 May 1871. (Pp. 456-457)

A. L. Foster and wife Mary E., Micajah Brown and wife Mary Ann, and E. T. Foster to J. L. Colvert a lot in the town of Smithville. 4 May 1871. (Pp. 457-458)

DEED BOOK K

Charles T. Yeargin and wife Florence to James M. Baird a lot in the town of Alexandria. 1 May 1871. (Pp. 458-459)

John A. Bass and wife Sarah to A. J. Yeargin and wife a tract of land they received by descent from Edward Robinson. 1 Jan 1869. (P. 460)

A. J. Yeargin and wife, Tabitha, to John A. Bass a tract of land that they drew in the estate of Edward Robinson. 15 Jan 1869. (Pp. 461-462)

(Fabson) Yeargin and wife Emily to Samuel Hooper a tract of land on Helton's Creek. 18 Mar 1871. (Pp. 462-463)

J. E. Warren and J. L. Calvert to Elijah J. Cass 100 acres in the 14th District. 14 Sep 1870. (Pp. 463-464)

John E. Warren to Alvin Medley 32 acres in the 14th District. 20 May 1871. (Pp. 464-465)

L. J. Magness and wife Melissa to W. H. Sellers and J. H. Dodd a tract of land in the 7th District. 20 May 1871. (Pp. 465-467)

M. M. Brien to Jane C. Richardson a tract of land in the 9th District on Fall Creek. 8 Sep 1859. (Pp. 467-468)

Eli Lefever to William C. Johnson two acres in the 8th District. 26 May 1871. (P. 468)

M. D. Sanderson to John H. Love a trust deed. 11 May 1871. (P. 469)

Lemuel Braswell to John H. ( ) a tract of land on Dry Creek. 12 May 1871. (P. 470)

Lemuel Braswell to John H. Savage a tract of land. 4 Mar 1871. (Pp. 471-472)

John Reynolds to William C. Avant my life interest in a tract of land in the 12th District containing twelve acres. 31 May 1871. (Pp. 472-473)

C. F. Yeargin and wife Florence to H. H. Luckey and Henry Schurer a lot in the town of Alexandria. 29 May 1871. (Pp. 473-474)

Aaron Frazer, Executor of Henry Frazer, to E. S. Walker a tract of land in the 6th District. 5 Jun 1871. (Pp. 474-475)

James K. Cantrell and wife Mary E. to B. A. Cantrell their interest in the estate of Green Cantrell. 6 Jun 1871. (Pp. 475-476)

Perry G. Magness to William G. Foster a lot in the town of Smithville. 1 Jul 1857. (Pp. 476-477)

Paris Driver and wife, Matilda, to James L. Colvert their interest in a tract of land in the 9th District. 9 Jun 1871. (Pp. 477-478)

Thomas Lawrence to Ezekiel W. Bass 40 acres in the 12th District. 20 Jun 1864. (Pp. 478-479)

DEED BOOK K

W. L. Driver and wife Nancy to L. J. Magness for the use and benefit of Melissa A. Magness and her children a tract of land in the 9th District. 23 Jun 1871. (Pp. 479-480)

John Merritt and wife Nancy to William H. Merritt 26 acres in the 16th District. 22 Apr 1871. (Pp. 480-481)

Perry G. Garner to William Austin 30 acres in the 16th District. 29 Jun 1871. (Pp. 481-482)

James H. Stark to Joshua Hollinsworth one acre in the 2nd District. 10 Jul 1871. (Pp. 482-483)

John J. Calicott and wife Ann H. J. to W. T. Robinson 100 acres in the 17th District. 11 Jul 1871. (Pp. 483-484)

David Calicott to John W. Bethel 13 acres in the 2nd District. 13 Jun 1871. (Pp. 484-485)

Aaron Frazer and wife Paralee to T. J. Williams 260 acres in the 4th District. 7 Jun 1871. (Pp. 485-486)

J. W. Hurd to J. D. Baird Lot No. 19 in the town of Alexandria. 11 Sep 1869. (Pp. 486-487)

J. M. Baird to J. D. Baird a house and lot in the town of Alexandria. 28 Jan 1871. (Pp. 487-488)

W. W. Griffith to J. D. Griffith a tract of land in the 1st District. 29 Mar 1871. (Pp. 488-489)

Fatha Etheridge, John Etheride and wife Rebecky to Andrew Allen 50 acres in the 10th District. 28 Jan 1871. (Pp. 487-488)

W. W. Griffith to J. D. Griffith 84 acres in the 1st District. 29 Mar 1871. (Pp. 488-489)

William F. Craven, trustee, to J. A. Nesmith. This deed is registered in Trust Deed Book A, pages 107-108, and 109. 17 Jul 1871. (P. 490)

Tennessee H. Hooper and wife Elizabeth A. to William C. Gilbert 100 acres in the 9th District. 30 Jun 1871. (P. 491)

James Allen to Tilman Adcock 90 acres in the 7th District. 17 Jul 1871. (Pp. 492-493)

John M. Lock to William Love a trust deed. 24 Jul 1871. (Pp. 493-494)

J. L. Colvert to John W. Shaw a quit claim to a tract of land in the 14th District. 15 Aug 1859. (Pp. 494-495)

John A. Mitchell to John D. Eldridge 50 acres in the 14th District. 20 Oct 1870. (Pp. 495-496)

William Barr and wife Rebecca to James H. Bozarth 168 acres on the Caney Fork. 20 Oct 1870. Said Barrs are residents of Edmonson County, Kentucky. (Pp. 496-497)

John L. Bond and others to Richard Barnabus Durham 64 acres in the 9th District. 28 Jul 1871. (Pp. 497-498)

Robert Cantrell and wife S. A. to B. A. Cantrell their interest of the estates of Green and Mary Cantrell. 22 Jul 1871.

(P. 499)

Cooper Milton and wife Mary G. to W. R. Wood a tract of land in the 9th District. 24 Jan 1871. (Pp. 500-501)

John T. Stokes to Mary Ann Starnes 130 acres in the 16th District on the Caney Fork. 20 Jul 1871. (Pp. 501-502)

John T. Stokes and wife Polina to Martha Jane Powell 80 acres in the 15th District. 21 Jul 1871. (Pp. 502-503)

Dabney M. League to H. S. Puckett six acres in the 8th District. 3 Jul 1871. (Pp. 503-504)

Clerk & Master to Elisha Cooper and Eli Cooper a tract of land belonging to the estate of F. T. Thweatt. 9 Aug 1871. (Pp. 504-505)

John J. Calicott and wife Ann to Aaron Frazer 446 acres in the 17th District. 24 Jun 1871. (Pp. 505-507)

Joshua J. Ford, Executor of Peter H. Clark, to William C. Clark a tract of land in the 3rd District. 6 Mar 1871. (Pp. 507-508.

William H. Magness to William C. Pettis two town lots in the town of Smithville. 31 Jul 1871. (Pp. 508-509)

Jesse T. Hollis, Commissioner, to the Clerk & Master for Thomas L. Sowell a tract of land. 17 Aug 1871. (Pp. 509-510)

Thomas L. Sowell to Micajah Brown a tract of land in the 9th District. 17 Aug 1871. (Pp. 510-511)

Articles of agreement between Thomas Christian and William E. Foutch. 2 Aug 1871. (Pp. 511-512)

William E. Foutch to John Blew a tract of land on Helton's Creek. 21 Aug 1871. (Pp. 512-513)

Samuel Warford and Helen Warford to Horace Hays 54 acres in the 11th District. 8 May 1871. (Pp. 513-514)

Clerk & Master to John Bethel Taylor a tract of land belonging to the estate of E. W. Taylor. 31 Aug 1871. (Pp. 514-516)

Clerk & Master to H. J. Yeargin a tract of land belonging to M. F. Hays, widow of William F. Hays. 2 Sep 1871. (Pp. 517-518)

Clerk & Master to Henry J. Yeargin a tract of land belonging to the heirs of James Yeargin, to wit, R. W. Yeargin and wife Tabitha, Isaac Cooper and wife Talitha, A. J. Yeargin, Sampson Yeargin, H. J. Yeargin, J. F. Yeargin, and Charles Yeargin. 2 Sep 1871. (Pp. 518-519)

Clerk & Master to John M. Hays a tract of land. Mentions Mariah F. Hays. 7 Sep 1871. (Pp. 519-521)

Clerk & Master to William H. Hays a tract of land belonging to Mariah F. Hays, widow of William F. Hays. 6 Sep 1871. (Pp. 522-523)

Clerk & Master to H. V. Hays a tract of land belonging to

Mariah F. Hays, widow of William F. Hays. 7 Sep 1871. (Pp. 524-525)

Clerk & Master to (Nancy P. Robinson) a tract of land belonging to Mariah F. Hays, widow of William F. Hays. 9 Sep 1871. (Pp. 526-527)

Rufus P. Kelly and wife Malissa, Mary Frances Lancaster and husband M. F., and William C. Gilbert the lot of land on which William C. Gilbert now lives. 10 Aug 1871. (Pp. 528-529)

Cantrell & Baird to R. D. Allen a tract of land belonging to Jasper Parker. 12 Sep 1871. (Pp. 529-530)

Clerk & Master to James M. Hays a tract of land belonging to Mariah F. Hays. 13 Sep 1871. (Pp. 531-532)

Clerk & Master to Levi R. Taylor a tract of land belonging to E. W. Taylor deceased. 20 May 1870. (Pp. 532-533)

William Malone and wife Rebecca to Yancy Malone a tract of land. 12 Sep 1871. (Pp. 533-534)

J. H. Kerr to S. H. Smith a tract of land. 24 Dec 1861. (P. 535)

M. M. Brien to John (Boid) a tract of land. 11 Jul 1871. (Pp. 535-536)

Samuel C. Duncan to Matthew S. West 52 acres in the 13th District. 25 Sep 1871. (Pp. 536-537)

D. P. Blankenship and wife M. L. to Isaac Drake a tract of land. 17 Sep 1871. (Pp. 537-538)

J. T. Hollis, special commissioner, to John Johnson a tract of land. 30 Sep 1871. (Pp. 538-539)

Jesse T. Hollis to Nathaniel Parker a tract of land belonging to the estate of S. S. Tyra. 30 Sep 1871. (Pp. 540-541)

E. W. Bass and wife Susan to W. T. Haskins a tract of land. 30 Oct 1871. (Pp. 541-542)

Yancy M. Malone to John B. Tubb a tract of land belonging to the estate of my grandfather William Malone. 2 Oct 1871. (Pp. 542-543)

William Wilmuth to William M. Jones a tract of land. 18 Jan 1868. (P. 543)

Samuel H. Batten to George W. Sanderson 110½ acres in the 21st District. 20 Jan 1859. (P. 544)

George W. Sanderson to L. (Hinson) a tract of land. 11 Oct 1871. (P. 545)

George W. Sanderson to David Kirby a tract of land in the 17th District. 4 Oct 1871. (P. 546)

William P. Kelly and wife Pamelia, and T. Kelly to (John) Henson a tract of land. 10 Aug 1869. (P. 547)

Gipson R. West and wife, Amanda, to James Griffith a tract

of land in the 13th District. 12 Oct 1871. (Pp. 547-548)

William H. Magness to T. J. Estes 50 acres in the 1st District. 21 Oct 1871. (Pp. 548-549)

T. C. Cantrell and wife Luisa and E. W. Cantrell to B. A. Cantrell their interest in the estate of Mary Cantrell. 19 Oct 1871. (Pp. 549-550)

Mary Hendrickson to Russell Spurlock 156 acres in the 9th District. 10 Dec 1870. (Pp. 551-552)

John D. Tittsworth and wife Elizabeth to Nathan T. Wall 65 acres. 24 Oct 1871. (Pp. 552-553)

W. T. Haskins and wife M. J. to John Hendrickson 51 acres in the 2nd District. 3 Apr 1871. (Pp. 553-554)

James McGuire to Lemuel G. Batten his interest in a tract of land fronting on Main Street. 31 Oct 1871. (Pp. 554-555)

W. T. Haskins to (Polis) Smith 153 acres on Smith Fork. 3 Jul 1871. (Pp. 555-556)

Lemuel G. Batten and wife Mary E. to Bill Cantrell a lot in the town of Smithville. 1 Nov 1871. (Pp. 556-557)

George Lamberson and wife, Dedamia, to John L. Ayers a tract of land. 4 Oct 1871. (Pp. 557-558)

William H. Magness to John L. Cripps 57 acres in the 7th District. 2 Nov 1871. (P. 559)

William C. Youngblood to William G. Evins his interest in a town lot in the town of Liberty. 3 Nov 1871. (Pp. 559-561)

A. T. Phillips to C. L. (Johnson) a tract of land. 6 Nov 1871. (Pp. 561-562)

William H. Whaley to Thomas G. Bratten 30 acres in the 2nd District. 31 Mar 1870. (Pp. 562-563)

Clerk & Master to J. J. Burnett the Caroline Wade house and lot in Smithville owned by M. T. Martin who died testate in the year 1862 or 1863. 16 Sep 1871. (Pp. 563-564)

John Mason and wife Eliza to John S. Ayers 21 acres. 15 Oct 1871. (P. 565)

Rody Kelly to George W. Lamberson 120 acres in the 17th District. 2 Jul 1870. (P. 566)

W. T. Robinson and wife Lucy J. to George W. Lamberson 150 acres in the 17th District. 2 Jul 1870. (P. 567)

James N. Eaton and wife, Eliza, to A. M. Robinson 222 acres in the 11th District. 1 Nov 1870. (Pp. 568-569)

O. B. Wright to W. H. Magness a tract of land in the 1st District. 6 Nov 1871. (P. 569)

William (Manard) and wife Louisa to Sarah Ann Manard and Adeline Manard a tract of land in the 8th District. 4 Oct 1869. (P. 570)

DEED BOOK K

William Garner and John Garner to James T. Garner their interest in 100 acres on Wolf Creek. 4 Nov 1871. (Pp. 570-571)

S. W. McClellan to J. D. Bone & Company a tract of land adjoining the town of Alexandria. 26 Sep 1871. (Pp. 571-572)

R. C. Bone to John D. Bone his one sixth interest in the Alexandria Mills. 14 Nov 1871. (Pp. 572-573)

D. M. Phillips to E. Warren 180 acres in the 9th District. 15 Nov 1871. (P. 573)

George W. Eastham to William Bass and Matilda McGinnis 100 acres in the 9th District. 15 Nov 1871. (P. 574)

William H. Magness and wife E. J. to William H. Hays a tract of land . 18 Nov 1871. (Pp. 574-575)

William H. Magness to M. L. Garrison 40 acres in the 1st District. 13 Mar 1871. (Pp. 575-576)

John P. Tittsworth and wife Elizabeth to John Jones 114 acres in the 7th District. 24 Oct 1871. (Pp. 576-577)

Thomas L. Sewell and wife Pheba Ann to Thomas H. Christian a tract of land in the town of Smithville. 21 Nov 1871. (Pp. 577-578)

John Manard to Gipson R. Manard a tract of land in the 5th District. 13 Nov 1871. (Pp. 578-579)

William H. Truett to William H. Measles and Thomas Grooms 134 acres in the 3rd District. 23 Nov 1871. (Pp. 579-580)

William Parker and wife Matilda B. to James H. Blackburn a tract of land in the 4th District. 24 Aug 1871. (P. 580)

Alexander Martin for love and affection to his grandson, A. T. Phillips, the northern portion of the Pistole tract which was deeded to me by Stephen Pistole in 1842. 31 Jul 1869. (P. 581)

William Manard to John Holla) a tract of land. 31 Aug 1865. (Pp. 581-582)

Gipson Manard and wife Elizabeth to William Manard a tract of land on Mine Lick Creek in the 5th District. 31 Oct 1871. (Pp. 582-583)

P. G. Magness, Sr. to Edward Warren 51 acres in the 5th District. 6 Dec 1871. (P. 583)

John Helmontoller and Joseph H. Helmontoller to Samuel H. Christian 102 acres in the 17th District. 1 Dec 1871. (Pp. 584-585)

J. W. Griffith and wife, E. J., to Martha Ann Scott 95 acres in the 2nd District. 18 Dec 1871. (Pp. 585-586)

C. W. L. Hale to William Vick a lot in the town of Liberty. 16 Dec 1871. (P. 586)

J. J. Ford to Wiley Jones a lot in the town of Alexandria. 20 Dec 1871. (P. 587)

Mary Fuson to Richard R. Hendrixson 12½ acres in the 10th District. 22 Nov 1871. (Pp. 587-588)

John B. Stark to William B. Preston and Robert (Gunn) 21 acres in the 3rd District. 25 Jun 1871. (Pp. 588-589)

A. F. Durham and L. K. Durham to E. C. Walker 100 acres in the 10th District. 16 Feb 1870. (Pp. 589-590)

John S. Bond and wife Nancy; Jonathan Hall and wife Rosanna to Vilina Jane Fuston 64 acres in the 9th District. 28 Jul 1871. (Pp. 590-591)

M. D. Smotherman to Thomas L. Sewell a trust deed. 4 Jan 1872. (Pp. 591-593)

James H. Camron and wife Ann Etta and E. T. Foster to James A. Nesmith their interest in a lot in the town of Smithville. 3 Oct 1871. (Pp. 593-594)

T. J. Williams, Administrator of Edward Robinson, to Daniel Jones a tract of land on the south fork in the town of Liberty. 17 Apr 1871. (P. 595)

James A. Nesmith to H. L. W. Capshaw a parcel of land in the town of Smithville. 9 Jan 1872. (Pp. 595-596)

T. J. Williams, Administrator of Edward Robinson, to G. Northcutt 41 acres in the 2nd District. 10 Jan 1872. (P. 597)

Russell Spurlock and wife Melinda to John D. Rigsby 156 acres in the 9th District. 10 Nov 1871. (Pp. 597-598)

T. H. Martin to his wife and son a tract of land in the 5th District. 8 Jan 1872. (P. 599)

William B. Sweeney and wife, Martha, to Joseph W. Gilbert three acres in the 9th District. 28 Dec 1871. (Pp. 599-600)

James H. Veach and wife, Mary Ann, to John C. Cannady 18 acres in the 9th District. 18 Nov 1869. (Pp. 600-601)

John C. Cannady to Mary A. Veach and husband James H. 36 acres in the 9th District. 18 Nov 1872. (P. 601)

Benjamin F. Davis to James W. Hicks a tract of land in the 14th District. 10 Jan 1872. (Pp. 602-603)

George H. Eastham to Lucinda Moore a title bond. 2 Dec 1871. (P. 603)

Thomas P. Jones and wife, Elizabeth, to James Eaton 134 acres in the 11th District. 22 Jan 1872. (Pp. 604-605)

Thomas P. Jones and wife, Elizabeth, to John V. Crowder 50 acres on Dry Branch of Helton's Creek in the 11th District. 22 Jan 1872. (Pp. 605-606)

E. Tubb and M. M. Brien, Jr., Executors of James Tubb, to Thomas Davis 23 acres in the 12th District. 14 Sep 1871. (Pp. 606-607)

George Beckwith to William D. Beckwith a tract of land on

Holmes Creek in the 9th District. 19 Jan 1872. (P. 607)

Shadrach Travel and wife Elizabeth to Elizabeth Garrison 200 acres in the 10th District. 13 Sep 1871. (Pp. 608-609)

Elizabeth Garrison to William H. Hendrickson a tract of land on Indian Creek in the 10th District. 27 Jan 1872. (Pp. 609-610)

William V. Jones to Benjamin Penager a tract of land in the 7th District. 5 Sep 1859. (Pp. 610-611)

Elizabeth Bailiff to James H. Eaton his interest in a tract of land in the 11th District. 22 Jan 1872. (Pp. 611-612)

Thomas B. Askew, trustee, to Thomas P. Jones a trust deed. (See Book J, page 443). 24 Jan 1872. (P. 612)

P. G. Magness, Clerk, to Wiley Chapman a tract of land belonging to the estate of Sampson Chapman who died intestate in the mouth of Jun 1871. (Pp. 612-613)

Sheriff James H. Blackburn to H. Harris a tract of land. 6 Jan 1872. (Pp. 614-615)

James W. Dodd to Nicholas Acuff a tract of land in the 5th District. 16 Jan 1871. (Pp. 615-616)

P. G. Magness, Clerk, to William Ellis a tract of land belonging to T. F. Everett who died testate on our about 1869. 5 Jan 1872. (Pp. 616-617)

William D. Pritchard and wife Minerva to Wilson Hendrickson the old Curtis place in the 10th District. 4 Dec 1871. (Pp. 617-618)

Thomas Sullins and wife Jutha Jane to Samuel S. Shelton a tract of land on Sink Creek in the 5th District. 7 Feb 1872. (Pp. 619-620)

G. B. Pedigo and wife Virginia to L. J. Love one half acre in the 9th District. 10 Feb 1872. (Pp. 620-621)

James Dildine died testate in White County about 1865. P. G. Magness, Clerk, to Mary Dildine a tract of land. 25 Dec 1871. (Pp. 621-623)

Jordan T. Stokes and wife Polina to Thomas Gill 27 acres in the 16th District. 20 Jul 1871. (Pp. 623-624)

F. M. Cantrell to Yancy Penager 90 acres. 15 Sep 1871. (Pp. 624-625)

William Goodman and wife Sarah to Elijah Hathaway their interest in a tract of land in the 7th District containing 80 acres. 6 Oct 1871. (Pp. 625-626)

P. G. Magness to G. W. Camron a tract of land belonging to Samuel H. Camron. 4 Feb 1872. (Pp. 626-627)

County Court Clerk to M. K. Smith 77 acres in the 5th District. 7 Dec 1871. (Pp. 627-628)

DEED BOOK K

Charles Hill and wife, Lucinda, to T. W. Fitts their interest in a tract of land in the 12th District. 27 Feb 1872. (Pp. 628-629)

M. A. Stark and wife, Sarah E., to Lemuel J. Bratten eight acres. 24 Feb 1872. (Pp. 629-630)

T. J. Williams to Edward Gothard one half acre. 7 Dec 1869. (Pp. 630-631)

W. J. Givin to G. M. (Bauers) 36 acres in the 1st District. 14 Dec 1871. (P. 631)

H. L. W. Turney to Caroline Jane Turney his interest in a tract of land in the 3rd District known as the dower of Mrs. Mary Turney, widow of Joseph Turney. 4 Dec 1871. (P. 632)

John B. Taylor and wife, Nancy, to T. W. Fitts a tract of land on the south side of Indian Creek in the 10th District. 6 Mar 1872. (Pp. 632-633)

(Pages 634 and 635 are blank)

Levi Nixon to James C. Fisher a tract of land in the 21st District. 3 Feb 1860. (P. 636)

DEED BOOK L

James N. Ray and wife Susan to Peyton S. Berry 117 acres in the 13th District. 22 Feb 1872. (Pp. 1-3)

Charles Rich and wife Nancy to John Gann and K. Gann 30 acres in the 11th District. 22 Feb 1872. (P. 4)

John W. Savage to Thomas C. Allen five acres. 9 Mar 1872. (P. 5)

Tabitha Williams to Thomas Leek 260 acres on Holmes Creek. 6 Jan 1872. (Pp. 6-7)

Berryman Avant to Sterling B. Prichard 231 acres on Smith Fork. 7 Apr 1851. (Pp. 7-8)

Reason Rowland and wife, Sarah, to Washington Reynolds 68 acres in the 11th District. 7 Apr 1871. (Pp. 8-9)

Jesse W. Scott to John Sandlin 50 acres on (Dismal) Creek. 4 Dec 1851. (Pp. 9-10)

David Reavis and wife Joyse M. to William C. Gilbert 20 acres in the 9th District. 22 Mar 1872. (Pp. 10-11)

H. L. W. Capshaw and wife Lucinda to P. T. Shores a lot in the town of Smithville. 25 Mar 1872. (P. 11)

E. W. Bass and wife Susan to Samuel Hathaway 40 acres. 28 Mar 1872. (P. 12)

John P. Tittsworth and wife Elizabeth F. to Elizabeth Penager 114 acres in the 7th District. 24 Oct 1871. (P. 13)

Allen Jones to Caroline White one and one half acres in the 11th District. 18 Dec 1869. (P. 14)

P. S. Berry and wife E. A. to Isaac Hayse a tract of land on the Caney Fork. 2 Apr 1872. (Pp. 14-15)

John H. French to Wiley Sanders his one eighth interest in a tract of land. 5 Oct 1865. (Pp. 15-16)

T. N. Christian to J. N. Ray a tract of land belonging to the estate of T. L. Compton. 2 Apr 1872. (Pp. 16-17)

James H. Blackburn and wife A. J. to W. T. Robinson a tract of land in the 4th District. 7 Feb 1872. (P. 17)

Daniel Gann and wife Martha to J. A. Nesmith one half acre, it being the land where we now live on Smith Fork. 15 Jan 1872. (P. 18)

George W. Eastham to his grandsons, to wit, J. S. Dunlap and J. F. Dunlap a tract of land in the 9th District. 12 Apr 1872. (P. 19)

Paris Driver and wife Matilda to John F. Gunn six acres in the 5th District. 3 Dec 1871. (Pp. 19-20)

Giles Driver to his daughter, Mary Briant, formerly Mary Driver, free from the control of her husband, William Briant, a tract of land. 14 Nov 1867. (Pp. 20-21)

R. R. Wamack, asinee of James M. Allen to A. T. Phillips a tract of land. 4 May 1872. (Pp. 21-22)

J. P. Hennessee to J. M. Green 73 acres in the 6th District. 9 May 1872. (P. 22)

Sheriff James H. Blackburn to H. Harris a tract of land. 11 May 1872. (Pp. 23-24)

Articles of agreement between Henry Adcock and James Barnes with regard to a title bond. 15 Dec 1867. (Pp. 24-25)

S. H. Lane and wife E., M. C. Foster, Sarah Lane, W. L. Foster, Isaac Bishop and wife Mary, Virginia Foster, A. C. Ferrell, and Martha Ferrell, the heirs of Epps Foster, quit claim to Elijah H. Foster 100 acres in the 16th District. 8 Feb 1868. (Pp. 25-26)

John Jones and wife Catherine to John Deadman 49 acres in the 1st District. 16 Dec 1871. (Pp. 26-27)

Clerk & Master to James C. Fisher a tract of land in the 17th District. 3 Jun 1872. (Pp. 27-28)

O. B. Wright to Rachel Garrison a tract of land in the 1st District. 13 Jun 1872. (Pp. 28-29)

Samuel T. Mottley to F. S. and W. H. Patterson 251 acres in the 1st District. 15 Jun 1872. (Pp. 29-30)

William G. Foster and wife Judia Ann to B. M. Cantrell Lot No. 71 in the town of Smithville. Bounded: corner of Church and Walnut Streets. 10 Jun 1872. (P. 30)

W. H. Whaley and wife Martha A. to C. W. L. Hale a lot in the town of Liberty known as Lot No. 10. Bounded: north side of the old Lebanon & Sparta Pike. 27 Jun 1872. (P. 31)

John D. Bone to O. B. Wright 18 acres. 20 Feb 1870. (Pp. 31-32)

John C. Cannady and wife Margrett A. to their daughter, Emma C. Dunlap, and her husband, J. S. Dunlap, about three acres in the 9th District. 25 Jun 1872. (Pp. 32-33)

John C. Cannady and wife Margrett A. to their daughter, Pheba Josephine Bomer, and her husband, Ruben C. Bomer, 41 acres in the 9th District. 25 Jun 1872. (Pp. 33-34)

Hardin Cantrell to Talitha Sanders for love and affection two tracts of land in the 5th District. 25 Jun 1872. (P. 34)

Obediah Rich to Milian Hicks and Paralee Hughs a tract of land in the 3rd District. 28 Aug 1870. (Pp. 34-35)

William Bates to Sarah Parkerson 26 acres in the 11th District. 9 Apr 1869. (Pp. 35-36)

W. E. Bartlett and wife Mary J., William H. Garner and wife Anna, heirs of Martha B. Smith to Felix H. Smith their interest in 75 acres on Wolf Creek in the 16th District. 25 Mar 1869. (Pp. 36-37)

Joseph H. Blackburn to Albert Porter a tract of land in the 2nd District. 4 Jul 1872. (P. 37)

DEED BOOK L

William H. Luckey and wife Martha M. to Martha Schurer, wife of J. H. Schurer, a house and lot in the town of Alexandria. 10 Apr 1872. (P. 38)

Susannah Lawrence to Thomas W. Lawrence a tract of land in the 12th District. 11 May 1872. (P. 39)

Morgan Lawrence to Tempy Lawrence and Sary Ann Lawrence a tract of land in the 12th District. 21 Mar 1872. (P. 40)

Tempy Lawrence and (Laury) Ann Lawrence to Morgan Lawrence 31 acres in the 12th District. 23 Mar 1872. (Pp. 40-41)

J. H. Dodd to J. W. Fowler 50 acres in the 9th District. 28 Mar 1870. (P. 41)

Walter Cantrell to A. W. Cantrell a tract of land in the 5th District. 31 Dec 1869. (P. 42)

George W. Eastham and Thomas J. Sneed enter into an agreement. 2 Jul 1872. (P. 43)

James H. Blackburn and James Blackburn to W. T. Robinson 12 acres in the 4th District. 27 Mar 1872. (Pp. 43-44)

John D. Bone, Administrator of A. Bone and also of W. Bone, filed suit against Abe Britton charging that said A. and W. D. Bone sold to said Britton a house and lot in Alexandria and that he has failed to pay for it. 15 Jul 1872. (Pp. 44-45)

George W. Eastham to William Smith 45 acres in the 9th District. 19 Jul 1872. (Pp. 45-46)

J. G. McIntire to A. J. McIntire a tract of land in the 10th District. 2 May 1872. (P. 46)

A. J. McIntire to M. S. McIntire and B. A. McIntire 150 acres in the 10th District. 19 Jul 1872. (P. 47)

Jane Cantrell and C. A. Cantrell to J. H. Dodd a tract of land in the 6th District conveyed to said Jane Cantrell by John A. Cantrell. 23 Jul 1872. (Pp. 47-48)

Lemuel G. Batten to Henry Johnson 50 acres in the 9th District. 15 Feb 1871. (Pp. 48-49)

Bluford Hendrix and wife Elizabeth of Benton County to J. B. Fowler a tract of land in the 4th District, it being a part of the land known as the Judiah Hunt tract. 29 Jul 1872. (Pp. 49-50)

Samuel Walker to Elizabeth Capshaw 50 acres. 1 Aug 1872. (Pp. 50-51)

William P. West to J. J. Ford her interest in a tract of land that belonged to his father, John F. West. My brother, Wiley B. West, also has a share. 3 Aug 1872. (P. 51)

J. C. Cannady to Rebecca B. Hendrickson and Wiley Hendrickson 175 acres in the 10th District. 30 Jul 1872. (P. 52)

William H. Magness to D. M. Adcock a tract of land in the 7th District. 22 Feb 1872. (Pp. 52-53)

DEED BOOK L

Clerk & Master to John F. Yeargin a tract of land belonging to the heirs of James Yeargin, to wit, Isaac Cooper and wife Talitha, A. J. Yeargin, Sampson Yeargin, H. J. Yeargin, J. F. Yeargin, and Charles Yeargin. 10 Aug 1872. (Pp. 54-55)

Jane Cantrell and husband C. A. Cantrell to D. W. Sanders 141 acres in the 6th District. 20 Nov 1869. (Pp. 55-56)

Thomas Shields to Henderson Green a tract of land in the 9th District. 24 Aug 1872. (P. 56)

Clerk & Master to Talitha Cooper a tract of land belonging to the heirs of James Yeargin. 31 Aug 1872. (Pp. 56-58)

James Hollinsworth and wife Elizabeth to C. W. L. Hale a tract ofland in the town of Liberty. 4 Sep 1872. (Pp. 58-59)

Nancy T. M. Davis to Samuel H. Davis a lot in the town of Alexandria. 20 Oct 1870. (P. 59)

E. H. Foster to W. L. Foster a tract of land. 31 Jul 1872. (P. 60)

A. J. Foster died intestate in 1863. James M. Lee was appointed administrator. County Court Clerk to W. L. Foster a tract of land in the 16th District belonging to the estate. 4 Sep 1872. (Pp. 60-61)

P. G. Magness, Sr. to R. B. Summers a tract of land in the 5th District. 23 Aug 1872. (Pp. 61-62)

Clerk & Master to Jesse W. Scott 76 acres known as the dower of Lucinda Hays. Said tract of land is 76 acres and is located in the 13th District. 3 Sep 1872. (Pp. 62-63)

James H. Dodd and wife Nancy to Joseph H. Dodd 108 acres on Sink Creek in the 5th District. 20 Jan 1872. (Pp. 63-64)

Isaac Whaley to John Parker 80½ acres in the 4th District. 13 Dec 1869. (Pp. 64-65)

Robert S. Alcorn to James Holley 55 acres in the 16th District. 14 Oct 1871. (P. 65)

James Holley and wife Leah to W. B. Winchester 171 acres in the 16th District. 9 Sep 1871. (Pp. 66-67)

John Atnip to Alexander E. Ferrell a tract of land in the 10th District. 6 Sep 1861. (P. 68)

P. H. Cantrell to B. A. Cantrell the portion of real estate which was allotted to me in the partition of my father, Green Cantrell. 16 Sep 1872. (Pp. 68-69)

John C. Cantrell to B. A. Cantrell his interest in the estate of his father Green Cantrell. 27 Dec 1871. (Pp. 69-70)

Lucian B. Allen, Administrator of Samuel Allen, versus John Moore and wife Mary J., Susan Allen, Luisa Allen, Samuel Allen, Wesley Cannady, Augusta Cannady, Floid Cannady, William Eastham, Charley Eastham, and Mary Eastham. County Court Clerk to Hiram Cantrell 100 acres belonging to the estate. 30 Aug 1872. (Pp. 70-71)

DEED BOOK L

Elijah Hathaway and wife Jane to W. S. Fitts 116 acres in the 14th District. 6 Oct 1871. (Pp. 71-72)

Perry G. Magness to E. N. Green 50 acres in the 6th District. 17 Oct 1871. (Pp. 72-73)

O. B. Wright, R. Cantrell, and J. S. Calvert to Whig Garrison and wife Elizabeth 111 acres in the 1st District. 25 Sep 1872. (Pp. 73-74)

Thomas B. Potter and wife S. D. to Micajah Brown a town lot in the town of Smithville. 11 Sep 1872. (P. 74)

James M. Baker to David B. Worley nine acres in the 9th District. 5 Oct 1872. (P. 75)

William Austin and wife Luisa to James T. Exum 25 acres in the 16th District. 14 Sep 1872. (Pp. 75-76)

The legatees of James Bond, to wit, Betie Bond, Nancy Bond, S. W. Bond, Ruthy Bond, A. J. Bond, John L. Bond, W. H. H. Bond, James M. Bond, G. W. Bond, T. A. Burton, W. E. Burton, Roxanna Hull, Jonathan Hull to A. J. Bond and W. H. Bond the home tract containing 290 acres. Said A. J. and W. H. Bond obligate themselves to take care of and support Ruthy Bond during her natural life. 17 Sep 1872. (Pp. 76-77)

Thomas Ferrell and wife Sintha to Greenberry Mullinax 21 acres in the 5th District. 7 Oct 1872. (Pp. 77-78)

H. H. Kidwell and wife Ellen to T. W. Goodner a house and lot on Church Street in the town of Alexandria. 9 Oct 1872. (Pp. 78-79)

Benjamin Forest and wife Mary to William H. Love 50 acres. 12 Oct 1872. (Pp. 79-80)

George W. Eastham to M. Green 30 acres in the 9th District. 25 Jul 1872. (P. 80)

The legatees of John Bond to George H. Bond the Foster tract on which he now lives. 22 Jun 1872. (Pp. 80-81)

Asa Driver and wife Tabitha to James M. Malone 30 acres in the 12th District. 18 Oct 1872. (Pp. 81-82)

Thomas Shields to William N. Wilson 19 acres in the 9th District. 24 Oct 1872. (P. 82)

Sheriff J. H. Blackburn to G. W. Persar a tract of land belonging to the estate of A. Bone. 23 Oct 1872. (Pp. 83-84)

E. Warren to J. M. Doak 188 acres in the 9th District. 26 Oct 1872. (Pp. 84)

George C. Drumgole to C. L. Gibson and wife Narcissa a tract of land for the benefit of the said Narcissa. 29 Oct 1872. (Pp. 84-85)

William G. Foster and wife Juda to James L. Calvert a title bond. 5 Oct 1872. (Pp. 85-86)

John Chapman and Roxanna Chapman by descent from Thomas Bailif to Columbus Bailiff the Simpson tract in the 1st District. 2 Jun 1871. (Pp. 86-87)

John J. Burton to Anna Duncan 40 acres in the 8th District. Bounded: the heirs of John Dyer. 28 Jul 1871. (P. 87)

A. J. Bennett to John Vannatta 65 acres in the 13th District. 26 Apr 1872. (P. 88)

P. P. Peterman, Caroline Peterman, Isabella Ford, California Culwell, and James Ford to George W. McCarty a tract of land in the 9th District. 1 Nov 1872. (Pp. 88-89)

John H. Savage to Isiah White a tract of land adjoining the town of Smithville. 1 Apr 1872. (Pp. 89-90)

Fuller Sanland and wife Peggy to Thomas Curtis 21 acres in the 11th District. 8 Aug 1872. (Pp. 90-91)

Joseph H. Blackburn and Jenny Blackburn to George Turner, colored, a tract of land. 3 Nov 1872. (P. 91)

William H. Atwell and John B. Atwell to Thomas Smith 79 acres in the 9th District. 11 Oct 1872. (Pp. 91-92)

Jeremiah Hendrickson and wife Sarah M. to David C. Taylor three acres in the 10th District. 9 Nov 1872. (Pp. 92-93)

William B. Stokes to his wife, Parilee A. Stokes, a deed of gift. (P. 93)

(Pages 94 and 95 are blank)

J. W. Bickers to H. C. McEwen two tracts of land. 12 Nov 1872. (Pp. 96-97)

Lorenzo V. Hass and wife Spira M. to George Little a tract of land in the 9th District. 26 Sep 1861. (Pp. 97-98)

S. J. Magness and wife Melisa A. to G. R. Smith 30 acres that he bought from W. S. Driver and wife. 8 Nov 1872. (P. 99)

G. R. Smith and wife Rebecca to S. Lucian J. Magness as trustee for Melisa A. Magness and her children by the said L. J. Magness a tract of land in the town of Smithville. 19 Oct 1872. (P. 100)

Isiah White and wife Lucy A. to Isaac Davis a tract of land adjoining the town of Smithville. 19 Nov 1872. (Pp. 100-101)

J. H. Dodd and wife M. E. to John J. Cantrell a tract of land in the 6th District on Sink Creek. 21 Oct 1872. (Pp. 101-102)

Isaac M. Pirtle and wife Mary R. to Levi B. Moore 43 acres in the 9th District. 22 Nov 1872. (P. 102)

H. E. McEwen to John C. Cannady 80 acres in the 9th District. 21 Nov 1872. (P. 103)

Aaron Frazer, Executor of Henry Frazer, to Barnabas Johnson a tract of land. 5 Mar 1872. (Pp. 103-104)

J. J. Williams and wife Mary to J. M. Tramell 50 acres.

29 Nov 1872. (Pp. 104-105)

John C. Cannady, Administrator of James Cantrell, to Samuel Cantrell, Lawson Cantrell, A. P. Cantrell, and Sarah Cantrell part of the tract of land purchased by James Cantrell from Samuel Hooper, 2 Dec 1872. (Pp. 105-106)

County Court Clerk to Isaac N. Fite a tract of land owned by Tilman Bethel who died intestate. 28 Nov 1872. (Pp. 106-107)

Henry Johnson and wife Levina to James C. Brien 50 acres in the 9th District. 27 Nov 1872. (Pp. 107-108)

Andrew A. Robinson and wife Mary to John C. Taylor 112 acres in the 9th District. 30 Nov 1872. (Pp. 108-109)

Carroll Cantrell and wife Martha J. to J. H. Dodd eight acres. 1 May 1872. (Pp. 109-110)

B. A. Cantrell and wife Darcus to B. L. Estes a tract of land in the 9th District. 7 Dec 1872. (Pp. 110-111)

Jeremiah Hendrickson to his wife, Sarah M., and children by her 55 acres in the 10th District. 9 Nov 1872. (P. 111)

James E. Burton to John J. Burton his one fifth interest in the lands owned by my father, Charles Burton, including my interest in my mother's dower. 14 Aug 1872. (Pp. 112-113)

William Robinson to Gipson R. West one half acre. Bounded: Amanda and Sarah Alexander. 15 Aug 1872. (P. 113)

J. J. Ford, Executor of Peter Clark, to Eliza Clark, the widow, a tract of land in the 13th District. 17 Dec 1872. (Pp. 113-114)

James M. Milom to Thomas H. Lawrence a tract of land in the 12th District. 18 Dec 1872. (Pp. 114-115)

William H. Magness to Harrell Byers 50 acres in the 5th District. 21 Dec 1872. (P. 115)

William H. Magness to Thomas B. Potter part of Lot No. 26 in the town of Smithville. 2 Jan 1873. (Pp. 115-116)

W. D. Irwin to L. D. Smith a tract of land on Fall Creek in the 7th District. 15 Oct 1872. (P. 116)

T. Parrish and wife Elizabeth to P. G. Byers a tract of land in the 9th District. 8 Jan 1873. (Pp. 117-118)

John C. Cannady and wife Margrett A. to Andrew A. Robinson and James Taylor 250 acres. 24 Dec 1873. (P. 118)

David Luis to Perry Adcock a tract of land in the 7th District, it being the same land laid off for the Charity Luis dower, the wife of Benjamin Luis. 18 Jan 1873. (P. 119)

S. T. Kelton to A. M. Kelton a tract of land in the 5th District. 28 Jan 1873. (Pp. 119-120)

Malicia Culwell to George and Luisa Manard a tract of land in the 9th District. 30 Jan 1873. (Pp. 120-121)

DEED BOOK L

Sanford Mann and wife Matilda to Samuel Barger a tract of land in the 2nd District. 11 Jan 1873. (P. 121)

Sanford Mann and wife to J. W. Hunt 109 acres in the 2nd District. 10 Jan 1873. (P. 122)

J. W. Hunt and wife Abigil to Sanford Mann 142 acres in the 2nd District. 10 Jan 1873. (P. 123)

Joseph P. Davis and wife, Amanda, to Thomas J. Davis 52 acres in the 12th District. 29 Jun 1872. (P. 124)

John R. Lawrence and wife Gracy to Anny Davis two acres in the 12th District. 16 Dec 1872. (P. 125)

James Beaty, John Beaty, and W. A. Beaty to William C. Avant a tract of land. 3 Dec 1873. (Pp. 126-127)

Jesse B. Farler and wife Lucinda to John T. Johnson ten acres in the 4th District on Dry Creek. 29 Jul 1872. (Pp. 127-128)

W. F. Dowell to John T. Johnson a tract of land in the 4th District. 5 Feb 1873. (P. 128)

M. Puckett, by S. F. Puckett, to H. F. Love 36 acres in the 8th District. 7 Feb 1873. (Pp. 128-139)

Simon Williams and wife Minerva to Mary E. Cantrell, wife of George W. Cantrell, 40 acres in Pigeon Roost Hollow in the 9th District. 8 Feb 1873. (Pp. 129-130)

Thomas Sewell and wife Pheba A. to Peter P. Johnson a lot in the town of Smithville on the main road running from Smithville to McMinnville. 8 Feb 1873. (Pp. 130-131)

George W. Earthan to William Foster eight acres in the 9th District. 6 Jan 1872. (P. 131)

Jason White and wife Nancy A. to John Willaby 123 acres in the 11th District. 7 Feb 1873. (Pp. 131-133)

Isaac Whaley and wife Nancy; William H. Whaley and wife Martha A.; S. M. Whaley and wife Mary; John D. Whaley and wife Letha; and Lemuel B. Whaley and wife Martha to Matilda Beckwith 94 acres in the 9th District. 12 Nov 1872. (Pp. 133-138)

J. S. Crips to W. G. Etheridge a tract of land. 25 Dec 1872. (Pp. 138-139)

Clerk & Master to William B. Stokes a tract of land in the 1st District. Said land was sold in the case of R. C. Bone, guardian of William T. Bone et als. 10 Feb 1873. (Pp. 139-140)

John Reavis to Robert Johnson a tract of land in the 5th District including his father's estate. 16 Jan 1861. (Pp. 140-141)

Robert Johnson and wife Mary A. to William C. Gilbert their interest in the lands belonging to the heirs of Thomas Reavis. 19 Feb 1873. (P. 141)

DEED BOOK L

John S. Harrison to James Ford 25 acres. 8 Feb 1873. (P. 142)

Watson Potter to James Ford to Tolton Parish 120 acres on Pine Creek. 10 Dec 1872. (Pp. 142-143)

W. N. McNamara to John C. Jones his interest in 136 acres. 2 Jan 1862. (P. 143)

John C. Jones to James C. Jones a tract of land in the 5th District. 19 Jun 1872. (P. 144)

Samuel C. Fish to George W. Jones a tract of land in the 9th District. 30 Dec 1871. (Pp. 144-145)

Joseph H. Mangrum and wife Martha J. to Bethel Parsley 75 acres in the 9th District. 6 Jan 1873. (Pp. 145-146)

Isaac Hays to Richard W. McGinnis 100 acres in the 9th District. 28 Dec 1867. (Pp. 146-147)

W. C. Cantrell and Martha J. Cantrell to Mary Elender Avery 67 acres in the 6th District. 11 Jan 1873. (P. 147)

G. N. Northcutt and wife Laury to Sanford Mann a tract of land. 17 Jan 1873. (P. 148)

Sanford Mann to J. W. White 12 acres in the 2nd District. 3 Feb 1873. (P. 149)

Benjamin F. Prim of the State of Texas to E. and A. S. Inglish 640 acres on Smith Fork. 27 Feb 1867. (Pp. 149-150)

B. A. Cantrell and wife Darcus and Mary Cantrell to Squire Warren one and one fourth acres in the 9th District. 10 Apr 1870. (Pp. 150-151)

B. A. Cantrell to W. L. Cantrell a tract of land in the 7th District containing 63 acres. 3 Dec 1872. (Pp. 151-152)

Wesley Overall to Elizabeth Parker one half acre in the 4th District. 16 Oct 1865. (P. 152)

John A. Fuson to Henry M. Fite 142 acres in the 4th District. (Pp. 152-153)

E. W. Taylor to James Hendrickson a tract of land. 22 Mar 1861. (Pp. 153-154)

David Jones to John A. Moss a tract of land in the 16th District. 4 Oct 1869. (Pp. 154-155)

M. S. McIntire, B. H. McIntire, Wilson H. Hendrickson and wife Frances to John M. Trammel 150 acres in the 10th District. 1 Aug 1872. (Pp. 155-156)

John M. Trammel, M. S. McIntire, B. H. McIntire to Wilson Hendrickson a tract of land in the 10th District. 1 Aug 1872. (Pp. 156-157)

William Robinson to Margrett A. Campbell two shares in her father's land. 22 Feb 1870. (Pp. 157-158)

Sampson Chapman died intestate in Jun 1870. County Court

Clerk to S. B. Harriman a tract of land belonging to the estate. 10 Feb 1873. (Pp. 158-159)

A. J. Edwards to Joseph Rollins a town lot in the town of Alexandria. 24 Apr 1871. (Pp. 159-160)

Margaret Jane Barnes to Thomas Park a tract of land. 3 Mar 1873. (P. 160)

Wiley Young and wife Elizabeth to Aaron Cantrell a tract of land in the 7th District. 26 Sep 1871. (Pp. 160-162)

Aaron Cantrell and wife Sarah to Wiley Young 30 acres in the 7th District. 26 Sep 1871. (P. 162)

James R. Beckwith and wife Matilda G. to John Lyles and John Pack 100 acres in the 9th District. 4 Mar 1873. (P. 163)

James B. Hollis, Trustee, to C. W. Anderson a tract of land containing 50 acres. 3 Mar 1873. (Pp. 164-165)

James R. Beckwith and wife Matilda G. to Lemuel B. Whaley their one sixth part of a tract of land in the 9th District derived to them from the estate of Elijah Whaley deceased. 12 Nov 1872. (Pp. 165-166)

Melissa J. Wall and husband T. M. Wall to N. T. Wall 155 acres in the 6th District. 11 May 1872. (Pp. 166-167)

N. T. Wall and Mary G. Wall to Melissa J. Wall 65 acres in the 7th District. 11 May 1872. (Pp. 167-168)

Barnabas S. Johnson and wife Nancy L. to W. J. Parsley a tract of land in the 4th District. 1 Mar 1873. (Pp. 168-169)

Barnabas S. Johnson and wife Nancy L. to J. K. Byford 30 acres in the 4th District. 1 Mar 1873. (P. 169)

Barnabas S. Johnson and wife Nancy L. to Daniel Johnson 100 acres on Dry Creek. 26 Mar 1873. (P. 170)

L. B. Hale and wife Elizabeth to Mary Connor a tract of land in the 3rd District. 6 Jan 1873. (P. 171)

B. F. Hale and wife Mary; L. B. Hale and wife Elizabeth to R. M. Dodd a tract of land in the 3rd District, it being the J. O. Connor tract of land. 8 Mar 1873. (P. 172)

James T. Allen and wife Lucy Ann to Jeremiah Coggin their interest in the real estate of Giles Williams deceased which is situated in the 16th District. 6 Jan 1873. (P. 173)

William Dodd and wife Charlotte to R. M. Dodd a tract of land in the 5th District. 17 Sep 1870. (Pp. 173-174)

J. Harrison Dodd and wife M. E. Dodd to Presley Adamson 75 acres. 6 Jan 1873. (Pp. 175-176)

Tilmon Jones and wife Elizabeth to John Corder 100 acres in the 15th District. 28 Dec 1868. (P. 176)

Sampson Bethel to P. C. Bluhn a tract of land in rhw 4rh District. 11 Feb 1873. (P. 177)

Thomas J. Sneed to Martha Schurer three fourth's of an acre in the 1st District. 13 Mar 1873. (Pp. 177-178)

Isaac K. Conyer to William Garner 40 acres in the 16th District. 11 Sep 1865. (Pp. 178-179)

John Hughes and Robert Smith to William Garner 20 acres in the 16th District. 10 Oct 1866. (P. 179)

Thomas Crips to Tilmon Jones and Elizabeth Jones 100 acres. 9 Aug 1871. (P. 180)

James Hale to H. G. and J. F. Hale 75 acres in the 3rd District. 23 Jun 1872. (Pp. 180-181)

James M. Baird of Alexandria, assignee in bankrupty of E. W. Bass to Wiley Odum and others a tract of land. 25 Oct 1872. (Pp. 182-183)

Elijah Hathaway and wife Jane; Solomon Goodman and wife Elizabeth to Willis M. Cutrell five acres. 11 Jan 1873. (P. 184)

William Whitson, George C. Drungole, and M. C. Whitson to Simon P. Elliott 800 acres in the 9th District. 5 Mar 1875. (P. 185)

John L. Crips to Peter Connor 106 acres in the 4th District. 28 Mar 1873. (Pp. 185-186)

John Hughes to William Garner two acres in the 14th District. 18 Mar 1873. (P. 186)

James Ford and wife Isabel to Emeline Curtis a tract of land in the 9th District. 13 Feb 1873. (P. 187)

By statute of dower, Charity Self is seized and possessed of two tracts of land. Said Charity to William T. Robinson her right of dower. 1 Mar 1871. (Pp. 187-188)

James M. Lee and wife Elizabeth H. to William E. Foster three quarter's of an acre in the 16th District. 15 Jun 1873. (Pp. 188-189)

Abraham Cantrell and wife Rebecca to William C. Gilbert 500 acres on Pine Creek in the 5th District. 10 Apr 1873. (Pp. 189-190)

P. G. Magness to Daniel G. Talley a tract of land in the 5th District. 7 Apr 1873. (P. 190)

J. L. Hollinsworth and wife M. A. to Augustus S. Redmon one acre in the town of Liberty. 30 Sep 1871. (P. 191)

W. J. Crawley to Charles H. Hall 25 acres on Pine Ridge. 15 Apr 1873. (P. 192)

Clerk & Master to John Parker a tract of land belonging to F. C. (Wroe). 18 Apr 1873. (Pp. 192-193)

W. G. Foster and wife Juda to J. H. and R. B. Capshaw a tract of land in the town of Smithville. 11 Apr 1873. (Pp. 193-194)

James T. Exum to William A) a tract of land. 18 Apr 1873. (Pp. 194-195)

Thomas S. Sewell, W. S. Tyree, and Isiah White for the use of Liberty Lady No. 77, Free and Accepted Masons to the said Lodge the Masonic Hall at the southwest corner of the Public Square of Smithville. 18 Apr 1873. (Pp. 195-196)

John C. Cannady to his daughter Mary Ann Veach, wife of James W. Veach 30½ acres in the 9th District. 24 Apr 1873. (Pp. 196-197)

County Court Clerk to John F. Bain a tract of land belonging to James A. Durham deceased. 25 Apr 1873. (P. 197)

County Court Clerk to Amanda Alexander and Sarah Alexander one acre belonging to William Robinson. 2 May 1871. (P. 198)

P. M. Wade and wife Nancy Ann to George W. Eastham a quit claim to a tract of land in the 9th District. 24 Apr 1873. (Pp. 198-199)

H. L. W. Capshaw and wife Lucinda to John C. Cannady as trustee for the use of his infant daughter, Maud W. Cannady, town lot No. 39 in the town of Smithville. 28 Apr 1873. (Pp. 199-200)

W. D. Beckwith to B. M. Cantrell in the 9th District. 17 Jan 1873. (Pp. 200-201)

H. L. W. Capshaw and wife Lucinda to John C. Cannady for the use of his infant daughter, Maud W. Cannady, a town lot in the town of Smithville. 9 May 1873. (Pp. 201-202)

John C. Cannady, trustee for Maud H. Cannady, to W. G. Crawley town lot No. 39 in the town of Smithville. 9 May 1873. (Pp. 202-203)

John Bethel Taylor and wife Martha to John C. Taylor and Lisk Taylor about five acres in the 10th District. 24 May 1873. (Pp. 203-204)

County Court Clerk to Paul D. Rhea, trustee of Ann Rhea, a tract of land belonging to M. T. Martin who died in 1863. 16 May 1873. (P. 204)

A. E. Frazer and wife Nancy A. to Jacob Atnip three acres in the 9th District. 7 Apr 1873. (P. 205)

Thomas Sneed and wife Ellen to James M. Baird seven acres on Hickman's Creek in the 1st District. 19 May 1873. (Pp. 205-206)

Nancy T. M. Davis to Samuel H. Davis a lot in the town of Alexandria. 14 Jan 1873. (P. 207)

F. M. Parkerson and wife Elizabeth to John T. Johnson 50 acres in the 4th District. 7 Sep 1871. (Pp. 207-208)

Green Cantrell died intestate about the 15th dan of Jan 1869. County Court Clerk to William H. Magness a tract of land belonging to the estate. 29 May 1873. (Pp. 208-209)

John (Hellum) to Elizabeth A. Hooper a tract of land in the 9th District. 17 Mar 1873. (Pp. 209-210)

George W. Eastham to W. W. Foster a tract of land in the 9th District. 23 Feb 1870. (Pp. 210-211)

Mathias T. Pennager to Mary J. Pennager, Charles Garrison Pennager, and Harty Anderson Pennager for love and affection 70 acres in the 7th District. 15 Feb 1873. (P. 211)

Lucy Woodson to F. W. Hobson 62½ acres in the 17th District. 28 Feb 1873. (Pp. 211-212)

Jonathan Denny, Timothy Denny, James Denny, Baley Woodson, Lucy Woodson, Catherine Huddleston, William Denny, and John Denny to F. W. Hobson 62½ acres in the 17th District. 1 Apr 1867. (P. 213)

F. W. Hobson and wife Mary F. to Yancy Malone 62½ acres in the 17th District. 29 May 1873. (P. 214)

Sheriff James H. Blackburn to William K. Durham 60 acres. 2 Jun 1873. (P. 215)

Eli Vick to Horace McGuire a tract of land. 5 Jun 1873. (P. 216)

L. J. Magness and wife Melissa A. to Havilla Dillard a town lot in the town of Smithville. Bounded: south by Main Street. 10 Jun 1873. (P. 217)

Joseph H. Blackburn and wife Jenny to Mary A. Turner a tract of land in the 4th District. 12 Dec 1871. (Pp. 217-218)

Sheriff James H. Blackburn to Thomas S. Sewell a tract of land containing one acre. 18 Jun 1873. (P. 219)

E. A. Bomer to R. C. Bomer Lot No. 75 in the town of Smithville. 20 May 1873. (P. 220)

J. D. Wheeler to Nelson Sneed one and one fourth acres in the 1st District. 30 Dec 1870. (Pp. 220-221)

John H. Allen to Pleasant Pistole three acres in the 3rd District. 3 Apr 1871. (Pp. 221-222)

William F. Dowell to Aaron Frazer one acre in the 4th District. 31 Oct 1870. (P. 222)

Samuel Warford to the Baptist Church of the old order at Helton's Creek a tract of land in the 11th District. 1 Apr 1871. (Pp. 222-223)

George W. Eastham to A. A. Foster 75 acres in the 9th District. 6 Jan 1872. (P. 223)

Nelson M. Bennett and wife Candes, formerly Candes M. Sandlin; Charity J. Butcher, formerly Charity J. Sandlin; and Mary Sandlin to John W. Sandlin their interest in the estate of Randolph Sandlin, it being land in the 1st District. 14 Apr 1871. (Pp. 224-225)

DEED BOOK L

James H. Blackburn and wife Jennie to Joseph H. Blackburn a tract of land in the 4th District. 15 Dec 1871. (Pp. 225-226)

J. J. Ford, Executor of Peter W. Clark, to Eliza Clark, widow of the said Peter W. Clark, Lot No. 3 in the division of the land between the several heirs of William Bennett. 24 Jun 1873. (Pp. 226-227)

Reuben C. Bomer and wife Pheba J. to John S. Harrison Lot No. 75 in the town of Smithville. 27 Jun 1873. (P. 227)

Alfred S. Hancock to C. W. Hale 25 acres in the 3rd District. 29 Apr 1873. (P. 228)

Alfred S. Hancock to S. Hale 130 acres in the 3rd District. 29 Apr 1873. (P. 229)

John Hendrickson and wife Martha to John W. Jacobs a tract of land in the 10th District. 22 Aug 1870. (Pp. 230-231)

Jeremiah Connor died in 1866 intestate. County Court Clerk to L. B. Hale and B. F. Hale Lot No. 1, except the dower. 15 Jul 1873. (Pp. 231-232)

William Waters to McAdoo Vannatta two acres on Smith Fork in the 2nd District. 8 Nov 1872. (P. 232)

Thomas Shields to Henderson Green, colored, eight acres in the 9th District. 23 Jul 1873. (P. 233)

John H. Savage to Hiram Cantrell eight and one half acres on Pine Creek in the 9th District. 21 Jul 1873. (Pp. 233-234)

M. S. McIntire and B. A. McIntire to John M. Tramell 150 acres known as the Curtis and Duncan lands. 29 Jul 1873. (P. 234)

Jeremiah Coggin to George McGee 75 acres in the 16th District. 4 Aug 1873. (P. 235)

L. G. Lish to T. N. Christian a town lot in the town of Smithville. 4 Aug 1873. (Pp. 235-236)

W. H. Tramell and wife S. E. to John W. Jacobs one and one fourth acres in the 11th District. 19 Dec 1871. (P. 236)

George Carter to William H. Brown 125 acres on the ridge lying between Mine Lick and Second Creek. 10 Dec 1872. (P. 237)

M. D. Smallman, trustee, to John L. Crips a tract of land north of Smithville containing about seven acres. 8 Aug 1873. (Pp. 237-238)

Richard Tittsworth to John P. Tittsworth and the other directors a tract of land in the 5th District for a school. 11 Aug 1873. (P. 239)

William C. Gilbert and wife T. A. to Nancy P. Puckett the old Thomas Reavis land in the 9th District. 11 Aug 1873. (Pp. 239-240)

Sidney Herren to his sons, William and David Herren, for taking care of me and paying my burial expenses 113 acres in the 9th District. 12 Aug 1873. (Pp. 240-241)

P. C. Garner to J. F. Stacy three acres in the 16th District. 15 Jan 1870. (P. 241)

John S. Crips and wife N. C. to David Worley seven acres in the 9th District. 16 Aug 1873. (P. 242)

J. H. Harris and wife Nancy and Sarah Pack to Isaac Cantrell and M. D. Smallman their interest in a tract of land in the 9th District. 19 Aug 1873. (P. 243)

John Fish and wife Matilda, G. W. Jones, Nancy Jones, William Fish, Caroline Fish, Edmun Fish, Nancy Fish, Sarah Fish, Caroline Fish to John C. Taylor 82 acres in the 9th District. 16 May 1873. (Pp. 244-245)

James A. Nesmith to T. N. Christian and G. G. Dillard a parcel of land on the west side of the Public Square in the town of Smithville. 21 Aug 1873. (Pp. 245-246)

T. N. Christian and wife Rebecca; G. G. Dillard and wife M. to Jesse T. Hollis a town lot in the town of Smithville adjoining John C. Cannady. 23 Aug 1873. (Pp. 246-247)

Jesse T. Hollis and wife H. B. to Amanda Davis the tract of land on which the said Jesse T. Hollis' law office now stands. 23 Aug 1873. (Pp. 247-248)

Joseph H. Blackburn and wife Eliza Jane to C. W. L. Hale 96 acres in the 2nd District. 25 Aug 1873. (P. 248)

Solomon Davis and wife Anny to G. W. Spencer 90 acres in the 12th District. 23 Aug 1873. (Pp. 249-250)

Sheriff to S. E. Tramell a tract of land. 1 Jul 1873. (Pp. 250-251)

Herbert C. Saddler and wife, Cynthia J., daughter of (Riley) League to Edmon R. League, William R. League, and Dabney M. League their interest in 200 acres in the 16th District. 28 Feb 1867. (Pp. 253)

Coleman Hellum and wife Mary B., daughter of Riley League, to Edmon R. League, William R. League, and Dabney M. League their interest in 200 acres in the 16th District. 18 Jan 1868. (Pp. 253-254)

Richard Tittsworth and wife Nancy to John P. Tittsworth 215 acres in the 5th District. 24 Aug 1873. (Pp. 254-256)

Peter Crips to Wiley Eastrage 26 acres in the 4th District. 29 Aug 1870. (P. 256)

Matilda Fish; John Fish and wife Matilda to John C. Taylor their interest in a tract of land. 27 Aug 1873. (Pp. 256-257)

Samuel M. Phillips by Dabney M. Phillips to Joshua D. Phillips a one sixth interest in a tract of land in the 9th District belonging to our father Martin Phillips. 30 Aug 1873. (Pp. 257-258)

John Hendrickson to J. W. George 52 acres in the 2nd District. 15 Aug 1873. (Pp. 258-259)

Thomas B. Potter and wife Samantha D. to P. T. Shores a tract of land in the 9th District. 1 Sep 1873. (Pp. 259-260)

C. T. Burton and wife S. B., daughter of Riley League and sister of D. M. League deceased; Coleman Hellum and wife Mary E. of the same relations to W. R. League and E. R. League their interest in 283 acres. 24 Sep 1872. (Pp. 260-261)

James W. Milton and wife Martha to James M. Pack a tract of land in the 9th District. 1 Sep 1873. (P. 262)

Moses A. Stark and wife, Sarah E., to Richardson Anderson 224 acres in the 3rd District. 2 Sep 1873. (P. 263)

John Fowler and wife Paralee to James H. Lyles 50 acres in the 9th District. 2 Sep 1873. (Pp. 263-264)

John Reavis to Sarah Reavis and Robert Johnson his interest in the old Tan Yard place in the 5th District in which my father, Thomas Reavis, died seized and possessed. 10 Oct 1857. (Pp. 264-265)

H. C. Sadler and wife, Cynthia, to W. R. League and E. R. League their interest in a tract of land owned by Riley League deceased. 15 Oct 1872. (Pp. 265-266)

Reuben C. Bomer and wife, J. P., to J. S. Dunlap Lot No. 69 in the town of Smithville. 18 Sep 1873. (P. 267)

Thomas L. Sewell and wife Phila Ann to W. N. Wilson a town lot in the town of Smithville. 22 Sep 1873. (Pp. 267-268)

Thomas N. Christian to Thomas B. Potter and the other trustees of the Christian Church at Smithville a lot along the edge of Lebanon & Sparta Road. 26 Sep 1873. (Pp. 268-269)

John H. Allen and wife, Eliza, to Thomas Givens 114 acres in the 3rd District. 25 Aug 1873. (Pp. 269-270)

John H. Allen and wife, Eliza, to Robert J. Givens a tract of land in the 3rd District. 25 Aug 1873. (Pp. 270-271)

James Allen and wife, Cinthia J., to John H. Allen 193 acres in the 2nd District. 23 Aug 1873. (Pp. 272-273)

Zenus Crips and wife Margaret Jane to John R. Corder 100 acres in the 15th District. 22 Aug 1868. (Pp. 273-274)

Riley McClure and wife Sarah Manda to John R. Corder 100 acres in the 15th District. 18 Aug 1873. (Pp. 274-275)

John R. Corder, Frances Corder, Jackson Corder, Mary Corder, Asa Corder, Mary Corder, James Robinson and wife Frances to John S. Close 100 acres in the 15th District. 9 Aug 1873. (Pp. 275-276)

William Truett and wife Tennessee to Marcus (Westing) 40

acres on Helton's Creek. 2 Jun 1873. (Pp. 277-278)

Martha Smith to T. C. Harper 20 acres in the 16th District. 21 Jan 1870. (Pp. 278-279)

Isaac Young and wife Elizabeth to William Pennegar 15 acres in the 7th District. 20 Sep 1873. (Pp. 279-280)

Sheriff to S. D. Blankenship 240 acres belonging to David M. Blankenship. 4 Oct 1873. (Pp. 280-281)

Samuel Braswell to his wife, Susan Braswell, 120 acres in the 9th District. 11 Oct 1873. (P. 282)

D. B. Winchester and wife Matilda to George W. Null and Sarah A. Winchester 68 acres in the 16th District. 14 Oct 1873. (P. 283)

William Blackburn to John T. Armstrong one acre in the town of Liberty. 9 Oct 1873. (Pp. 283-284)

Commissioners proceeded on the 14th, 15th, and 16th days of Jun 1838 to sell lots in the town of Smithville. The Commissioners sold the north half of Lot No. 87 and set apart the south half of said lot for a church lot to belong to the religious denomination that built first on said lot. The Methodist Episcopal Church South did first take possession of said lot. They built a house of public worship on said lot and a regular Board of Trustees for said church was kept up for about nineteen years. The Trustees to George W. Camron their interest in the south half of Lot No. 87. Bounded: east by Market Street. 18 Oct 1873. (Pp. 284-285)

William Barr and wife, Mary J. and Matilda McGinnis to William H. Pedigo 100 acres in the 9th District. 20 Oct 1873. (Pp. 285-286)

Crawford Rankhorn to his living children, to wit, Ellen M. Tippitt, Anne J. Robinson, Crawford M. Rankhorn, Jr., Cintha M. Rankhorn and also to his grandchildren who are the children of his son, G. B. Rankhorn deceased, to wit, Nancy F. Rankhorn, John H. Rankhorn, Martha G. Rankhorn, Ellen M. Rankhorn, and E. T. Rankhorn, also to Melinda M. Rankhorn, daughter of Miles Rankhorn deceased, 262 acres in the 6th District on which I now live. 9 Jun 1873. (Pp. 286-287)

A. D. Cantrell and wife Mary A. to William Marsh 90 acres in the 6th District. 1 Nov 1873. (Pp. 287-288)

John Reynolds and wife Mary to Adam Tittle 35 acres in the 4th District. 16 Aug 1873. (P. 288)

Preston Turner and wife Sarah E.; Harry Turner and wife Sarah C. to William Pennegar 28 acres on the Caney Fork in the 7th District. 15 Sep 1873. (Pp. 289-290)

James A. Nesmith and wife Elizabeth J. to Polly Wilson a title bond. 27 Oct 1873. (Pp. 290-291)

John A. Cantrell and wife Nancy to Isaac D. Cantrell 72 acres in the 7th District. 3 Dec 1872. (Pp. 291-292)

DEED BOOK L

Henry Adcock to Marshal E. Adcock 50 acres in the 7th District. 1 Nov 1873. (Pp. 292-294)

Reuben C. Bomer and wife, Pheba, to A. T. Phillips a title bond. 1 Nov 1873. (P. 294)

M. F. Doss and wife Martha E. to John C. Garrison a town lot in the town of Alexandria. 8 Nov 1873. (P. 295)

W. R. Parish and wife Seneth to Steven G. Hankins 125 acres in the 5th District. 21 Oct 1873. (Pp. 295-296)

William R. Parish and wife Seneth to John L. Byers five acres in the 5th District. 22 Mar 1873. (Pp. 296-297)

William Pennegar and wife Elizabeth to Levi Pennegar ten and one half acres in the 7th District. 6 Nov 1873. (P. 297)

James Hollinsworth to Elijah J. Britton two acres in the 2nd District. 25 Jun 1862. (P. 298)

County Court Clerk to Elijah Whaley a tract of land belonging to the heirs of Tilman Bethel deceased. John H. Bethel and others had filed suit against C. F. Bethel and others. 10 Nov 1873. (Pp. 298-299)

John Wilson to William H. Magness Lot No. 37 in the town of Smithville. 6 Nov 1873. (Pp. 299-300)

Harris A. Overall and wife, Caroline, to Robert J. Givens 57¼ acres on Clear Fork. 20 Oct 1873. (Pp. 300-301)

Harris Overall and wife, Caroline, to Ada Dennis 44 acres on Clear Fork on what is known as the Adams' Branch. 20 Oct 1873. (Pp. 301-302)

Mathias T. Pennegar and wife, Mary J., to William R. Durham 30 acres in the 7th District. 17 Nov 1873. (Pp. 302-303)

Mathias T. Pennegar and wife, Mary J., to Johne Pennegar ten acres in the 7th District. 12 Nov 1873. (Pp. 303-304)

County Court Clerk to John H. Nichols a tract of land belonging to Nicholas Parsley deceased. 19 Nov 1873. (Pp. 304-305)

County Court Clerk to Sarah J. Gosham 70 acres belonging to the estate of Green Cantrell who died intestate on 15 Jan 1869. (Pp. 306-307)

E. F. Reece to M. F. Doss a tract of land in the town of Alexandria. 13 Nov 1873. (P. 307)

James M. Allen and wife Elizabeth; A. T. Phillips and wife Emma to George W. Camron a tract of land. 26 Nov 1873. (Pp. 307-308)

James M. Allen and wife Elizabeth; Alexander T. Phillips and wife Emma to George Parker one acre in the 9th District. 15 Nov 1873. (Pp. 308-309)

Isiah White to Elizabeth White 33 acres on Dry Creek in Smith County. 16 Mar 1853. (P. 309)

DEED BOOK L

Robert Cantrell of Wilson County to John E. Warren two tracts of land in the 14th District on the Caney Fork. 2 Dec 1873. (Pp. 309-310)

N. M. Burnett and wife Candes Melissa to Hyram Cantrell a tract of land in the 9th District. 28 Feb 1871. (Pp. 310-311)

James H. Capshaw to Mary J. Capshaw Lot No. 68 in the town of Smithville. 21 Oct 1873. (Pp. 311-312)

Sheriff to Turney & Ward a tract of land in the 2nd District. 13 Dec 1873. (Pp. 312-313)

Nicholas Acuff and wife Rebecca to R. B. Ware 250 acres in the 5th District. 3 Oct 1873. (Pp. 313-314)

Chesley Turner and wife Darcus M. to Henry Turner a tract of land in the 7th District. 25 Dec 1873. (P. 314)

Chester Turner and wife Darcus M. to John C. Lu) 50 acres in the 7th District. 5 Dec 1873. (P. 315)

A. J. Hunt and D. W. Hunt; James R. Agee; Louisa Ricketts and Isaac Ricketts; M. L. Agee; Permelia M. Welch and J. M. Welch; Jonathan Colger; Frances M. Sandlin and S. R. Sandlin to Frances L. Foutch 82 acres in the 18th District. 21 Oct 1873. (Pp. 315-316)

John C. Cannady and wife Margret A. to James George 100 acres in the 4th District. 15 Dec 1873. (Pp. 316-317)

John C. Cannady and wife Margret A. to Mary A. Veach and James H. Veach a tract of land in the 7th District. 15 Dec 1873. (P. 317)

County Court Clerk to Sebaston Williams a tract of land belonging to William D. Adamson who died intestate about the year 1865. (P. 318)

Perry G. Magness, Sr. to the Common School Directors of the 5th District a lot on the right hand of the road leading from my dwelling house to the Short Mountain up Sink Creek. This land is to be used for school purposes and no other. If it should be used for other purposes, then this deed is void. 8 Dec 1873. (Pp. 318-319)

Blakely Allen to Jackson Allen, in consideration of a promise to support Blakely Allen, Hannah Allen, and Parlina Allen during their natural lives and provide for Artamesa and Amanda should they live single and subject themselves to his care, 90 acres in the 6th District. 20 Dec 1873. (Pp. 319-320)

Blakely Allen to his beloved son, William Allen, 100 acres in the 6th District. 20 Dec 1873. (Pp. 320-321)

Blakely Allen to his son, Hesekiah Allen, 50 acres in the 6th District. 9 Aug 1873. (Pp. 321-322)

Blakely Allen to his oldest son, Winslow Allen, a tract of land in the 6th District. 9 Aug 1873. (P. 322)

Blakely Allen to his beloved son, Amos Allen, 83 acres in

the 6th District. 9 Aug 1873. (Pp. 322-323)

John and Susan (Starne) to Calvin and Adeline King 55 acres in the 5th District. 1 Nov 1873. (Pp. 323-324)

James M. Baird to Thomas D. Fite 92½ acres in the 1st District. 15 Sep 1871. (Pp. 324-325)

W. H. Truett and wife Martha T. to A. J. E. Marler and wife Julia A. a tract of land in the 1st District. 13 Oct 1873. (Pp. 325-326)

Isaac D. Griffith and wife, Sallie D., to William G. Rawling a tract of land in the 1st District. 22 Nov 1873. (Pp. 326-327)

J. H. Dodd to W. D. Lovin a tract of land in the 7th District. 8 Oct 1870. (Pp. 327-328)

John H. Savage to A. D. Cantrell a title bond. 20 Dec 1873. (Pp. 328-329)

(Meful) Hendrix and wife, Lucy C., to Jesse B. Farler a tract of land in the 4th District. 9 Aug 1872. (P. 329)

Henry L. Puckett and wife, Anna J., to George H. Null 67 acres in the 16th District. 10 Nov 1873. (P. 330)

Mary M. Woods for love and affection to L. F. Woods Lot No. 5 in the town of Liberty. 27 Nov 1873. (P. 331)

F. M. Cantrell to Benjamin F. Hicks 60 acres. 20 Nov 1868. (Pp. 331-332)

William Johnson to James M. Driver 35 acres. 19 Jan 1874. (P. 332)

W. T. Robinson and wife L. J. to T. L. and W. R. Scutter 55 acres in the 17th District. 21 Jan 1873. (Pp. 332-333)

James T. Garner to Samuel Lankford 40 acres in the 16th District. 3 Jan 1874. (Pp. 333-334)

Byrd Douglass and Hugh Douglass of Davidson County to Preston Turner 60 acres. 2 Oct 1873. (Pp. 334-335)

Jesse T. Hollis to Robert Cantrell, J. J. Ford, and M. D. Smallman a lot in the town of Smithville just south of a lot now owned by the heirs of W. A. Dunlap. 23 Jan 1874. (P. 335)

Leonard Adcock to William R. Durham 135 acres in the 6th District. 15 Dec 1853. (P. 336)

Robert Cantrell and J. J. Ford to Jesse T. Hollis a lot in the town of Smithville known as the R. Cantrell old law office lot. 2 Feb 1874. (Pp. 336-337)

J. J. Ford to George McNelly about one and one half acres in the 1st District. 24 Nov 1873. (Pp. 337-338)

Mathew Wilson and wife, Polly, to George Smith a tract of land in the 9th District. 4 Feb 1874. (P. 338)

William Woldridge and wife Mary J. to W. D. Petty 50 acres

in the 9th District. 9 Feb 1874. (P. 339)

David Durham, Sr. and wife, Tirsey, to David Durham, Jr. one half interest in 300 acres in the 6th District known as the place formerly owned by William Adcock and the place where Captain David Adcock now lives. 10 Feb 1874. (Pp. 339-340)

Clerk & Master to Martin Foutch a tract of land belonging to George Beckwith. 2 Jan 1874. (Pp. 340-341)

Martin Foutch to B. M. Cantrell two town lots in the town of Smithville. 2 Jan 1874. (P. 341)

William C. Clark and wife Caroline T. to Allen Wilson and wife Elizabeth 65 acres in the 3rd District. 15 Feb 1874. (P. 342)

Isaac H. Hayse and wife Jebeline to David J. Taylor, Jr. 108 acres in the 10th District. 18 Feb 1874. (P. 343)

Hirum B. Smith and wife, Susan H., to R. C. Bone 365 acres in the 1st District. 12 Jan 1874. (Pp. 344-345)

W. W. Foster to Martha Foster 50 acres in the 9th District. 1 Nov 1873. (P. 345)

John C. Clark and wife, Mariah A., to William M. Pack their one sixth interest in 140 acres where William M. Pack and Bartamus Pack now live. 21 Feb 1874. (P. 346)

J. J. Ford to J. M. Baird one fourth of an acre in the 6th District. Bounded: the tan yard finishing shop. 10 Mar 1874. (P. 347)

E. C. Walker to William R. Durham 30 acres in the 6th District. 7 Nov 1865. (Pp. 347-348)

Samuel L. Walker to William R. Durham 25 acres in the 6th District. 22 May 1867. (p. 348-349)

Henry J. Yeargin and wife, Rachel, to L. M. Scott 52 acres, it being lot number three in the division of the lands belonging to the heirs of James Yeargin deceased. 13 Mar 1874. (Pp. 349-350)

J. L. Hollinsworth and wife, Mary, to James Allen a lot in the town of Liberty. 25 Sep 1873. (Pp. 350-351)

W. T. Hoskins and wife, Melissa J., to J. L. Ayers 50 acres in the 12th District. 25 Dec 1873. (Pp. 351-352)

William Wood and wife, Octavia, to P. L. Wood a lot in the town of Alexandria. 23 Feb 1874. (Pp. 352-353)

P. L. Wood and wife, Amanda, to William Wood part of the tract of land I now live on. 7 Mar 1874. (Pp. 353-354)

A. J. Allen to John Rawlings his fee simple interest in remainder to take effect after the youngest child of Julia Rawlings deceased arrives at the age of twenty-one years in 160 acres in the 1st District. 16 Mar 1874. (P. 354)

J. A. Fuson to John Reynolds a tract of land. 2 Jan 1873.

(p. 355)

G. W. Eastham and W. C. Eastham to James Willis 75 acres in the 14th District. 13 Aug 1873. (Pp. 355-356)

J. M. Allen and wife Elizabeth to the Aldermen of the town of Smithville a certain tract of land 253 yards long along the east side of our house. 28 Mar 1874. (P. 356)

Mary Chapman to William W. Wade my interest in 300 acres, my interest being about 90 acres or my dower of Sampson Chapman. 19 Mar 1874. (P. 357)

Sally Adcock, widow of Lafayette Adcock, to John P. Tittsworth my interest in the estate of my father, John Wilmuth. 28 Mar 1874. (Pp. 357-358)

T. L. Seawell and wife Pheby Ann to Mayor and Aldermen of Smithville a tract of land near the south west corner of the Corporation of Smithville. 9 Mar 1874. (P. 358)

Corporation officers of the town of Smithville to J. A. Nesmith a lot of land. 21 Feb 1874. (Pp. 358-359)

Robert Cantrell to Samuel Botts, colored, 50 acres in the 4th District. 16 Mar 1874. (P. 360)

Allen Wilson and wife, Elizabeth, to Moses H. Fite four acres in the 3rd District. 1 Apr 1874. (P. 360)

John L. Bass to J. E. Goodner and T. H. Goodner one half acre in the town of Alexandria. 30 Dec 1870. (Pp. 361-362)

J. M. Allen and wife Elizabeth; A. T. Phillips and wife Emma to M. E. Foster and wife A. L. one acre in the 9th District. 2 Apr 1874. (Pp. 362-363)

J. H. Griffith to Hinton A. Hill a title bond. 28 Dec 1874. (Pp. 363-364)

Thomas Goodner and wife Julia to J. E. Goodner a tract of land in the 1st District. 30 Mar 1874. (Pp. 364-365)

James H. Schurer and wife Mattie to Jesse T. Hollis a tract of land. 4 Apr 1874. (Pp. 365-366)

Jesse K. Cantrell and wife Elizabeth to A. J. Fuson 95 acres in the 9th District. 14 Apr 1874. (Pp. 366-367)

Isaac H. Hayse and wife Iblene to A. J. Fuson their interest in the lands of Jonathan Fuson. 31 Jan 1874. (Pp. 367-368)

Thomas C. Francis and wife Eliza to A. J. Fuson their interest in the lands of Jonathan Fuson. 21 Dec 1873. (Pp. 368-369)

H. T.Hoskins and wife M. J. to Thomas D. Bass, Jr. 474 acres in the 12th District. 16 Mar 1874. (Pp. 369-370)

Copy of decree of the Chancery Court. Emeline T. Lamberson versus Helen A. Lamberson. Ex Parte. 12 Sep 1868. (Pp. 370-371)

DEED BOOK L

James Goodner of Williamson County, Tennessee to James M. Baird of DeKalb County and James N. Cartwright of Williamson County a tract of land that Jacob Fite and James Goodner purchased from Daniel Coggin. 5 May 1874. (Pp. 371-372)

Mary Cantrell to William H. Magness 70 acres including the mansion house and buildings alloted to the said Mary, madam of Green Cantrell. 9 May 1874. (Pp. 372-373)

Isaac Tittsworth and wife Caroline to John P. Tittsworth 15 acres near John Tittsworth's barn. 6 May 1874. (P. 373)

Isaac Tittsworth and wife T. C. to Miles Tittsworth and wife Mary T. 34 acres in the 5th District. Apr 1874. (P. 374)

Miles Tittsworth and wife Mary to Isaac Tittsworth 30½ acres in the 5th District. Apr 1874. (P. 375)

John A. Robinson to Marcus C. (Rittenberry) 32½ acres in the 13th District. 10 Apr 1874. (P. 376)

David Griffith and wife Susannah W. to J. D. Griffith a tract of land in the 13th District. 9 Jan 1874. (Pp. 376-377)

James M. Baird, Assignee of E. W. Bass, to J. W. Hunt a tract of land. 25 Oct 1872. (P. 378)

D. A. Parker to William F. Dowell one acre in the 4th District. 1 Jun 1874. (Pp. 378-379).

James Goodner to William Eller 46 acres in the 1st District. 15 May 1874. (Pp. 379-380)

Giles Driver to Susan Davis, my daughter and wife of Louis Z. Davis, the place in the 9th District about three fourth's of a mile from and south of Smithville, it being the place where the said Davis now lives. 14 Jun 1869. (Pp. 380-381)

John W. Lamberson to Martha A. Whaley one acre in the 2nd District. 29 Aug 1873. (Pp. 381-382)

William Adamson to Lorenzo D. Jacobs 20 acres in the 4th District. 22 Aug 1870. (Pp. 382-383)

Alford Suthren to J. D. Tramel 50 acres in the 6th District. 12 Jun 1874. (P. 383)

James G. Terry and wife Martha to J. P. Terry 42 acres. 1 Oct 1873. (P. 384)

John M. Foster and wife Martha; Jesse Hale; T. C. Harper and wife Sarah; Mary Hale; James M. Hale; Elizabeth Baker; Jeremiah Hale; and J. K. Haile to Elizabeth S. Hale and Susan Hale their interest in the dower of Jane Hale, widow of Linton Hale. 12 Sep 1870. (Pp. 385-386)

James Hale to Christopher (Fountin) Owen 66 acres in the 3rd District. 18 Apr 1874. (Pp. 386-388)

Clark Sanders and wife Elizabeth to Robert A. Tramel a tract of land in the 5th District containing 54 acres. 29 May 1874. (Pp. 388-389)

Clark Sanders and wife, Elizabeth, to William E. Bain a tract of land in the 6th District. 29 May 1874. (Pp. 389-390)

Clark Sanders and wife, Elizabeth, to John Bain 70 acres in the 6th District. 31 May 1873. (Pp. 391-392)

Joshua J. Ford, Executor of John W. Clark, to Allen Wilson two acres in Districts 3 and 13. 4 Jul 1874. (P. 392)

John Ayers and wife, Della, to John Mason 21 acres in the 15th District. 7 Feb 1874. (Pp. 392-393)

John E. Robinson and wife, M. E., to Newton Reynolds three fourth's of an acre in the 15th District. 6 Jul 1874. (Pp. 393-394)

William W. Estes and wife, Elizabeth, to Thomas Grooms 20 acres in the 13th District. 14 Apr 1874. (P. 395)

William H. Luckey and wife, Martha M., to Thomas Grooms two acres in the town of Alexandria. 1 Jun 1874. (P. 396)

David Kelly for love and affection for the Primitive Order of the Baptist of the Round Lick Association to the Primitive Order of Baptist for church and school purposes and for no other a tract of land in the 12th District. 24 Apr 1874. (Pp. 396-397)

David M. Hays and wife, Elizabeth, to Mariah L. Hays 280 acres in the 14th District. 27 Jul 1874. (Pp. 397-398)

John P. Tittsworth and wife, Elizabeth, to Vinson Bailey a tract of land on Pine Creek in the 7th District. 28 Jul 1874. (Pp. 398-400)

Thomas E. Neal and wife, Elizabeth M., to E. H. Butterbaugh eight acres on Fall Creek in the 9th District. 1 Aug 1874. (Pp. 400-401)

Newton Reynolds and wife, Mary, to J. F. Turner a tract of land in the 15th District. 15 Jul 1874. (Pp. 401-402)

Charles Duay and wife, Rilla, of Marshall County, Tn. to Jesse Farler their interest in 150 acres in the 4th District, it being the same tract of land willed by Matthew Hunt to Judah Hunt. 30 Mar 1874. (Pp. 402-403)

Susannah Brim and Matilda Brim, heirs of Thomas Brim, to William R. Durham the home place on which Thomas Brim lived and containing 48½ acres. 28 Oct 1873. (P. 403)

William R. Durham and wife, Nancy, to M. J. Pennager 90 acres in the 4th District. 23 Jun 1874. (P. 404)

William E. Ferrell to Algina Hildreth 70 acres. 2 Feb 1870. (Pp. 404-405)

T. C. Allen and wife, Roda W.; A. B. Cheatam and wife, J. E.; and Elizabeth Grace to A. E. Ferrell their interest in 80 acres in the 10th District. 7 Aug 1874. (Pp. 405-406)

DEED BOOK L

John L. Bond and wife, Nancy, to A. J. Lockhart and John Lockhart 70 acres in the 9th District. 4 Mar 1873. (Pp. 407-408)

J. J. Ford to William J. Clouse 100 acres in the 7th District. 4 Aug 1874. (P. 408)

J. J. Ford to J. W. Fowler 50 acres in the 9th District. 1 Jul 1874. (P. 409)

James S. Dunlap and wife, Emma, to William G. Foster a town lot in the town of Smithville, it being Lot No. 69. 12 Sep 1873. (Pp. 409-410)

G. P. M. Williams to S. A. Williams and E. F. Williams 12 acres in the 2nd District. 9 Jul 1874. (P. 410)

Richard Tittsworth to R. M. Tittsworth a tract of land in the 5th District. 31 Jan 1874. (P. 411)

H. B. Douglass to William Pennegar 90 acres in the 7th District. 6 Mar 1874. (Pp. 411-412)

J. L. Colvert, Mayor, and the Aldermen of Smithville to G. W. Camron a lot in the town of Smithville. Bounded: Masonic Hall and Widow Nuld's lots. 13 Apr 1874. (Pp. 412-413)

John B. Robinson, Clerk & Master, to Thomas B. Potter a tract of land belonging to the heirs of William Hale. 10 Jun 1874. (Pp. 413-414)

R. B. Ware to J. W. Britton and E. R. Northcutt 250 acres in the 5th District. 16 Dec 1874. (P. 415)

John A. Cantrell and wife Nancy to Thomas Griffith 125 acres in the 5th District. 10 May 1873. (P. 416)

John K. Gorham and wife Sarah J. to Joseph Cantrell 70 acres in the 5th District. 22 Nov 1873. (Pp. 416-417)

Clerk & Master to Andrew Allen 50 acres in the 10th District. 12 Aug 1874. (Pp. 417-418)

James M. Hale to Mary H. Hale his interest in a tract of land purchased by my father, William M. Hale, from Spencer Bing. My part is one fifth. 30 Oct 1866. (Pp. 418-419)

Burta Hendrickson, Jane Hendrickson, William C. Hendrickson, Samantha Hendrickson, Wiley Hendrickson, Margret Hendrickson, F. M. Hendrickson, M. A. Hendrickson, Jery Smith, Matilda Smith, Nathaniel Hendrickson, M. E. Fuston, and Thomas Fuston, heirs of James Hendrickson, to James Debenport their interest in 18 acres in the 10th District. 13 Mar 1874. (Pp. 419-420)

John T. Johnson and wife, Elizabeth, to Daniel Gann a tract of land in the 4th District. 19 Aug 1874. (Pp. 420-421)

Peter Connor to J. L. Crips 75 acres in the 4th District. 21 Aug 1874. (P. 421)

William Measles and wife Nancy, formerly Nancy Truett; James Truett; Wingate Truett; William Truett; John Truett;

William Adamson and wife Partheny; Henry Smith and wife Tennessee to Thomas Grooms their interest in 129 acres in the 3rd District, it being land in which Elijah Truett died seized and possessed. 14 Apr 1874. (Pp. 422-423)

The heirs of L. B. Vick, to wit, Frances Jane Vick, William P. Vick, William Vick, Robert Yeargin and wife Celinda, Sampson Yeargin and wife Rebecca, John J. Evins and wife Lucindy, Jonathan Griffith and wife Jane, and Augustine M. Vick, a minor, to J. H. Griffith the tract of land in the 2nd District that L. B. Vick died seized and possessed. Eli Vick is the administrator of both L. B. Vick and Rhoda Vick. 30 Sep 1873. (Pp. 423-425)

A. H. Robinson and wife, Rebecca, to W. A. Parker 55 acres in the 4th District. 22 Mar 1874. (Pp. 425-426)

N. M. Hays and wife, Mira, to John E. Atnip 25 acres on Holmes Creek in the 9th District. 3 Aug 1874. (Pp. 426-427)

Paris Driver and wife, Matilda to J. D. Givins a tract of land on Pine Creek in the 5th District. 21 Aug 1874. (Pp. 427-428)

R. C. Bone and wife, Anna F., to Hiram B. Smith 309 acres in the 1st District. 26 Aug 1874. (Pp. 428-429)

James Murphy and wife, Candice, to James Young their interest in the Judith Hunt tract of land in the 4th District. 22 Aug 1874. (Pp. 429-430)

Isiah Bain died intestate some time before 1867. J. H. Roberts, Administrator, to Rawling Gootson a tract of land belonging to the said Isiah Bain. The dower was laid off the widow, Anna Bain. 28 Aug 1874. (Pp. 430-431)

Paris Driver and wife, Matilda, to James L. Colvert and George H. Colvert 90 acres in the 9th District. 9 Aug 1874. (Pp. 431-432)

A. B. Hicks to W. C. Yeargin a tract of land in the 13th District. 4 Nov 1873. (Pp. 432-433)

Samuel H. Bratten to John S. Harrison a tract of land on Holmes Creek in the 9th District. 28 Jun 1869. (Pp. 433-434)

Enoch Jones to John Stoner a tract of land in the 5th District. 20 Mar 1869. (P. 434)

James Redman and wife, Esther, to Aaron Cantrell 75 acres in the 9th District. 29 Aug 1874. (P. 435)

John P. Tittsworth and wife, Elizabeth, to the school directors of the 5th District a tract of land made to us by Richard Tittsworth in 1873 which was given for school purposes and for no other purpose. 4 Aug 1874. (Pp. 435-436)

Richard W. McGinnis and wife, Mary, to Gipson R. McGinnis a tract of land in the 10th District. 3 Sep 1874. (P. 437)

Eli Vick to M. A. Walker a tract of land sold for tax

purposes. Said Vick is the tax collector. 4 Sep 1874. (P. 438)

Darcus Cantrell to William H. Magness 70 acres in the 5th District. 4 Sep 1874. (Pp. 438-439)

James Cantrell died intestate prior to the May Term of the County Court 1870. Martha Cantrell and others filed suit for the sale of land. John C. Cannady, Administrator, to Jesse T. Hollis and B. M. Cantrell a tract of land in the 9th District. 28 Aug 1874. (Pp. 439-440)

John H. Savage to John C. Cannady a tract of land. (See Book C, page 30). 5 Sep 1874. (P. 441)

James K. Fisher to George Blankenship 50 acres on the Caney Fork. 1 Jul 1873. (Pp. 441-442)

John Blare and wife, Susan Caroline, to John Garrison and John C. Garrison 78 acres in the 1st District. 13 Mar 1872. (Pp. 443-444)

Charles Ferrell and wife, Mary, to G. W. Purser 50 acres in the 9th District. 8 Sep 1874. (Pp. 445-446)

W. T. Blackburn and wife, Mary E., to Barzel Taylor 50 acres in the 4th District. 18 Sep 1874. (Pp. 446-447)

H. B. Smith and wife, Susan H. Bridges, to W. Bridges a tract of land in the 1st District. 4 Sep 1874. (Pp. 448-449)

James Turner died on 29 Jul 1869 intestate. The heirs of the said James Turner, to wit, Susie A. Paschal, Harriet Paschal, John M. Paschal whose mother was a sister of the deceased; James Turner, Amanda Sykes, Candace P. Evans, Harriet Caroline Terry, J. F. Turner, and W. A. Turner whose father was a brother of the deceased; James Turner, William Turner, and Edward Turner, and Peter M. Turner who were brothers of the deceased, and Hulda B. Hollis, a sister of the deceased, and Taliferro Turner, also a brother to E. and P. M. Turner a tract of land. 19 Dec 1874. (Pp. 449-453)

John Bethel Taylor and wife, Martha, to John C. Taylor their interest in Anna Taylor's dowery containing about 120 acres and located in the 10th District. 29 Sep 1874. (Pp. 453-455)

Sheriff to Fite Anderson a tract of land. 6 Jul 1874. (Pp. 456-457)

W. H. Magness and wife, E. J., to B. A. Cantrell and wife Darcus the remainder dower interest of Mary Cantrell. 12 Oct 1874. (Pp. 457-458)

Benjamin Cantrell and wife, Darcus, to William H. Magness nine eleventh's interest in a tract of land belonging to Mary Cantrell. Other heirs: B. A. Cantrell, P. H. Cantrell, T. J. Cantrell, Robert Cantrell, Leonard Cantrell, John Cantrell, W. L. Cantrell, Louis K. Cantrell and wife Mary E., John Gorham and wife Sarah J. 12 Oct 1874. (Pp. 459-460)

W. G. Foster and wife, Juda Foster the Gay Tract in the

2nd District. 15 Oct 1874. (Pp. 460-461)

A. L. Foster and wife Mary E., and E. T. Foster to W. H. Tyree two acres in the 9th District. 19 Oct 1874. (Pp. 461-462)

James C. Brien and wife, Nancy, to T. N. Christian 50 acres in the 9th District. 28 Oct 1874. (Pp. 462-463)

Leonard Lamberson to William Thompson one acre in the 2nd District. 2 Nov 1874. (Pp. 463-464)

M. A. Starke and wife, Sarah E., to L. J. Bratton a tract of land in the 3rd District. 24 Oct 1874. (Pp. 464-465)

A. L. Foster and wife, Mary E., to E. T. Foster two acres. 19 Oct 1874. (Pp. 466-467)

Miles Tittsworth and wife, Mary, to Russell Spurlock and wife 34 acres in the 5th District. 15 Oct 1874. (Pp. 467-468)

Leander Jackson to Hinton A. Hill my interest in part of the land belonging to Nancy Foutch and was sold from her for her lifetime and taken away from her, the same being willed to her and her legal heirs by my father in North Carolina and brought to Tennessee, Smith County. 28 Jan 1856. (Pp. 469-470)

Thomas Oakley filed suit in Chancery Court against Sophronia Hall and others for the sale of one third of a tract of land belonging to the heirs of Margarett Simpson and Sophronia Hall deceased. Clerk & Master to H. Oakley the tract of land. Other heirs: Sophronia C. Hall, William Hall, Martha Hall, Laura Simpson, Luella Simpson, and Ralph Simpson. 4 Nov 1874. (P. 471)

Leonard Moore to Malissa Alexander, Samuel H. Alexander, Anson F. Alexander, Margaret E. Alexander, James M. Alexander, Ester A. Alexander, William B. Alexander 50 acres in the 9th District. 5 Dec 1870. (Pp. 472-473)

Thomas Fuson and wife, Elizabeth, to A. J. Fuson their interest in the land of J. Fuson in the 9th District. 31 Oct 1874. (Pp. 473-474)

Alexander L. Walker to Thomas W. Jones the Alexander Walker, Sr. land in the 6th District. 10 Mar 1874. (P. 475)

Julene Walker, wife of Alexander L. Walker, appeared privately and apart from her husband to acknowledge the above written deed. 9 Nov 1874. (P. 476)

John M. Love to Love's heirs, James Love's heirs, William Love, Rebecca Turner, Marian Love, Rachel Love, and Sally Cantrell a title bond. 1 Oct 1874. (Pp. 476-477)

J. J. Ford to Harriet W. Howard a town lot in the town of Alexandria. 6 Oct 1874. (Pp. 477-478)

William B. Arler and wife, Elizabeth to Stephen Sellars 31 acres in the 4th District. 9 Aug 1873. (Pp. 478-479)

G. R. West Et Als to John T. Bass a tract of land in the 11th District. 6 Jan 1873. (Pp. 479-480)

Jackson West and Adaline West, his wife, to Amandy Hudson for the consideration of her undivided interest in the Anna West tract of land on the Caney Fork 204 acres. 15 Dec 1873. (Pp. 480-482)

J. D. Wheeler to Thornton Saunders two acres in the 1st District. 5 Nov 1874. (Pp. 482-483)

John T. Stokes and wife, Perlina, to Nancy J. Stokes 60 acres in the 15th District. 14 Mar 1874. (Pp. 483-484)

John Robinson and wife, Eliza, to William Avant and the other trustees two acres in the 15th District for the building of a place of worship for the Southern Methodist Episcopal Church. 2 Aug 1873. (Pp. 484-486)

Jesse Frazier to his mother, Charity Frazier, his interest in the north half of a 15 acre tract in the 9th District. 6 May 1874. (Pp. 486-488)

William Alexander and wife Nancy; William Ervin and wife Malissa Paralee; Joseph Pack and wife Anna; Johnson Pack and wife Matilda to Jonathan Hall their interest, amounting to two third's interest, in 100 acres in the 9th District. 9 Sep 1873. (Pp. 488-489)

Edward Hudson and wife Amanda to Jackson West their interest, it being one fifth, in the land of Anna West deceased. 15 Dec 1873. (Pp. 490-492)

James Page and wife, Mary, to their beloved son, Thomas J. Page, a tract of land in the 10th District. 14 Nov 1874. (Pp. 492-493)

James Page and wife, Mary, to their beloved son, James M. Page, 85 acres in the 10th District. 14 Nov 1874. (Pp. 493-495)

James Page and wife, Mary, to their beloved son, Rowland L. Page, minor, 86 acres in the 10th District. 14 Nov 1874. (Pp. 495-496)

James Page and wife, Mary, to their beloved son, Barney R. Page, 85 acres in the 10th District. 14 Nov 1874. (Pp. 496-497)

James Page and wife, Mary, to their beloved son, Richard Page, minor, 85 acres in the 10th District. 14 Nov 1874. (Pp. 498-499)

A. L. Foster and wife, Mary E., to W. G. Foster 700 acres in Cumberland County. 21 Nov 1874. (Pp. 499-501)

Yancy Malone and wife, Dora Ann, to Dobson Yeargin a tract of land in the 17th District. 17 Mar 1871. (Pp. 501-502)

Thomas Yeargin to C. H. Yeargin his interest in a tract of land in the 17th District. 28 Jul 1874. (Pp. 502-503)

DEED BOOK L

C. H. Yeargin and wife, Sarah, to George W. Gregston a tract of land in the 17th District. 16 Nov 1874. (Pp. 503-504)

Abraham Cantrell and wife, Rebecca, to William A. Nesmith 65 acres in the 9th District. 11 Nov 1874. (Pp. 505-506)

John A. Foutch to W. E. Foutch his interest in the estate of his father William Foutch. 2 Dec 1874. (P. 507)

W. B. Stokes and wife, Paralee A., to W. T. Robinson Et Als 707½ acres in the 12th District. 15 Dec 1874. (Pp. 507-509)

J. H. McHaffy and wife, Margaret E., to W. M. Pack 140 acres in the 9th District. 22 Aug 1874. (Pp. 510-511)

Green Cantrell died intestate on 15 Jan 1869. Mary Cantrell was appointed Administrator. It was agreed by the parties involved that the personal property was sufficient to pay off all the debts. It appears to the County Court that Isaac Cantrell and the mother of Missouri Potter had been advanced in lands in the life time of Green Cantrell and his widow, Mary Cantrell, had waived her dower in said land. The Court ordered that the land be partitioned between the widow and several heirs. Heirs: Isaac Cantrell, Missouri Potter, Thomas J. Cantrell, Thomas C. Cantrell, Wiley Cantrell. 26 Dec 1874. (Pp. 511-513)

Joseph Cantrell and wife, Quelin, to L. C. and E. W. Cantrell 45 acres in the 5th District. 26 Dec 1874. (Pp. 513-514)

J. H. Baird and wife, Amanda R., to Thomas B. Brown a town lot in the town of Alexandria. 15 May 1874. (Pp. 514-515)

Elijah Yeargin to Thomas B. Brown a house and lot in the town of Alexandria. 7 Feb 1872. (Pp. 515-516)

William H. Luckey and wife Martha M.; Henry Schurer and wife Martha to Thomas B. Brown a house and lot in the town of Alexandria. 21 Apr 1872. (Pp. 517-518)

Henry D. McDonald to Thomas B. Brown a town lot in the 1st District. 10 Oct 1870. (Pp. 518-520)

J. J. Bennett to Elizabeth Dunlap a town lot and house in the town of Smithville. Bounded: Caroline Wade lot where W. W. Wade now lives. Dec 1874. (Pp. 520-521)

Elizabeth White and Caroline White to John Willoby 33¼ acres in the 11th District. 3 Dec 1874. (Pp. 521-522)

Mary Corder to J. S. Close her interest in the old Asa Corder land in the 15th District. 18 Nov 1874. (Pp. 522-523)

Thomas C. Cantrell and wife, Louisa B., to Samuel C. Duncan and wife, Sarah P., 45 acres in the 5th District. 28 Dec 1874. (Pp. 523-524)

Priscilla Pack to Thomas Pack 17 acres. 26 May 1874. (Pp. 524-525)

DEED BOOK L

T. W. Shields to Priscilla Pack 26 acres in the 9th District. 8 Jan 1875. (P. 526)

L. W. Goodner and wife Angilla; J. E. Goodner and wife E. J. to T. W. Eason a lot on the corner of Main and Church Streets in the town of Alexandria. 11 Sep 1874. (Pp. 526-528)

William Eller to J. M. Baird 46 to 50 acres in the 1st District. 25 May 1874. (Pp. 528-529)

O. M. Turner to Edward Turner his one half interest in a house and lot in the town of Alexandria. 7 Dec 1874. (Pp. 529-530)

Edward Turner to P. M. Turner a tract of land in the 1st District. 14 Dec 1874. (P. 531)

J. M. Baird and wife, Amanda R., to P. M. and E. Turner 50 acres in the 1st District. 26 Oct 1874. (Pp. 532-533)

J. H. Schurer and wife, Mattie, to B. F. Bell three fourth's of an acre in the 1st District. 14 Dec 1874. (Pp. 533-534)

James W. Hicks to J. W. Anderson a tract of land in the 13th District. 10 Sep 1872. (Pp. 534-535)

T. N. Christian and wife, Rebecca J., to Moses Pack 50 acres. 13 Jan 1875. (P. 536)

Luetta Scott to Jesse W. Scott her power of attorney to receive any money coming to her from the estate of her grandfather, Benjamin Burnett. 14 Oct 1874. Said Luetta is a resident of St. Frances, Missouri. (P. 537)

Daniel P. Searcy and wife, M. L., to John W. Hunt a town lot in the town of Liberty. 21 Oct 1874. (Pp. 537-539)

James Baker, trustee of William H. Baker, to George W. McCarty his interest in 50 acres in the 9th District. 1 Feb 1875. (P. 539)

G. W. McCarty and wife, Mary, to W. W. Foster a tract of land in the 3rd District. 1 Feb 1875. (P. 540)

John L. Starks and wife, Perlina, to the trustees of the Methodist Church a tract of land in the 15th District. 1 Oct 1873. (Pp. 541-542)

Clerk & Master Robinson to Mary A. C. Harvey and S. M. Harvey a tract of land belonging to George Beckwith. 9 May 1868. (Pp. 543-544)

P. P. Johnson and wife, Lucinda, to A. B. Cheatham 100 acres in the 9th District. 23 Feb 1875. (Pp. 544-545)

John Bridges and wife Sally to Samuel Allison their interest in the personal estate of Thomas Bridges deceased. 23 Oct 1868. (Pp. 545-546)

F. B. Nolner to Peter Starnes 124 acres in the 16th District. 23 Sep 1873. (Pp. 546-547)

DEED BOOK L

L. F. Woodside and wife, Harriet, to J. G. Squires Lot No. 5 in the town of Liberty. 26 Nov 1873. (Pp. 548-549)

J. G. Squires to W. P. Smith Lot No. 5 in the town of Liberty. 3 Dec 1874. (Pp. 549-550)

J. H. Lamberson to Liberty Academy in the 2nd District six poles. 20 Feb 1875. (Pp. 550-551)

H. A. Overall to Jordan W. Goggin 63 acres in the 3rd District. 1 Jan 1875. (Pp. 551-552)

Jordan W. Goggin to J. H. Lamberson ten poles in the 2nd District for DeKalb Lodge No. 398. 20 Feb 1875. (Pp. 552-553)

William Durham and wife, Nancy, to David Durham, Jr. 100 acres in the 6th District. 18 Sep 1874. (Pp. 553-554)

Amos Griffith died testate about Dec 1863. William T. Griffith was appointed Administrator. Said Administrator and others filed suit to sell a tract of land. County Court Clerk to J. J. Griffith Et Als 67 acres. 1 Mar 1875. (Pp. 554-555)

David Kelley to E. M. Jacobs ten acres on Dry Creek. 29 Apr 1874. (Pp. 556-557)

Sanford Mann and wife Matilda to C. W. L. Hale three acres in the 2nd District. 26 Feb 1875. (Pp. 557-558)

Martha Elizabeth Cantrell to Nancy M. Vanhooser and Barba S. Vanhooser a tract of land in the 5th District. 16 Mar 1875. (Pp. 558-559)

Sampson Chapman died intestate in the month of Jun 1870. William Keeth was appointed administrator. County Court Clerk to James T. Claburn a tract of land. 3 Mar 1875. (Pp. 559-560)

W. H. Whaley died intestate in the month of Dec 1872. W. G. Carnes was appointed Administrator. County Court Clerk to Walter Eason a lot in the town of Liberty. 17 Mar 1875. (Pp. 560-561)

J. D. Rowland, A. J. Harlon, Julia A. Harlon, W. G. Rowland have title to 40 acres in the 1st District. 14 Aug 1873. (Pp. 562-563)

Amos Griffith died testate some time about the year 1863. Thomas Griffith was appointed Administrator. County Court Clerk to A. J. Caplinger 68 acres. 1 Mar 1875. (Pp. 563-565)

STATE OF TENNESSEE Grant No. 12677 to Atwell and White 14 acres. 15 Dec 1869. (Pp. 565-566)

The death of Thomas R. Whaley was suggested. M. D. Smallman was appointed Administrator. County Court Clerk to James Beckwith a tract of land. 5 Apr 1875. (Pp. 566-568)

William H. Magness and wife, E. J., to T. M. Hooper a lot in the town of Smithville on the north side of the Public Square. 27 Mar 1875. (Pp. 568-569)

J. S. Harrison to R. B. West the western half of two lots, numbers 62 and 63, in the town of Smithville. Bounded: on the alley where South Street crosses the alley. 15 Apr 1875. (Pp. 569-570)

Harbard Smith and wife, Sarah, of Gonzales County, Texas to John B. Robinson their interest in the Alexander Robinson land in the 4th District. Their interest is one seventh. 24 Oct 1874. (Pp. 570-571)

Elisha Monroe and wife Kitty, to George H. Walton eight acres in the 10th District, it being an island in the Caney Fork River. 15 Mar 1875. (P. 572)

William Horace Hays and wife, Rutha, to Rufus Johnson 39¼ acres in the 1st District. 3 Sep 1873. (Pp. 573-574)

Rufus Johnson and wife, Rachel, to James A. Walker 21 acres in the 1st District. 1 Aug 1874. (Pp. 574-474)

Rufus Johnson and wife, Rachel, to J. H. Schurer 45 acres in the 1st District. 9 Dec 1874. (Pp. 575-577)

J. J. Pitts and wife, Estilene H., to John F. Luckey a lot in the town of Alexandria. 19 Apr 1875. (Pp. 577-578)

G. F. Dunlap to Harriet A. Dunlap about one half acre in the town of Smithville. 27 Apr 1875. (Pp. 578-579)

Thomas Fisher and wife, M. J., to Harriet C. Terry 63 acres in the 16th District. 20 Apr 1875. (Pp. 579-580)

Leroy Fuston and wife, Lucinda, to George Hathaway three acres in the 4th District. 16 Sep 1874. (Pp. 581-582)

W. C. Tippitt and wife, Elen, to Levi Haney and Ellen Haney eight acres in the 6th District. 17 Oct 1873. (Pp. 582-583)

Clerk & Master to L. J. Magness a tract of land belonging to James M. Allen. 26 Apr 1875. (Pp. 583-585)

W. W. Sellars and wife, Sarah E. A., to James T. Kelton, trustee of his wife, Mollie W. Kelton, of Warren County a tract of land in the 6th and 7th Districts. 26 Apr 1875. (Pp. 585-588)

R. C. Bone to W. B. Bridges 33 acres on the west side of the Statesville Road. 29 Apr 1875. (Pp. 588-590)

Robert Smith for love and affection to his daughter, Helen Merritt, 100 acres in DeKalb and Putnam Counties. Bounded: beginning on a beech standing in Robert Smith's north boundary line in the head of the graveyard. 10 Aug 1871. (Pp. 590-591)

M. T. Martin died testate in the year 1862 or 1863. Samuel L. Tyree was appointed Administrator. County Court Clerk to L. J. Magness a tract of land belonging to the estate. 20 May 1875. (Pp. 591-592)

Thomas & Robinson, lawyers, to Dexter A. Hawkins a tract of land. 19 Apr 187?. (Pp. 593-596)

DEED BOOK L

J. H. Dodd and wife, M. E. to James W. Dodd 150 acres in the 6th District. 2 Dec 1872. (Pp. 596-598)

John M. Foster and wife, Martha, to W. M. Hale 74¼ acres in the 16th District. 3 May 1875. (Pp. 598-599)

G. W. Purser and wife, Mary, to J. H. Bains about 40 acres in the 9th District. 2 Jan 1875. (Pp. 499-600)

Elenor Smellage to F. H. Smith and J. F. Stacy 43 acres in the 16th District. 24 Nov 1875. (P. 601)

Reuben Plunkett and wife, Nancy A., to Felix H. Smith 75 acres on Wolf Creek in the 16th District. 20 Jun 1874. (Pp. 602-603)

John F. Stacy and wife, Nancy, heirs at law of Martha B. Smith, to Felix H. Smith their interest in a tract of land on Wolf Creek in the 16th District belonging to the said Martha B. Smith. 15 Jan 1874. (Pp. 603-604)

William H. Whaley died intestate in 1872. W. D. Carnes was appointed Administrator. County Court Clerk to George Childress and Tennessee Childress a tract of land. 16 Jun 1875. (Pp. 605-606)

Abraham Cantrell and wife, Rebecca, to H. C. Eastham 26 acres in the 9th District. 17 Jun 1875. (Pp. 606-607)

D. P. Searcy and wife, M. L. to John B. Robinson their one seventh interest in a tract of land in the 4th District on which Alexander Robinson died seized and possessed. 8 Jun 1875. (Pp. 608-609)

David B. Worley and wife, Mary E., to John B. Atwell a tract of land in the 9th District adjoining the town of Smithville. 19 Jun 1875. (Pp. 609-610)

J. H. Dodd and wife, M. E., to Amy Smith 50 acres on Fall Creek in the 9th District. 21 Jun 1875. (Pp. 610-611)

Thomas Mason died intestate on 14 Oct 1864. John Linder was appointed Administrator. County Court Clerk to H. L. and H. T. Judkins 19 acres in the 7th District. 2 Jul 1875. (Pp. 611-613)

Frederick Starnes and Bennet Braswell to the trustees of the Methodist Church one and one half acres in the 16th District on Long Branch. 2 Sep 1868. (Pp. 613-614)

Nathaniel Wilson and wife, Mary, to E. J. Evans a lot in the 9th District. 2 Jul 1875. (Pp. 614-615)

Thomas L. Seawels to his wife, Phila Ann, and children, now living or which hereafter may be born, five acres in the 9th District. 10 Jul 1875. (Pp. 616-617)

J. H. Delong (also appears as W. J. Delong) to J) Delong his interest in a tract of land belonging to the estate of James Delong, it being one fourth of a 250 tract acre. 12 Nov 1873. (Pp. 617-618)

George W. Walker and wife, R. L., to Robert D. Walker and wife, Adeline, their one eighth interest in the personal property known in a deed of gift made by Samuel L. Walker deceased to Gilley Walker, George Walker, Robert D. Walker, and Mary E. L. D. Walker. 13 Feb 1875. (Pp. 618-619)

Nancy E. Turney, daughter of Joseph Turney and Mary, to George Turney her interest in the dowery of Mary Turney, widow of Joseph Turney. 18 Nov 1871. (P. 620)

County Court Clerk to Barnes & Christian a tract of land for tax purposes. 21 Jul 1875. (Pp. 621-622)

J. H. Dodd to Amy Smith 50 acres in the 9th District. 2 Oct 1871. (Pp. 622-623)

Hardy Johnson to Robert Johnson 100 acres in the 4th District. 10 Feb 1868. (Pp. 623-624)

John D. Rigsby and wife, Ann, to B. M. Cantrell a tract of land in the 9th District. 31 Jul 1875. (Pp. 624-625)

Thornton Sanders and wife, Manda, to George Rollings 43 poles in the 1st District. 1 Mar 1875. (Pp. 625-626)

O. B. Wright to G. L. Bowers 23 acres in the 1st District. 22 Mar 1875. (P. 627)

Thornton Sanders and wife, Manda, to Martha Baker a lot in the 1st District. 1 Aug 1875. (Pp. 627-628)

C. A. Cantrell and wife, Jane, to Mary J. Youngblood a tract of land in the 9th District. 2 Aug 1875. (Pp. 629-630)

John Jones, Executor of ?. B. Foutch and Mary Foutch to William E. Foutch 53 acres. Others named in the petition to sell the land were Monroe Foutch, Thomas H. Foutch, Elizabeth Foutch, M. L. Foutch, Adalade Foutch, and William B. Foutch. 8 Sep 1871. (Pp. 630-631)

Wiley R. Wood and wife, M. V., to J. L. Colvert 97 acres in the 9th District. 11 Aug 1875. (P. 632)

J. L. Colvert and wife Martha M. to William H. Magness a tract of land in the 9th District. 17 Aug 1875. (P. 633)

W. T. Robinson and wife, Lucy J., to Mary A. Farmer two acres in the 4th District. 2 Oct 1875. (P. 634)

J. L. Parsley and wife S. J.; Francis M. Hendrickson and wife Mary A. to J. J. Millican a tract of land in the 10th District belonging to Jeremiah C. Mullican deceased. 18 Aug 1875. (Pp. 635-636)

James Cantrell died intestate prior to the May Term of County Court 1870. John C. Cannady was appointed Administrator. County Court Clerk to J. T. Hollis and B. M. Cantrell 250 acres belonging to the estate. 29 Aug 1874. (Pp. 636-637)

W. J. Givins to William Turner a tract of land on Helton's Creek in the 1st District. 24 Jul 1875. (Pp. 637-638)

R. C. Bone and wife, Anna F., to James P. Doss 16¼ acres in the 1st District. 10 Apr 1875. (Pp. 638-639)

Jane Richardson to Harriet Tubb 50 acres in the 9th District. 11 Oct 1873. (Pp. 639-640)

M. C. Rowland to A. J. C. Marler and W. T. Rowland a tract of land that the said M. C. received by deed from Eli Rowland. 22 Mar 1875. (Pp. 640-641)

J. D. Rowland to A. J. C. Marler his interest in a tract of land that the said J. D. received from Eli Rowland. 11 Oct 1873. (Pp. 641-642)

John R. Lyles and wife, Mary, to J. M. Bailiff a tract of land on Dry Creek in the 4th District. 1 Sep 1875. (Pp. 643-644)

Moses Pack and wife, N. A., to John R. Lyles 50 acres. 21 Aug 1875. (Pp. 644-645)

T. L. Shields to L. R. Lawson 53 acres in the 9th District. 2 Sep 1875. (Pp. 645-646)

S. D. Blankenship and wife, M. E., to E. Warren 185 acres in the 9th District. 13 Sep 1875. (Pp. 646-647)

Nancy M. and Barbra S. Vanhooser of Warren County wish to restore a land trade which was made by themselves and Martha Elizabeth Cantrell. Said land is located in DeKalb County on Pine Creek. 17 Mar 1875. (Pp. 647-648)

Thomas Sneed, Sr. to W. G. Crawley a title bond. 5 Feb 1874. (Pp. 648-649)

Watson Potter to Esquire Warren a title bond. 10 Sep 1867. (Pp. 649-650)

Esquire Warren and wife, Margarett J., to L. J. Magness 142 acres in the 9th District. 10 Apr 1870. (Pp. 651-652)

John Robinson to Isaac Hays a tract of land in the 15th District. 18 Mar 1875. (Pp. 652-653)

Eliza J. Robinson, wife of John Robinson, acknowledges the above written deed. Oct 1875. (P. 653)

Lucresa Stanford to Jerry Fisher and wife Helen, formerly Helen Stanford, her interest in 100 acres in the 4th District. 28 Jun 1875. (P. 654)

James M. Pack and wife, Mary Jane, to G. W. McCarley 25 acres in the 9th District. 4 Oct 1875. (P. 655)

W. C. Tippit and wife, Elen M., to Levi Haney their one sixth interest in the estate of Crawford Rankhorn deceased. 17 Oct 1873. (Pp. 656-657)

John Young, Sr. and wife, Elizabeth, to B. C. Vaughn their interest in nine acres in the 7th District. 21 Aug 1875. (Pp. 657-658)

Isaac Johnson and wife, Barbee, to J. N. Hays 11 acres in

the 2nd District. 8 Apr 1874. (Pp. 658-659)

George W. Eastham and William Smith to (Monroe) Green a tract of land in the 9th District. 13 Jul 1875. (P. 660)

Aaron Cantrell to L. H. Bain a tract of land on Pine Creek in the 9th District. 11 Nov 1875. (Pp. 660-661)

T. C. Cantrell and wife L. B., and E. W. Cantrell to Joseph Cantrell 25 acres in the 5th District. 26 Sep 1874. (P. 662)

W. L. Driver and wife, Nancy W., to W. G. Crawley three acres in the 9th District. 28 Sep 1875. (P. 663)

Obediah Hollinsworth and wife, Martha Alice, to G. W. Martin 35 acres. 29 Sep 1875. (P. 664)

G. W. Jones and wife, Nancy, to Joe Devenport their interest in a tract of land in the 10th District. 4 Oct 1875. (Pp. 665-666)

S. J. Sneed, Sr. and wife, Ellen, DeKalb County Agricultural & Mechanical Association three acfes in the 1st District. Bounded: the north bank of Hickman Creek opposite the mouth of Church Street Alexandria. 4 May 1872. (Pp. 666-668)

B. C. Bowman and wife, F. J., to Lucy N. Bowman a town lot in the town of Alexandria in the 1st District. 3 Jun 1875. (Pp. 668-669)

M. H. Lacks to J. C. Loring a tract of land in the 5th District. 11 Sep 1875. (Pp. 669-670)

E. N. Trail and wife, Sarah E., to M. R. Smith 40 acres in the 5th District. 29 Dec 1873. (Pp. 670-671)

A. T. Phillips and wife, E. V., to J. M. Allen a town lot in the town of Smithville. Bounded: the place where the said A. T. Phillips now lives. 5 Mar 1875. (Pp. 671-672)

G. W. Eastham to G. W. McCarty a lot in the 9th District containing 20 acres. 28 May 1875. (P. 672)

Benjamin Bennett, Sr. died intestate in the year 1873. Josiah Griffith was appointed Administrator. County Court Clerk to Asberry Hays 41 acres belonging to the estate. 19 Oct 1875. (Pp. 673-676)

Elizabeth S. Haile and Susan Haile to James M. Foster for taking care of us in a reasonable and comfortable manner a tract of land in the 16th District. 29 Sep 1875. (Pp. 676-678)

John A. Evans to Martha J. Evans his interest in two tracts of land in the 9th District. 5 Oct 1875. (P. 678)

J. M. Bains and wife, M. J., to G. W. Purser 40 acres on Harriman Creek in the 9th District. 12 Oct 1875. (P. 679)

William McDowell and wife, Josephine, formerly Josephine Sandlin, to J. M. Sandlin their interest in the estate of Randolph Sandlin. 15 Jul 1875. (Pp. 680-682)

DEED BOOK L

William Page and wife, Leanna, to John H. Tramel their interest in the land in which (Andrew) Page died seized and possessed in the 10th District. 4 Nov 1875. (Pp. 682-684)

William Rich for love and affection for the Baptist Church at M. T. Mariah one acre. Said church is located in the 3rd District. 11 Nov 1875. (Pp. 684-685)

Aaron Frazier to W. T. Hoskins 219 acres in the 12th District. 3 Nov 1875. (Pp. 685-686)

William Austin to Felix W. Garner 20 acres in the 16th District. 6 Oct 1875. (Pp. 686-687)

W. T. Hoskins to Aaron Frazier 47 acres in the 12th District. 3 Nov 1875. (Pp. 687-688)

Thomas B. Brown to John W. Fakes a house and lot in the town of Alexandria. 15 Nov 1875. (Pp. 688-690)

Margaret Garrison to A. E. Bowers 15 acres in the 1st District. Bounded: Widow Palmer's dower. 6 Sep 1873. (Pp. 690-691)

J. T. Hollis, trustee; T. W. Fitts and wife Isabella; C. Hill and wife Lucinda to F. M. Close and Thomas N. Close 140 acres in the 12th District. 15 Nov 1875. (Pp. 691-692)

James Devenport and wife, Malinda, to G. W. Taylor 18½ acres in the 10th District. 15 Oct 1875. (Pp. 692-693)

Mary E. Worley to John Bullin one acre. 25 Nov 1875. (P. 694)

Fred Starnes and wife, Polly, to Joseph A. Starnes 220 acres in the 15th District. 5 Sep 1874. (Pp. 695-696)

J. L. Colvert and wife, Martha M., to Lafayette Kirby 50 acres in the 14th District. 3 Dec 1875. (P. 697)

W. N. Wilson and wife, Frances M., to Mary Jane Capshaw 12 acres in the 9th District. 27 Nov 1875. (Pp. 698-699)

W. P. Smith to W. B. Stokes a house and lot. 6 Dec 1875. (Pp. 699-700)

William (Riely) died testate many years ago. He left certain lands to H. G. and Neal (Reily) at the death or marriage of Mary Reily, his widow. Said Mary has died. A suit has been filed asking partition of the land. 7 Dec 1876. (Pp. 700-701)

H. G. Reily and Elizabeth Reily to Herd Cope a tract of land on the Caney Fork in the 7th District. 6 Dec 1875. (Pp. 701-702)

G. W. Eastham to Jehu Cantrell a title deed. 5 Nov 1875. (Pp. 702-703)

John H. Savage to James Ferrell 61 acres. 6 Sep 1875. (P. 704)

Levi Harvey and wife, Ellender, to Robert W. N.ely 227 acres. 30 Oct 1875. (Pp. 705-706)

W. T. Bone to J. S. Bone his interest in lot numbers 3 and 4 known as the Bone Farm. 1 Dec 1875. (Pp. 706-707)

County Court Clerk to W. C. Gilbert a tract of land belonging to the heirs of A. Bevert. 15 Dec 1875. (Pp. 707-708)

J. P. Winchester and wife, L. P., to J. M. Pullum 30 acres in the 16th District. 25 Aug 1873. (Pp. 709-710)

Bartamus Pack and wife, Elizabeth, formerly widow of Esaw Pack, to William T. Shields a tract of 30 acres in the 7th District, it being the interest of the said Elizabeth laid off to her as the widow of Esaw Pack. 31 Aug 1875. (Pp. 710-711)

W. T. Shields to Isaac Cantrell a tract of land, it being formerly the dower interest of Elizabeth Pack. 20 Dec 1875. (Pp. 711-712)

A. T. Phillips and wife, Emma, to R. C. Hays a town lot in the town of Smithville. 23 Dec 1875. (P. 712)

J. M. Pack and wife, Kanadgo, to William M. Pack 140 acres in the 9th District. 24 Dec 1875. (Pp. 713-714)

Isaac N. Drake and wife, E. R., to J. M. Gowen a title bond. 18 Dec 1875. (Pp. 714-715)

Sheriff to W. B. Stokes a lot of land in the town of Alexandria belonging to Yandle Woods. 20 Dec 1875. (Pp. 716-717)

Commissioners to G. F. and W. W. Patterson a tract of land in the 1st District. 27 Apr 1872. (P. 717)

J. W. Reynolds and wife, Elizabeth, to William L. Malone a tract of land in the 11th District. 14 Aug 1873. (Pp. 718-719)

Wiley Hendrickson and wife, Mary; James Hickman and wife Susan; Benjamin Bennett and wife Levina; Francis Smith and wife Mary Jane; and Matilda Smith, heirs of Paralee Smith, formerly Paralee Hendrickson to ?. W. Taylor a tract of land in the 10th District. 1 Jan 1876. (Pp. 719-720)

DEED BOOK M

James P. Doss for love and affection to his wife, Mattie M. Doss, and children, Callie, Bettie, and Sallie, and any other children we may have hereafter Lot No. 1 of the landed estate of J. C. Doss deceased partitioned between his heirs, it being the land drawn by Carline Quarles and sold to me by her and husband James P. Quarles. Also, the interest I now have in the dower of Priscilla Doss. 8 Jun 1867. (P. 1)

G. M. Fite to Mrs. G. A. Trapp, wife of M. Trapp a deed of gift of about 13 acres, excluding one fourth of an acre. 9 Jan 1875. (P. 2)

Sintha Botts to J. B. Farler one acre in the 4th District. 24 Nov 1875. (Pp. 2-3)

William Simpson and wife Caroline to J. J. Adcock 160 acres in the 7th District. 14 Jan 1876. (Pp. 3-4)

David Fisher and wife, Harriett, to Ferdinand P. Fisher 38 acres in the 6th District. 6 Oct 1874. (Pp. 4-5)

W. C. Gilbert for love and affection to his wife, T. A. Gilbert, and his children several tracts of land including 100 acres in the 9th District. 19 Jan 1876. (Pp. 5-7)

Fern Marford to A. P. Cantrell a tract of land accrued to us under a decree of the Cnancery Court. 20 Jul 1869. (P. 7)

T. P. Christian to Jackson Malone 227 acres belonging to the estate of William Malone. (Pp. 8-9)

J. B. Robinson to A. P. Cantrell a tract of land in the 6th District. 17 Mar 1875. (Pp. 10-11)

William Bates and wife, Cynthia, to James Oakley 25 acres in the 11th District. 6 Dec 1874. (Pp. 11-12)

William Bates and wife, Cynthia, for love and affection to their son, C. G. Bates, 75 acres in the 11th District. 6 Dec 1875. (Pp. 12-13)

Lewis E. Finley to Wile W. Jackson of Trigg County, Kentucky his interest in the estate of William Foutch deceased, my interest being one undivided fifth of that part of said estate that would have descended to my mother, Nancy Mahaly Finley, who was one of the children of the said William Foutch. 28 Dec 1874. (Pp. 13-14)

G. W. McClellan and John F. Ray to Aaron Williams, colored, three fourth's of an acre o the 1st District on Hickman's Creek. 26 Jan 1876. (Pp. 14-15)

James M. Baird to Robert Johnson 100 acres in the 4th District. 6 Dec 1875. (Pp. 15-16)

John Harper to Benjamin Harper a tract of land lying partly in Smith County and partly in DeKalb County. 7 Feb 1876. (Pp. 16-17)

W. H. Hays and wife, R. S., to J. A. Walker a tract of land in the 1st District containing 12 acres. 17 Sep 1876.

(Pp. 17-18)

J. T. Hollis and wife, H. B., to A. Calhoun a house and lot in the town of Alexandria. 8 Feb 1896. (Pp. 18-19)

E. Tubb and M. M. Brien, Executors of James Tubb, to C. M. Williams two tracts of land in the 12th District. 14 Sep 1870. (Pp. 19-20)

A. L. and E. T. Foster to W. J. Shields one acre in the 7th District. 12 Feb 1876. (Pp. 20-21)

Joseph Hollinsworth and wife, Sarah, of Cannon County to W C. Gilbert, trustee for T. A. Gilbert, their interest in 200 acres known as the Thomas Reaves land on Pine Creek. 16 Feb 1876. (P. 21)

G. L. Barnes and wife, Martha F., to Levi Foutch 16¼ acres in the 1st District. 4 Jan 1876. (Pp. 22-23)

William H. Magness and wife, E. J., to M. J. Carnes a tract of land in the 9th District. 7 Feb 1876. (P. 24)

William G. Crawley, W. J. Carnes and wife, Mary J., to J. A. Nesmith a tract of land in the town of Smithville. 11 Feb 1876. (P. 25)

Daniel Gann and wife, Martha, to James A. Hathaway a tract of land in the 4th District. 3 Apr 1875. (P. 26)

J. A. Walker for love and affection to E. J. Walker 80 acres in the 1st District. 16 Feb 1876. (P. 27)

Clerk & Master W. T. Hoskins 112 acres. 17 Feb 1876. (Pp. 27-28)

T. J. Williams to John B. Robinson five acres in the 4th District. 17 Feb 1876. (P. 29)

John B. Robinson to T. J. Williams 22 acres in the 4th District. 18 Feb 1876. (Pp. 29-30)

James J. Bennett binds himself to Bartamus Pack and others in the penal sum of $800. 29 Oct 1875. (Pp. 30-31)

Robert Johnson to Isaac C. Johnson 50 acres in the 4th District. 18 Feb 1876. (Pp. 31-32)

G. H. Gray and wife, Matilda, to W. H. Magness a tract of land on the south side of the town of Smithville. 7 Jan 1876. (Pp. 32-33)

William H. Magness and wife, E. J., to S. H. Gray 77 acres in the 9th District. 7 Jan 1876. (Pp. 33-34)

Henry Adcock and wife, Mercy J., to A. E. Adcock a title bond. 19 Feb 1876. (Pp. 34-35)

L. K. Lawson and wife, Susan, to J. H. Mangrum 53 acres in the 9th District. 29 Feb 1876. (Pp. 35-36)

James T. Quarles and wife, Darthula, to James P. Doss their interest in 88 acres. 20 Aug 1875. (Pp. 36-37)

DEED BOOK M

James T. Quarles and wife, Darthula, to James P. Doss 88 acres in the 1st District, it being their interest in the dower of Priscilla Doss. Their interest is five sixth's of one sixth. 20 Aug 1875. (Pp. 38-40)

Sheriff M. F. Doss to W. V. Winchester a tract of land in the 16th District belonging to the heirs of J. M. Null. Mentions Elizabeth Winchester. 6 Mar 1876. (Pp. 40-42)

Ellis H. Buterbaugh and wife, Samantha, to Lucinda H. Force 78 acres in the 9th District. 14 Feb 1876. (Pp. 42-43)

Clerk & Master to J. S. Harrison a tract of land belonging to Elick Tubb. 7 Mar 1876. (Pp. 43-45)

B. L. Estice to Mary Estice a trust deed on 93 acres in the 9th District. 6 Mar 1876. (Pp. 45-46)

Susan Brim, L. P. Goff and wife Sarah, Elizabeth Fitts, J. R. Brim, Nancy A. Brim, and Matilda Brim to R. A. Trammel 40 acres in the 6th District to J. J. Trammel and wife conveyed to Thomas Brim. 31 Jul 1875. (Pp. 46-48)

O. B. Wright to Elizabeth J. Palmer a town lot in the town of Alexandria. 18 Dec 1868. (Pp. 48-49)

Clerk & Master to John W. Groom a tract of land belonging to the heirs of Joseph Turney. 7 Mar 1876. (Pp. 49-50)

J. A. Walker, T. B. Walker, and Martha J. Walker to John M. Walker their interest in 80 acres in the 1st District. 8 Nov 1873. (P. 51)

Henry Adcock and wife Mary J. to James L. Baines and Elyza Baines 57 acres in the 9th District. 8 Feb 1876. (Pp. 52-53)

William Pack and wife Paralee to Jasper N. Hayes a thirty foot wide strip of land for a road through so much of their land. 4 Sep 1875. (Pp. 53-54)

W. C. Gilbert and wife, T. A., to Jacob Potter and wife Margaret ten acres in the 9th District. 15 Mar 1876. (Pp. 54-55)

J. W. Henderson to Joseph H. Fite 36 acres in the 13th District. 25 Sep 1875. (Pp. 55-56)

A. P. Hayes and wife, Parmelia, to Isaac Cooper eight acres in the 2nd District. 19 Sep 1874. (Pp. 56-57)

James M. Baird of Alexandria, assignee of E. W. Bass who was adjudged bankrupt, to W. T. Hoskins a tract of land in the 12th District. 26 Oct 1872. (Pp. 57-58)

Mc Vanata and Sarah Vanata to C. W. L. Hall two acres in the 2nd District. 19 Jan 1875. (Pp. 58-59)

James Hale to Isaac Shehane 50 acres in the 3rd District. 23 Oct 1875. (Pp. 59-60)

James R. Beckwith and wife, Matilda J., to Seth M. Whaley

their one seventh interest in a tract of land in the 9th District descended to us from the estate of Elijah Whaley. Mentions the undivided interest of Thomas R. Whaley deceased. 25 Mar 1876. (Pp. 61-62)

A. T. Fisher and wife, Mary, to George Blankenship 12 acres on the Caney Fork in the 7th District. 22 Feb 1875. (Pp. 62-63)

J. C. Cannady and wife, Margaret A., to J. G. Dunlap and wife 200 acres in the 4th District. 1 Apr 1876. (Pp. 63-64)

George McGee and wife, Catherine, to A. R. Dunham 25 acres in the 16th District. 19 Aug 1874. (Pp. 64-65)

James Willis and wife, Elizabeth, to James H. Briggs and others a trust deed on 145 acres in the 14th District. 6 Mar 1876. (Pp. 66-67)

Sheriff to David Dunham and Thomas Potter 300 acres on Sink Creek. 21 Mar 1876. (Pp. 67-68)

David Dunham to William B. Barns 93 acres in the 6th District. 1 Feb 1876. (Pp. 68-69)

W. W. Malone and wife, Rebecca, to Catharine Malone, wife of Y. M. Malone "as long as she remains a lawful wife or widow" a tract of land in the 11th District. 3 Feb 1875. (Pp. 69-70)

Milton C. Dodd and wife Rebecca to George Turney their interest in the dowery of Mary Turney, widow of Joseph Turney. 9 Sep 1871. (P. 71)

Joseph Hendrickson to Wesley Vantrease 50 acres on Dry Creek. 19 Aug 1852. (Pp. 72-73)

A. L. Foster and E. T. Foster to G. A. Bing 71 acres in the 9th District. 26 Apr 1876. (P. 73)

Alexander Martin for love and affection to his daughter, Martha P. Allen, 50 acres on the Caney Fork River. 9 Oct 1875. (P. 74)

B. M. Cantrell, Sophia Cantrell, and Benjamin Cantrell to John Lyles eight acres in the 9th District. 10 Mar 1876. (Pp. 74-75)

W. Lawrence Driver and wife, N. W., to John Crowder four acres in the 9th District. 5 May 1876. (Pp. 75-76)

Samuel T. Hooper and wife, Mary, to Charles W. Cameron 85 acres. 21 Jan 1877. (Pp. 76-77)

John Jones to John Dedman 18 acres in the 1st District. 25 Nov 1875. (Pp. 77-78)

T. L. Seawell to J. Q. Seawell a tract of land in the town of Smithville. 22 Feb 1876. (Pp. 78-79)

William Adamson to Mary A. Covington during her natural life and then to her bodily heirs, to wit, Elizabeth Covington, Mary Covington, Miles J. Covington, Jr., and Tessy Covington

50 acres in the 1st District. 14 Jun 1875. (Pp. 79-80)

Shedrick Tramel and wife, Elizabeth, to William B. Tramel and wife a tract of land in the 10th District for supporting and keeping me and my wife in food and clothing as long as we both shall live. 22 May 1876. (Pp. 80-81)

A. J. Edwards and S. W. McClellan to D. W. Dinges and W. H. Lincoln a store house and lot in the town of Alexandria. 28 Nov 1870. (Pp. 81-82)

T. W. Eason and wife, Emma, to G. W. Dinges one and one half acres in the town of Alexandria. Bounded: east corner of the parsonage lot. 1 Jan 1876. (Pp. 83-84)

John Blew and wife, Susan Caroline, to D. W. Dinges a lot in the town of Alexandria containing two acres. 20 Apr 1874. (Pp. 84-85)

Thomas Potter and wife, Falama, to P. G. Magness 25 acres on the north side of Sink Creek. 20 Apr 1876. (Pp. 85-86)

Melviny Merritt to A. J. Fuston my interest in the lands of Jon Fuson. 24 Apr 1876. (Pp. 86-87)

William Johnson for love and affection to his children, to wit, Louisa Magness, wife of G. W. Magness; Nancy Johnson; Carrol Johnson; Catharine Young, wife of Joe Young; Parilee Fowler, wife of Johnathan Fowler; Tabitha Ann Johnson, Allen Johnson, Susan Johnson, William Johnson, and Elizabeth Johnson a tract of land in the 9th District reserved as my home place. 31 May 1876. (Pp. 87-88)

A. L. Foster and wife, Mary E., to G. W. Camerson their one half interest in 28 acres. 20 May 1876. (Pp. 88-89)

Purtaman Puckett and wife, Martha Ann, for love and affection to their daughter, Amanda G. Burton, a tract of land on the Caney Fork River. 8 Jun 1876. (P. 89)

Giles L. Bowers and wife, Martha F., to R. Marler 23 acres in the 13th District. 8 Apr 1876. (Pp. 90-91)

William A. Braswell to G. M. McGee 23 acres on the west side of the Caney Fork. 9 Nov 1875. (Pp. 91-92)

Frederick Starnes to William A. Braswell a small lot in the 16th District. 25 May 1876. (Pp. 92-93)

Clerk & Master of Smith County has a suit pending in the Chancery Court at Carthage in the case of Catron versus White. Sheriff of DeKalb County to Ira W. King a tract of land. 12 Jun 1876. (Pp. 93-94)

Morgan Lawrence to W. T. Robinson 268½ acres in the 12th District. 15 May 1874. (Pp. 95-96)

Corporation of Smithville to J. J. Smith the tract of land that J. J. Smith purchased of B. M. Cantrell. 12 Jun 1876. (Pp. 96-97)

George G. Dillard and wife, H., to T. N. Christian a lot in the town of Smithville. 17 Jun 1876. (Pp. 97-98)

DEED BOOK M

Theodore Staley died testate testate some time in the year 18__. It was necessary to sell his one half interest in a tanyard. County Court Clerk to T. H. Richardson the one half interest. 20 Jun 1876. (Pp. 98-99)

Samuel Warford, Administrator of David Malone, and William A. Robinson and wife Mary E. on 8 Jan 1868 filed suit in Chancery Court against Mary J. Malone, Claiborn Malone, Mary Warford, David Warford, Elijah Warford, Paralee Warford, William J. Robinson, Monroe Malone, Robert Malone, and James Malone, minors. Clerk to J. P. Eaton 30 acres in the 11th District. 2 Dec 1870. (Pp. 100-101)

W. J. Evans to J. A. Evans, Jr. his interest in a tract of land in the 9th District. 26 Jun 1876. (Pp. 101-102)

Allen G. Mullican and wife Amanda, and K. H. Mullican to J. J. Mullican a tract ofland in the 16th District belonging to Jeremiah Mullican deceased. 27 Jun 1876. (Pp. 102-103)

Mathew Wilson and wife, Mary, to Edna Hooper a lot on the Lebanon & Sparta Publick Road. 1 Jul 1876. (P. 103)

Mary Lockhart to William Johnson a tract of land on Short Creek in the 9th District. 6 Dec 1875. (P. 104)

John M. Lane to his son, Frances M. Lane, 118 acres in the 7th District. 7 Feb 1876. (Pp. 104-105)

John T. Stokes and wife, Perlina, to John A. Wright 16 acres on Smith Fork. John A. Wright's wife, Mary, is also named on the deed. 8 Aug 1873. (Pp. 106-107)

James Bates to John A. Wright and wife, Mary, a tract of land in the 7th District. 21 Apr 1876. (Pp. 107-108)

J. Q. Seawel and wife, Sarah Alice, to P. T. Shores a lot in the town of Smithville. 10 Jul 1876. (P. 109)

William Rich to B. F. Hale a tract of land in the 3rd District. 5 Jan 1876. (Pp. 110-111)

T. B. Brown and wife, Annie, to D. W. Dinges a tract of land in the 1st District. 16 Jun 1876. (Pp. 111-112)

T. L. Seawel and wife, Fily A., to J. Q. Seawel a tract of land in the 9th District south of Smithville. Jul 1876. (Pp. 112-113)

B. M. Cantrell and wife, Sophie C., to J. J. Smith a house and lot in the town of Smithville. 25 Jul 1876. (Pp. 113-114)

W. W. Wade and wife, Bettie, to John Crowder a tract of land in the 9th District. 1 Jan 1876. (Pp. 114-115)

Charles Ferrell and Mary Ferrell to G. W. Perser a tract of land in the 9th District. 16 May 1876. (Pp. 115-116)

Jane Williams, Nancy Williams, James Williams, John S. Williams, and H. B. Williams to William H. Jones 50 acres in the 16th District. 26 Dec 1868. (Pp. 116-117)

James N. Veach and wife, Mary A., to Mary L. Blankenship 30 acres in the 9th District. 15 Nov 1873. (Pp. 117-118)

John Pack and wife, Emeline, to Thomas Pack their interest in the estate of Bartemus Pack deceased. 29 Mar 1874. (Pp. 118-119)

Benjamin M. Merritt and Margaret Merritt to John Merritt the tract on which the said Benjamin M. now lives in the 16th District. 26 Feb 1875. (Pp. 119-121)

Elias Lane, Sr. for love and affection to his son, Elias Lane, Jr. the place where I now live including the old mansion house. 22 Jan 1869. (Pp. 121-122)

P. J. Lee and wife, Barthena, to J. L. Colvert and H. C. Earthman part of the Morgan tract in the 9th District. 4 Aug 1876. (Pp. 122-123)

J. S. Dunlap and wife Emma; James H. Seawel and wife Amanda; R. C. Bomer and wife Josie to J. H. Veach and wife, Mary A., a quit claim to a tract of land that John C. Cannady made to his wife and her children. 5 Aug 1876. (Pp. 123-125)

M. M. Brien to T. W. Fitts ten acres. 10 Aug 1876. (P. 126)

J. W. Hunt and wife, Abigail, to Jasper Rule a lot in the town of Liberty. 27 Jan 1874. (Pp. 126-127)

William Wood and wife, Octavia, to J. W. Wood a lot on the western boundary of the town of Alexandria. 18 Feb 1876. (Pp. 127-128)

S. S. Hooper and wife, Mary A., to A. C. Hooper a tract of land in the 9th District. 17 Aug 1876. (Pp. 128-129)

J. C. Loving and others to John P. Titsworth their interest in the school land that was deeded to the commissioners by Richard Titsworth near the McMinnville Road. 3 Jul 1876. (P. 130)

R. C. Hayes and wife, Masoria M., to Isaac Drake a lot in the town of Smithville. Bounded: Main Street and Mountain Street. 3 Jul 1876. (P. 131)

David Fisher and James R. Fisher to Alfred Bain 30 acres in the 6th District. 18 Aug 1876. (P. 132)

P. J. Lee and wife, Bethenia, to H. C. Eastham five acres in the 9th District. 1 Jan 1876. (P. 133)

Thomas Potter and wife, Fatimer, to Daniel Potter 35 acres. 21 Jun 1876. (Pp. 133-135)

E. Warren and wife, S. E., to E. Lish and wife 23 acres in the 9th District. 26 Aug 1876. (P. 135)

Daniel Smith to William T. Jones a tract of land in the 7th District. 12 Jul 1866. (P. 136)

Joshua L. Jennings and wife Martha J.; Robert T. Smith and

wife, Amanda F. Smith; James P. Doss; and M. F. Doss to James T. Quarles, he being the husband of our sister, Caroline, who died about the year 1858 or 59, a quit claim to a tract of land in the 1st District that descended to the said Caroline from her father, J. C. Doss, and set apart as the dower of Priscilla Doss, wife of the said Jonathan C. Doss. 19 Jan 1874. (Pp. 136-140)

W. J. Hale and J. R. Hale to W. T. Robinson a title bond. 24 Aug 1871. (Pp. 140-141)

Thomas Bane and wife, Elizabeth, to Starlin Wisdom four acres in the 2nd District. 11 Aug 1876. (Pp. 141-142)

Amanda T. Davis to William R. Smith a lot in the town of Smithville. 6 Nov 1873. (Pp. 142-143)

Christopher C. Wright and wife, Anna, to William Wright, their son, for love and affection 100 acres in the 6th District. 16 Aug 1876. (Pp. 143-144)

Christopher C. Wright and wife, Anna, to Christopher C. Wright, Jr., their son, for love and affection 104 acres in the 6th District. 12 Sep 1876. (Pp. 144-145)

W. V. Winchester and wife E. E.; J. M. Winchester and wife G. A.; V. M. Williams and wife M. F., all heirs of Jacob and Jane Null, to J. W. Null their interest in 87¼ acres. 24 Aug 1876. (Pp. 145-149)

Christopher Wright and wife, Anna, to Ferdinand P. Fisher five acres in the 6th District. 6 Feb 1875. (P. 150)

James Goodner to C. L. Barton a tract of land adjoining the town of Alexandria. 21 Aug 1876. (Pp. 151-152)

J. M. Baird to B. F. Bell a tract of land in the 1st District. 14 Apr 1876. (P. 152)

W. C. Avant and wife Nancy to C. C. Avant a tract of land. 3 Jan 1876. (Pp. 152-154)

P. J. Lee and wife, Bettenia, to Levi Harvey a tract of land in the 9th District. 2 Aug 1876. (Pp. 154-155)

James H. Blackburn and Robert Cantrell to Giles L. Bower 16 acres in the 1st District. 16 Sep 1876. (Pp. 155-156)

Clerk & Master to Fatima Potter a tract of land belonging to the heirs of Tilman Potter. Mentions Lucy Parish, Jane Martin, Mary Mulican, Sarah Cantrell, Elizabeth Davis, Annie Marsh, and Thomas Potter. 20 Sep 1876. (Pp. 156-158)

Francis Turner of Wilson County to William and Joseph H. Blackburn 330 acres. 4 Aug 1876. (Pp. 158-160)

M. H. Pack and wife, Martha, to Isaac Cantrell a tract of land in the 9th District. 31 Mar 1876. (Pp. 160-161)

William Bains and N. C. Bains to A. M. Allen 78 acres in the 6th District. 11 Sep 1876. (Pp. 161-162)

DEED BOOK M

Abraham Cantrell and wife, Rebecca, to (Neton) Fowler 30 acres in the 9th District. 2 Oct 1876. (Pp. 162-163)

Robert Johnson to John Miller 50 acres in the 4th District. Mary H. Johnson is the wife of the said Robert Johnson. 9 Feb 1876. (Pp. 163-164)

P. J. Lee and wife, Bethena, to E. J. Wright 15 acres in the 9th District. 2 Aug 1876. (Pp. 164-165)

O. B. Wright to R. V. Wright 40 acres in the 1st District. 12 Sep 1876. (Pp. 165-166)

William H. Hayes to John M. Hayes, trustee, for the use of the Methodist Episcopal Church one half acre in the 14th District. If at any time the church should be abandoned, then the land reverts back to the said William H. Hayes. 7 Oct 1876. (P. 167)

A. C. Hooper to T. M. Hooper a tract of land. 9 Oct 1876. (Pp. 167-168)

Daniel Gan and wife, Martha, to A. M. Robinson their one half interest in a steam saw and grist mill located on Dry Creek in the 4th District. 14 Oct 1876. (Pp. 168-169)

Joseph Mangrum and wife, Martha J., to Henry Evins 53 acres in the 9th District. 15 May 1876. (Pp. 169-170)

H. E. Staley and wife, C. L., to Litterer & Calibar 50 acres in the 9th District. 14 Oct 1876. (Pp. 170-171)

J. Q. Seawel and wife, Alice, to John Jones four acres in the 9th District. 25 Sep 1876. (Pp. 171-172)

W. B. Tramel and wife, Elizabeth, to John H. Tramel 50 acres in the 10th District. 3 Nov 1876. (Pp. 172-173)

Horace Foster and wife, Hattie N., to D. J. Carnes and T. N. Christian 25½ acres in the 3rd and 4th Districts. 1 Nov 1876. (Pp. 173-174)

D. G. Talley and wife, E. T., to M. N. Smith a tract of land in the 5th District. 16 Oct 1876. (Pp. 174-175)

T. W. Fitts and wife, Isabel, to Jack Rice a tract of land in the 15th District. 6 Nov 1876. (Pp. 175-176)

Robert V. Wright of Davidson County to John Garrison Lot No. 10 in the town of Alexandria. 12 Jan 1875. (Pp. 176-177)

Moses Walker and wife, N. J., to Marcus P. Badgett and James R. Badgett 300 acres. 11 Aug 1876. (Pp. 177-178)

John Merrett and wife, Nancy, to Benjamin M. Merrett the tract of land on which the said John Merrett now lives and is located in the 16th District. 26 Feb 1873. (Pp. 178-180)

Joseph Mitchell to Letha McRay 101 acres. 13 Feb 1872. (Pp. 180-181)

John H. Savage to William T. Wright 30 acres in the 6th District. 19 Sep 1876. (Pp. 181-182)

John Wilaby and wife, Anna, to A. B. Allen two acres in the 11th District. 28 Aug 1876. (Pp. 182-183)

Edward Turner to O. D. Williams two acres in the town of Alexandria. 12 Nov 1875. (Pp. 183-184)

M. M. Brien and wife, Mary; Elick Simpson and wife Martha to William Oakley 282 acres in the 12th District. 1 Sep 1875. (Pp. 184-186)

Jackson Malone and wife, Harriet, to William E. Foutch 19½ acres in the 11th District. 15 Sep 1876. (Pp. 186-187)

James M. Lee and wife, Elizabeth, to Coleman Helm 250 acres in the 16th District. 20 Oct 1876. (Pp. 187-189)

Obediah Rich to Viney Ratcliff a deed of gift of all my property. The transfer takes effect at my death and the death of my old lady. The said Viney Ratcliff has lived with me for twenty-seven years. 16 Oct 1870. (P. 189)

David Fisher to J. A. Cantrell 50 acres. 20 Nov 1876. (P. 190)

Henry Bullard in DeKalb County about the first of the year 1870 intestate. Mary Bullard filed a petition asking for dower to be laid off to her as the widow and for the real estate to be partitioned among the several heirs. The heirs are Mary Bullard, Elizabeth Bullard, William Bullard, Henry Bullard, Susan Bullard, (Juttia) J. Sullins, and Albert Bullard. County Court Clerk to Rachel Hibdon their interest in Lot No. 6. 28 Nov 1876. (Pp. 190-191)

Aaron Frazer, Executor of Henry Frazer, to Martha Pack a tract of land in the 9th District. 17 Dec 1874. (Pp. 192-193)

M. H. Pack and wife, Martha, to M. E. Cantrell 35½ acres in the 9th District. 27 Nov 1876. (Pp. 193-194)

W. G. Crawley to W. W. Wade a lot in the town of Smithville. Bounded: southeast corner of the Academy lot. 27 Nov 1876. (Pp. 194-195)

M. H. Pack and wife, Martha, to Thomas Pack a title bond. 27 Nov 1876. (P. 195)

Jere. Keel and wife, Solona, to Roena Delilah Blythe, daughter of J. W. Scott, 150 acres in the 4th District for $300. 30 Nov 1876. (Pp. 196-197)

Taxes were assessed against W. M. Manard on a certain tract of land. They land is sold to W. C. Dyer for taxes. 5 Dec 1876. (Pp. 197-198)

Green Cantrell died intestate on 15 Jan 1867. Clerk & Master to J. J. Summers a tract of land belonging to the said intestate. 8 Dec 1876. (Pp. 198-199)

William Braswell to Aaron Braswell his interest in the lands belonging to Nathan Braswell. 29 Jul 1876. (P. 200)

R. B. Capshaw to Mary J. Capshaw his interest in Lot No. 68 in Smithville for ten dollars. 12 Sep 1876. (Pp. 200-201)

Samuel Warford and wife, Rachel Ann, to William E. Foutch a tract of land in the 11th District. 11 Aug 1875. (Pp. 201-202)

John C. Cannady, Trustee for his daughter Maud H. Cannady, to Potter and Smith part of Lot No. 39 in the town of Smithville. (W. C. Potter and George K. Smith). 14 Nov 1876. (Pp. 202-203)

B. H. Pack and wife, Melvina, to William M. Pack their interest in 140 acres in the 9th District, it being a one seventh interest. It is the place where William Pack and B. H. Pack now live, it being the place deeded to Mariah Pack on 21 Apr 1862. 14 Dec 1876. (Pp. 203-204)

G. Blankenship and wife, M. C., to W. H. Magness a tract of land in the 9th District. 14 Nov 1876. (Pp. 204-205)

Nelson Bryan to S. W. Bryan a tract of land in the 5th District. 16 Aug 1872. (Pp. 205-206)

William Foutch died testate some time before the first of Feb 1874. William E. Foutch filed suit against James M. Foutch asking for a sale. County Court Clerk to Thomas (Custice) a tract of land belonging to the estate. 21 Dec 1876. (Pp. 206-208)

County Court Clerk to William E. Foutch 113 acres belonging to the estate of William Foutch. 22 Dec 1876. (Pp. 208-209)

County Court Clerk to Robert Cantrell a tract of land belonging to the estate of Green Cantrell. 28 Dec 1876. (Pp. 209-210)

Aaron Braswell and wife, Mahaley, to W. B. Baines 134 acres in the 4th District. 16 Aug 1876. (P. 211)

B. H. Cantrell to Benjamin Cantrell a tract of land. 27 Dec 1876. (Pp. 212-213)

Benjamin Cantrell to Martin Foutch eight acres in the 9th District. 28 Dec 1876. (Pp. 213-214)

John H. Gray to Frederick (Starnes) a tract of land. 27 May 1874. (Pp. 214-215)

H. P. Cantrell and wife, Hannah, to E. B. Hicks part of the land that the said H. P. Cantrell now live on. 22 Aug 1872. (Pp. 215-216)

County Court Clerk to Mary E. Cantrell the interest that the heirs of Green Cantrell have in a tract of land. Jan 1877. (Pp. 216-217)

William Vick to J. G. Squires a corner of Lot No. 22 in the town of Liberty. 1 Jan 1873. (P. 218)

A. W. Walker and wife, Mary, to R. P. Goodson twelve acres

in the 6th District. 3 Dec 1876. (Pp. 218-219)

A. P. Cantrell and wife, Martha Jane, to Joseph Cantrell and wife, Cynthia, 120 acres. Mentions Mary E. Cantrell, John A. Cantrell, and Joseph Cantrell. 6 Dec 1876. (Pp. 219-221)

P. T. Shores to Nancy Tyree and W. G. Tyree a tract of land in the 9th District. 15 Jan 1877. (Pp. 221-222)

T. L. Seawel and wife, P. A., to T. N. Christian 23 acres. 17 Jan 1877. (Pp. 222-223)

G. W. Martin to William C. Davis 35 acres in the 4th District. 17 Jan 1877. (P. 224)

T. L. Seawel and wife, Phila A., to H. L. Haney about three acres in the 9th District. 1 Aug 1876. (Pp. 224-225)

Louis F. Cantrell and wife, Mary E., to Peter Cantrell 35 acres in the 5th District. 5 Jan 1877. (Pp. 225-226)

John Phillips and wife, Polina; Lucy Bomer; Lizzie Wood; and J. M. Wood to D. W. Dinges their one fourth interest in a town lot in the town of Alexandria. 7 Oct 1876. (Pp. 226-227)

T. N. Christian and W. G. Carnes to G. T. Morris 100 acres in the 3rd District. 16 Oct 1876. (Pp. 227-228)

Robert Cantrell and wife, Letha, to Louis K. Cantrell a tract of land on Pine Creek in the 9th District. 4 Jan 1877. (Pp. 228-229)

John J. Burton and wife, Nancy, to M. A. Manard their one fifth interest in the land of Charles Burton deceased. 10 Nov 1873. (Pp. 229-231)

Ezekiel Manard and wife, M. A., to J. S. Burton their one fifth interest in the land of Charles Burton deceased. 10 Nov 1873. (Pp. 231-232)

G. T. Potter to R. B. West a lot in the town of Smithville. 25 Jan 1877. (P. 233)

R. B. West and wife, Hattie J., to G. W. Cameron a lot in Smithville on Mountain Street. 15 Jan 1877. (Pp. 233-234)

Elijah Hathaway to Angeline Manard 150 acres in the 8th District. 4 Jan 1869. (Pp. 234-235)

William F. Botts to White Myers a town lot in the town of Alexandria known as the Sarah Browning lot No. 23. Bounded: Main Street. 23 Mar 1872. (Pp. 235-236)

Bethel Parsley and wife, Selina, to E. D. Warren their interest in the lands of John H. Parsley deceased. 23 Jan 1877. (P. 237)

Ezekiel Maynard for love and affection to his wife, Mahala A. Maynard, and their present children, Sarah Frances Maynard, Sophronia Maynard, Bill Maynard, and James N. Maynard and any other children which may be born some personal property. 31 Jan 1877. (Pp. 238-240)

W. C. Cantrell and wife, Martha, to T. M. Reynolds their interest in a tract of land in the 6th District. 15 Jan 1877. (P. 241)

G. W. Williams and wife, Delilah, to J. E. Robinson their interest in their grandmother's estate which is one half of one share. 29 Sep 1876. (P. 242)

J. J. Tramel and James Ray enter into an agreement and compromise pertaining to their land. 27 Jan 1877. (P. 243)

Eveline Tramel, formerly Eveline Fuson, quit claim her interest in a tract of land to E. W. Taylor. 1 Jul 1873. (P. 244)

Henry Hoss to D. A. Parker 50 acres in the 4th District. 5 Feb 1877. (Pp. 244-245)

Thomas Parsley and wife, Caldonia, to Edward Warren and wife, M. A., their interest in the dower of Nancy Parsley, widow of John H. Parsley. 6 Feb 1877. (Pp. 245-246)

G. W. Cameron and wife, Prudence, to R. B. West for his two children, Leilia W. West and W. C. West, a tract of land in the town of Smithville. 25 Jan 1877. (Pp. 246-247)

Joseph Clark, having heretofore purchased at Sheriff's sale all the lands of John L. Cripps, to Mrs. Catherine Cripps all the interest I have in said land. 9 Nov 1875. (Pp. 247-248)

J. B. Robinson, Clerk & Master, to Thomas J. Kidwell a tract of land belonging to L. L. Cantrell. 9 Feb 1877. (Pp. 249-250)

Pleasant Watts and wife, Nancy, to Tilmon B. Foster 100 acres in the 9th District. 10 Feb 1877. (Pp. 250-251)

William H. Magness to James Moores his interest in a tract of land. 10 Feb 1877. (Pp. 251-252)

Crawford Rankhorn died intestate prior to the 1st of Nov. The Administrator, C. M. Rankhorn, has filed petition for the sale of the real estate. 14 Feb 1877. (Pp. 252-253)

J. L. Trammell and wife, Nancy, to John P. Tittsworth the Alford southern half of 51 acres in the 5th District. 23 Aug 1876. (Pp. 253-254)

James Jones and wife, Mary J., to John P. Tittsworth the Jackson Place in the 5th District. 17 Nov 1876. (Pp. 254-255)

T. F. Parsley and wife, Caldonia, to Joseph Mangrum their interest in the lands of John H. Parsley in the 5th District. 5 Feb 1877. (P. 256)

Russell Spurlock and wife, Malinda, to the school commissioners of the 5th District a tract of land on McNamara Road for a school. Bounded: on the southeast corner of the old school lot. 16 Aug 1876. (Pp. 256-257)

John J. Johnson to N. T. Stewart 50 acres in the 4th District. 15 Jan 1877. (Pp. 257-258)

Thomas Bradford departed this life in 1859 or 1860 intestate. Clerk & Master to E. J. Evans a tract of land in the 7th District. 22 Feb 1877. (Pp. 258-260)

For the consideration of $1200 paid to our mother, Helen Schurer, Oscar P. Hill and wife, Josephine, to T. B. Potter their interest in 35 acres in the 9th District. 12 Apr 1876. (Pp. 260-261)

Samuel Hooper to Sarah Hutchins 80 acres. 6 Feb 1877. (Pp. 262-263)

George Bowers to G. L. Bowers his interest all of his remainder interest in the estate of his father and the interest that he purchased of Bartlett James and wife, Eliza. 16 Sep 1876. (Pp. 263-264)

William Warren and wife, L. J., to Joseph Mangrum their interest in the land of John Parsley deceased. 23 Sep 1876. (Pp. 264-265)

J. M. Baird to B. F. Bell one and one half acres in the 1st District. 5 Mar 1877. (Pp. 265-266)

Samuel Braswell to L. S. Braswell three acres. 15 Feb 1877. (Pp. 266-267)

Nancy Bailiff has a fee simple interest in remainder to take effect after the death of myself who has a life estate in 100 acres called the Baliff old place. Nancy Bailiff to C. A. Bailiff her fee simple interest. 13 Dec 1875. (Pp. 267-268)

H. G. Kerby and wife, Elizabeth, to Herd Cope 50 acres in the 7th District. 7 Mar 1877. (Pp. 268-269)

H. G. Kerby and wife, Elizabeth, to John C. Atnip 50 acres in the 7th District. 7 Mar 1877. (Pp. 269-270)

David Jones and wife, Mary, to Joe M. Lee a title bond. 30 Jan 1877. (Pp. 270-271)

R. A. Tramel and wife, Delilah, to G. W. Walker a title bond to a tract of land in the 6th District. 4 Aug 1875. (Pp. 271-272)

E. N. Trail and wife, Sarah, to W. H. Hayes 190 acres in the 5th District. 8 Mar 1877. (Pp. 273-274)

James M. Baird of Alexandria, assignee of E. W. Bass, to F. M. Turner a tract of 81 acres. 26 Oct 1872. (PP. 274-275)

Aaron Frazier and wife, Paralee, to E. T. Rose a tract of land in the 17th District. 9 Feb 1874. (Pp. 276-277)

W. T. Robinson and wife, Lucy J., to W. T. Hoskins their interest in 114 acres in the 12th District where the said Hokins now lives. 18 Jul 1876. (Pp. 277-278)

Margaret Garrison to W. H. Hayes 17 acres in the 1st District. 2 Dec 1876. (P. 279)

Abe Britton and wife, Jane W. to Jerome Goodner a house and lot in the 1st District. 2 Jan 1874. (Pp. 279-280)

John M. Love and wife, Susan, for love and affection to their son, William 700 acres in the 7th District. 26 Feb 1877. (Pp. 280-281)

John M. Love for love and affection to his wife, Susan, and his son, H. E. Love, a tract of land in the 7th District. 26 Feb 1877. (Pp. 281-282)

Moses H. Fite, Administrator of Thomas C. Fite, to H. B. Groom 24 acres in the 3rd District. 24 Jan 1877. (Pp. 282-283)

Thomas Ferrell and wife, Cinthia, to G. D. Mullican 15 acres in the 5th District. 10 Feb 1877. (Pp. 283-284)

Sheriff to William Literer a tract of land belonging to James H. Blackburn. 15 Mar 1877. (Pp. 284-287)

Clerk & Master to Sarah Roland a tract of land belonging to John Simpson. 15 Mar 1877. (Pp. 287-288)

Tilman Haney and wife, Mary, to H. S. Hathaway a tract of land in the 6th District. 5 Mar 1877. (Pp. 288-289)

Robert Cantrell to G. W. Cameron a lot in the town of Smithville. 20 Mar 1877. (P. 290)

Tilman Haney to John P. Haney a tract of land in the 6th District. 15 Mar 1877. (Pp. 290-291)

Daniel Johnson and wife, Sarah, to H. H. Morris the tract of land in the 3rd District, it being the land that Daniel Johnson bought of his father, Barney Johnson. 10 Mar 1877. (P. 292)

W. L. Waters, President of the Lebanon & Sparta Turnpike Company to George Johnson a tract of land. 1 Dec 1875. (P. 293)

Nicholas Smith and wife Penelopy, to John Mason in the 15th District. 12 Sep 1876. (Pp. 293-294)

The heirs of Jefferson Cantrell deceased, to wit, Isaac Cantrell, E. J. Lefever and with Rutha, Hannah Cantrell, Martha J. Cantrell, P. G. Cantrell, Samantha Cantrell, A. M. Cantrell, and Mourning Cantrell to Watson Cantrell and wife Polina their interest in a tract of land belonging to Jefferson Cantrell deceased. 31 Mar 1877. (Pp. 295-296)

Watson Cantrell and wife, Polina, to Caroline McWherter 44 acres on Sink Creek. 5 Apr 1877. (Pp. 296-297)

W. J. Parsley to Monroe Blair 25 acres in the 4th District. 6 Apr 1877. (Pp. 297-299)

County Court Clerk to J. J. Summers a tract of land belonging to the estate of Green Cantrell. 10 Apr 1877. (Pp. 299-300)

W. B. Barnes and wife, Mary J., to James Moore a tract of land in the 6th District. 26 Jul 1876. (Pp. 301-302)

James R. Beckwith and wife Matilda G; George Beckwith and wife Fannie M.; Harriet B. Hill; James Beckwith and wife Elizabeth J.; and W. D. Beckwith, heirs of James Beckwith, to J. L. Colvert & Company a town lot in the town of Smithville known as Lot No. 44. Bounded: Main Street, it being the same lot that James Beckwith deceased bought from William Hackett. 26 Oct 1876. (Pp. 302-304)

Samuel Hooper and wife to F. F. Rigsby 43 acres. 8 Mar 1877. (Pp. 304-305)

Richard Lamberson and wife, Tabitha, formerly Williams, to H. G. Crawley a tract of land in the 7th District. 13 Apr 1877. (Pp. 305-306)

Priscilla Pack to Martha Pack a tract of land in the 9th District. 10 Jan 1876. (P. 307)

W. B. Barnes and wife, M. J., to George Norton 75 acres on Dry Creek in the 4th District. 14 Feb 1876. (Pp. 307-308)

Harriet M. Howard to Stephen Goodner, colored, a tract of land in the 1st District. Bounded: Mrs. Howard's plank fence. 10 Mar 1877. (P. 309)

J. W. Keel and wife Mary J.; J. L. Neal and wife Nancy E.; A. D. Young and wife Mary J.; Chesley Rigsby and wife Luraney; Catherine Young; and Elizabeth Young to John L. Young their interest in 100 acres in the 7th District with one half acre excepted as a graveyard. 10 Feb 1877. (P. 310)

John P. Tittsworth and wife, Elizabeth, to William Pinegar the Wilmoth land in the 7th District. 11 Nov 1876. (Pp. 311-312)

County Court Clerk to L. J. Magness, trustee of Malicia Magness a tract of land belonging to Jesse Allen deceased. 12 May 1877. (Pp. 312-315)

John Conley and wife, Mary J., to W. P. Smith and wife, Mary S., a tract of land in Liberty. 2 Sep 1876. (Pp. 315-316)

W. J. Shields; T. W. Shields and wife, Susan E., to their mother, R. E. Shields, a tract of land in the 9th District. Said land is intended as a loan to the said R. E. Shields during her natural life or widowhood. 28 Apr 1877. (Pp. 316-317)

James Robinson mineral contract on 275 acres. 5 Feb 1877. (Pp. 318-320)

Mineral contracts. (Pp. 321-324)

Joseph Bozarth to George M. Colvert a tract of land as a lease. 21 Dec 1876. (Pp. 325-327)

Mineral contracts. (Pp. 324-383)

P. M. Turner to E. Turner 50 acres in the 1st District.

27 Apr 1877. (Pp. 383-384)

William C. Gilbert for love and affection to his wife, T. A. Gilbert, and his children, Mary Haney and her husband Lawson Haney some personal property. 4 Jun 1877. (Pp. 384-385)

Henry Bullard and wife; and William Bullard to B. M. Cantrell and A. Avant, attornies, a tract of land and some personal property. 7 Jun 1877. (Pp. 386-387)

Miles J. Covington and wife, Mary A., to J. J. Ford a tract of land in the 1st District. 29 Nov 1876. (Pp. 387-388)

G. L. Bowers and wife to J. J. Ford a tract of land in the 1st District. 11 Sep 1876. (Pp. 388-390)

Thomas E. West and wife, Elizabeth M., to James H. Blackburn and Robert Cantrell their interest in a tract of land in the 1st District. Said land is encumbered by the life estate of Fannie Bowers, widow of Hezekiah Bowers. 24 Jul 1871. (Pp. 390-391)

Giles L. Bowers to Robert Cantrell and James H. Blackburn all of his interest in a tract of land belonging to his father, Hezekiah Bowers. 15 Sep 1876. (Pp. 392-393)

J. L. Colvert and wife M. M., and S. D. Blankenship and wife M. E. to R. H. Lee a lot in the town of Smithville known as Lot No. 44. Bounded: west by the hotel lot, north by the lot on which the hotel stable now stands, and south by Main Street. 20 Mar 1877. (Pp. 393-394)

J. W. Hudson of Alexandria for love and affection to John F. Ray, son of my deceased wife, the property which came to his wife by her first husband D. B. Ray. 20 Jun 1877. (Pp. 394-395)

J. J. Burton for love and affection to his wife, Nancy Burton, a tract of land in the 8th District. 2 Jul 1877. (Pp. 395-396)

E. J. Evans to W. W. Wade a title bond. 6 Jul 1877. (Pp. 396-397)

William P. Kelly, Permelia Kelly, and Tabitha C. Kelly to George P. Kelly a tract of land in the 17th District. 27 Sep 1875. (Pp. 397-398)

William Foutch died testate some time in the year 1874. County Court Clerk to L. L. Foutch a tract of land belonging to the said William Foutch. 10 Jul 1877. (Pp. 398-399)

John E. Jones is now prosecuted in the Circuit Court for the killing of Dr. Fletcher. The said Jones has now employed John H. Savage and F. R. Davis to defend him against said charge. John Jones and wife, Catharine, to Savage and Davis four acres. 10 Jul 1877. (P. 400)

John W. Bethel and wife, Sarah to James H. Lamberson nine

acres in the 2nd District. 7 Aug 1876. (Pp. 401-402)

Joseph Mangrum and wife Martha J. to Jerry Cantrell, colored, 15 acres in the 9th District. 6 Dec 1875. (Pp. 402-403)

Isaac N. Drake and wife, E. R., to John G. Harrison a lot in Smithville. Bounded: the old home place of T. Staley deceased and the Female Academy lot. 16 Jul 1877. (Pp. 403-404)

Robert Cantrell of Wilson County to William V. Jones 370 acres in DeKalb County. 10 Aug 1871. (P. 404)

Mineral rights. (Pp. 405-415)

James Stark and wife, Mary P., to the Directors of the Lebanon & Sparta Road five and one half acres in the 2nd District. 11 Jan 1877. (Pp. 416-417)

E. T. Foster to T. W. Shields two acres in the 9th District. 21 Jul 1877. (P. 417)

J. W. Griffith to S. R. Sandlin a tract of land in the 2nd District. 30 Sep 1876. (Pp. 418-419)

Robert Cantrell of Wilson County to James W. Foutch 100 acres at the top of Snow's Hill where Elizabeth Johnson now lives and known as the Wroe Place. 17 Jul 1877. (Pp. 419-420)

John Hughes to James Alexander 25 acres in the 16th District. 18 May 1868. (Pp. 420-421)

James A. Walker and wife, E. J., to M. O. Schurer 33 acres in the 1st District. 26 Jul 1877. (Pp. 421-422)

Anna West to T. P. West one half the farm on which I now live in the 7th District for the consideration of paying to Wiley Young and their youngest children twenty-five dollars each. T. M. Young is guardian of the said children. 24 May 1877. (Pp. 422-423)

W. B. Stokes to W. T. Hoskins 86 acres in the 12th District. 4 Jun 1877. (Pp. 423-425)

W. R. Smith and wife, Connie, to Robert Black a lot in the town of Smithville. Bounded: Amanda Davis. 2 Sep 1876. (Pp. 425-426)

J. H. C. Burton to Sarah E. Burton his interest in a 200 acre tract, it being two-fifth's, owned by my father Charles Burton deceased. 19 Jul 1877. (Pp. 426-427)

M. M. Brien to J. S. Dunlap a tract of land in the 9th District near Smithville. 17 Dec 1875. (Pp. 427-428)

John Bully Taylor and wife, Nancy, to Henry R. Taylor 149 acres on Indian Creek in the 10th District. 11 Aug 1877. (Pp. 428-429)

John Bully Taylor and wife, Nancy, to P. G. Taylor 12 acres on Indian Creek in the 10th District. 16 Jul 1877. (Pp. 429-430)

Harvey P. Force and wife, Lucinda H., to Asaph L. Sherrell 153 acres in the 9th District. 21 Dec 1876. (Pp. 430-431)

Susan Davis, once the wife and widow of Pleasant H. Wade; and her daughter, Mary Jane Wade, the only child and heir of the said Pleasant and Susan Wade, to H. L. Haney 14 acres in the 7th District. 23 Dec 1876. (Pp. 431-432)

H. L. Haney and wife, M. E., to Tilman Haney 14 acres in the 9th District. 13 Aug 1877. (Pp. 432-433)

Mary Jane Wade to Tilman Haney 66½ acres in the 9th District. 14 Aug 1877. (Pp. 433-434)

Christopher Wright and wife, Anna, to Eveline Adcock 70 acres in the 6th District. 19 Jan 1877. (Pp. 434-436)

Christopher Wright and wife, Anna, to Alice Mullins 27½ acres in the 6th District. 12 Jan 1877. (Pp. 436-437)

Christopher Wright and wife, Anny, to Frances Wright, our daughter, 27 acres in the 6th District. 19 Jan 1877. (Pp. 437-438)

Christopher Wright and wife, Anna, to Catherine Wright, our daughter, 27 acres in the 6th District. 19 Jan 1877. (Pp. 438-439)

Catherine Izabella Fite, Executrix of Samuel M. Fite, to W. E. Burton a tract of land in the 16th District. 30 May 1870. (Pp. 439-442)

Christopher Wright for love and affection to his wife, Anna, 52 acres in the 6th District. 17 Jan 1877. (Pp. 442-443)

Christopher Wright of White County, to his daughter, America Jones, a tract of land in the 6th District. Bounded: at the spring where Jo Jones now gets water, and the old Widow Bains dower. 2 Apr 1877. (Pp. 443-444)

J. Q. Seawel and wife, Alice, to P. T. Shores 36 acres in the 9th District. 12 Dec 1876. (P. 445)

P. T. Shores and wife, Maggie, to F. B. Nollner 36 acres in the 9th District. 24 Aug 1877. (Pp. 446-447)

Thomas Page and wife, Emeline, to John H. Tramel their interest in the lands of Andrew Page deceased. 29 Aug 1877. (Pp. 447-448)

J. M. Braswell for love and affection to his wife, Amanda, and his children viz. James Sidney Braswell, Mina Susan Braswell, and Adah Jane Braswell and any other children which may be born to me in lawful wedlock a tract of land in the 4th District. 3 Aug 1877. (Pp. 448-450)

John Hays and wife, Elizabeth, to Isaac Cantrell three acres in the 9th District. 15 Apr 1877. (Pp. 450-451)

Isaac Cantrell and wife, Mourning, to John Hays nine acres in the 7th District. 15 Apr 1876. (Pp. 451-452)

Clerk & Master to Pat Garret a tract of land belonging to the heirs of Mathew Sellars. 8 Nov 1876. (Pp. 452-454)

J. M. Bailiff a deed of gift to his wife, Eliza J., and his children, to wit, William M., Monza F., and Francis Bailiff a tract of land in the 4th District on the waters of Dry Creek. 4 Sep 1877. (Pp. 454-455)

George W. Colbert of Campbell County to H. L. Taylor a land lease. 25 Aug 1877. (Pp. 455-457)

Catherine Fite, Executrix of S. M. Fite, to Lavinia Johnson part of the land lying on the left hand side of Wolf Creek. 9 Mar 1870. (PP. 457-458)

Pleasant Watts and wife, Nancy H., to John Foster a tract of land heretofore sold to Tilman Foster. 11 Sep 1877. (Pp. 458-459)

John K. Bain and wife, Sarah L., to Nancy E. Jaco 64 acres in the 9th District. 6 Sep 1873. (Pp. 460-461)

George W. Eastham to G. W. Eastham 12 acres in the 9th District. 6 Dec 1875. (Pp. 461-462)

P. T. Shores and wife, Maggie, to S. R. Shanks a lot on Mountain Street in the town of Smithville. 13 Sep 1877. (Pp. 462-463)

G. W. McCarty and wife, Mary, to B. F. Wilkerson 150 acres in the 9th District that I purchased of James Baker, Administrator of William Baker. 13 Sep 1877. (Pp. 463-464)

W. W. Wade and wife, Betty, to Eli J. Evans one acre adjoining the town plan of Smithville. 17 Sep 1877. (Pp. 464-465)

J. J. Smith and wife, Lollie, to G. R. Shanks a town lot in the town of Smithville on the A. L. Davis Road. 21 Jul 1877. (Pp. 465-466)

William Literer, surviving partner of Literer & Cobler, to Mary E. Staley his one fourth interest or the interest of E. D. Staley in Lot No. 87 in the town of Smithville. 31 Dec 1877. (Pp. 466-467)

G. W. Eastham to Narcissas Pack a title bond. 20 Apr 1877. (Pp. 467-468)

Clerk & Master to P. T. Shores a store house and lot in the town of Smithville belonging to P. W. Whaley, the widow of G. B. Whaley. 30 Aug 1877. (Pp. 468-470)

J. S. Dunlap and wife, Emma, to W. G. Crawley 80 acres in the 9th District. 17 Sep 1877. (Pp. 470-471)

James J. Maxwell and wife, Elizabeth J., to E. L. Hutchings 85 acres. 18 Aug 1873. (Pp. 471-472)

John R. Corder and wife, Frances, to E. L. Hutchings the one sixth interest of 85 acres. 13 Aug 1873. (Pp. 472-473)

P. T. Shores and wife, Maggie, to J. J. Potter a lot on

the street that runs through the north side of the Square and east by the street that runs through the west side of the Square. 20 Sep 1877. (Pp. 473-474)

John C. Cannady on the 4th day of Dec 1869 made a settlement on his wife and children of all his real estate as found in Deed Book K, page 118. Said Cannady and wife had one other child named Maud born to them after the date of said deed. John C. Cannady, Margaret A. Cannady, J. H. Seawel, Amanda Seawel, J. S. Dunlap, Emma Dunlap, R. C. Bomar, and Josie Bomer to Maud H. Cannady their interest in a small tract of land in Smithville. Bounded: the Sligo Turnpike. 21 Mar 1877. (Pp. 474-475)

Aaron Frazier to Harden Denney a title bond. 14 Jan 1875. (Pp. 475-476)

William Marsh and wife, Mindia, to John Goodson 21 acres in the 6th District. 15 Nov 1876. (Pp. 476-477)

Aaron Frazier to J. H. White a tract of land on Dry Creek in the 4th District. 29 Sep 1873. (Pp. 477-478)

Aaron Frazier to Sampson Yeargin a title bond. 16 Oct 1876. (Pp. 478-479)

Elizabeth Moss to H. G. Stevens 113 acres in the 5th District. 27 Sep 1877. (Pp. 479-480)

John P. Crowder and wife, Sophronia, to William Eaton 50 acres in the 11th District. 24 Sep 1873. (Pp. 480-481)

J. L. Davis and wife, H. E., to Amanda E. Davis the tract of land and house where the widow, Amanda E. Davis, now lives and adjoining the town of Smithville. 11 Jul 1876. (Pp. 481-482)

G. W. Purser and wife, M. A., to Henry (Bess) 55 acres in the 4th District. 17 Mar 1875. (Pp. 482-483)

James J. Jones and wife, Josephine, to Susan Campbell 101 acres in the 5th District. 26 Oct 1875. (Pp. 483-484)

Nicholas Chambers and wife, Elizabeth, to L. D. Hollinsworth 55 acres in the 5th District. 6 Oct 1877. (Pp. 484-485)

Nicholas Chambers and wife, Elizabeth, to Ed Parsley 45 acres in the 5th District. 6 Oct 1877. Pp. 485-486)

Nicholas Chambers and wife, Elizabeth, to H. W. and T. E. Boatwright 50 acres in the 5th District. 6 Oct 1877. (Pp. 486-487)

Daniel Smith for love and affection to his daughter, Sarah E. Sellars, wife of William Sellars, his real and personal property. 10 Oct 1877. (P. 487)

P. T. Shores to his wife, Maggie, a deed of gift of his interest in the Hollis and Magness old tanyard in Smithville. 11 Oct 1877. (Pp. 487-488)

Barziel Taylor and wife, Frances M., to Martha J. Robinson 50 acres in the 4th District. 19 Jul 1875. (Pp. 488-489)

John P. Tittsworth to Freeling Turner a part of the William Baker land. 15 Oct 1877. (Pp. 489-490)

County Court Clerk to G. W. Elkins a tract of land belonging to William Adcock deceased. 15 Oct 1877. (Pp. 490-491)

R. R. Lamberson and Tabitha, to William Lockheart 100 acres in the 9th District. 23 May 1876. (Pp. 491-492)

Nancy Taylor for love and affection to her step sons, to wit, William E. Taylor, H. C. Taylor, and Horace Taylor her interest in the dower tract of land that D. C. Taylor died seized and possessed of. Bounded: John C. Taylor. 16 Oct 1877. (P. 493)

William Lindsley to John Chapman 90 acres. 9 Dec 1874. (Pp. 494-495)

W. H. McClellan and wife, Mary E., to E. A. Coggin their interest, it being one fourth, in the lands of Lafayette McClellan. 22 Oct 1877. (Pp. 495-496)

John Harrison and wife, Mary, to T. N. Christian a lot in the town of Smithville. Bounded: Academy Street. 20 Oct 1877. (Pp. 496-497)

Amman Parsley and wife, Mary J., to James J. Jones 101 acres in the 5th District. 24 May 1873. (Pp. 497-498)

William H. Pedigo and wife, Amanda, to Eliza James 86 acres in the 9th District. 31 Oct 1877. (Pp. 498-500)

Eliza James to William H. Pedigo 23 acres in the 9th District known as the William Ball tract. 31 Oct 1877. (Pp. 500-501)

William H. Pedigo for love and affection to his wife, Amanda some personal property. 31 Oct 1877. (Pp. 501-502)

William Jones to W. B. Farley his interest in a tract of land now in the possession of my mother, Elizabeth Jones, who has a life estate. 3 Nov 1877. (Pp. 502-503)

Sarah J. Hale and Sarah F. Hale to Catherine Malone, wife of M. Malone, ten acres in the 11th District. 1 Nov 1877. (Pp. 503-504)

Isaac Burton to Henry Johnson ten acres in the 16th District. 2 Jan 1872. (Pp. 504-505)

David Dollar to John Q. Dollar, my son, a tract of land with the condition being that he take charge of Martha, Nancy J., William, Rachel, Margaret, me, and Martin until the youngest of the above named reaches maturity. 20 Oct 1877. (Pp. 505-506)

John Reynolds died intestate some time before the 19th of Nov 1869. County Court Clerk to David Payne a tract of land belonging to the said Reynolds. 30 Oct 1877. (Pp. 506-508)

William Oakley and wife, Polly, to James M. Foutch 112 acres in the 11th District. 23 Oct 1874. (Pp. 508-509)

John V. Crowder to the Mayor and Aldermen of Smithville three acres in the 9th District and excluding one acre and ten poles that John C. Cannady has this day made to said Mayor and Aldermen as a deed of gift to what is known as the Cannady graveyard. I also give to the said Mayor and Aldermen a right of way to said land. 2 Nov 1877. (Pp. 509-510)

David Adcock and wife, Sarah, to John H. Savage a tract of land on Sink Creek. 21 Aug 1875. (Pp. 510-511)

Coleman Helm and wife, Mary, to Felix Helm 250 acres in the 16th District. 12 Nov 1877. (Pp. 511-512)

Barthena Moore to W. C. Potter and the other school directors of the 9th District one acre. Said land is to be used for school purposes and no other. When said land ceases to be used for said purposes, the land is to be sold and I am to have the preference of said land at ten dollars, giving said school the privilege of removing said house. 4 Sep 1877. (Pp. 512-513)

Survey of the land of Nancy Webb. 2 Nov 1877. (Pp. 513-514)

Nicholas Chambers and wife, Elizabeth, to W. V. Wilson three acres in the 9th District. 12 Nov 1877. (Pp. 515-516)

E. J. Evans and wife, Eugenia, to L. J. Potter and wife, Delia, for the consideration of house and lot joining the Public Square in the town of Smithville one half of our lot purchased from W. W. Wade on the south side of said lot. 13 Nov 1877. (Pp. 516-417)

Francis Hendrickson and wife Angeline; Wiley Hendrickson and wife Peggy; William Hendrickson and wife Samantha; Jerry Smith and wife Matilda; Thomas Fuson and wife Betsy; and Nathaniel Hendrickson to D. W. Taylor two acres in the 10th District. 24 Mar 1877. (Pp. 518-519)

W. V. Wilson and wife, Frances, to Nicholas Chambers two lots in the 9th District. 12 Nov 1877. (Pp. 519-520)

Nicholas Chambers and wife, Elizabeth, to John J. Spurlock 103 acres in the 5th District. 17 Oct 1877. (Pp. 520-521)

Sheriff to E. A. Coggins a tract of land belonging to E. D. Fish. 19 Nov 1877. (Pp. 521-522)

John C. Cannady for the effection that I have for the dead and dying to the Mayor and Aldermen of Smithville one acre in the 9th District. Bounded: north by Crowder, south by Crowder, east by Crowder, and west by Crowder. Reserving a family lot of sufficient size to bury my entire, to wit, beginning near an oak stump between the head of an old grave and the foot of Adam Dale's grave. . . beginning including the Ward and Cannady family and their connections. The proceeds arising from the sale of said lot for family graves be appropriated to the improvement of that portion of the burial ground. 2 Nov 1877. (Pp. 522-523)

E. Heald to O. T. Heald a lot in Smithville on the west side of the Square. I reserve to myself a life estate in the said lot. 12 Nov 1877. (Pp. 523-524)

J. N. Drake and wife, E. R., to J. J. Smith the Shanks farm in the 6th District of White County. 21 Jul 1877. (Pp. 524-525)

P. T. Shores to W. M. Shores a lot of Main Street in the town of Smithville. 28 Nov 1877. (P. 525)

J. J. Bennett to Jesse Petty 50 acres. 22 Mar 1877. (Pp. 526-527)

M. R. Smith, guardian of Rachel Tennessee Smith, to Ed Warren a one thirteenth remainder undivided interest in the dower of Nancy Parsley. 26 Nov 1877. (P. 527)

W. T. Robinson and wife, L. J., to Aaron Frazier 295 acres in the 17th District. 28 May 1873. (Pp. 527-528)

Thomas Adcock and wife, Frances, to A. E. Adcock their interest in 40 acres in the 7th District. 1 Dec 1877. (Pp. 529-530)

C. C. Murphy and wife Betty; A. L. Foster and wife Mary; and E. T. Foster to E. J. Evans a lot in the 9th District. 3 Dec 1877. (Pp. 530-532)

G. W. Eastham to H. C. Eastham a tract of land in the 9th District. 13 Dec 1877. (P. 532)

C. C. Wright and wife, Anna, to Susan Jones 35 acres in the 6th District. Said transaction is for the love and affection we have for our daughter, the said Susan Jones. 19 Jan 1877. (P. 533)

Daniel Jones and wife, Susan, to F. P. Fish four acres in the 6th District. 23 Jul 1877. (Pp. 533-534)

Christopher C. Wright and wife, Anna, to Louisa Fisher 35 acres in the 6th District. Said transaction is for the love and affection we have for our daughter, the said Louisa Fisher. 19 Jan 1877. (Pp. 534-535)

Nancy Webb to Ferdinand P. Fisher four acres in the 6th District. 26 Oct 1877. (Pp. 535-536)

Elizabeth Braswell to William A. Braswell 65 acres in the 16th District. 17 Apr 1876. (Pp. 536-537)

H. E. Staley and wife, C. T., to Jasper Fowler three acres in the 9th District. 17 Dec 1877. (P. 537)

Calvin Kersey and wife, Adeline, to Josiah Malone 55 acres in the 5th District. 26 Nov 1877. (P. 538)

E. Warren, F. D. Warren, John Elrod and wife M. E., A. M. Warren, R. B. Montgomery and wife Amanda, M. J. Durham and wife Lou, and W. T. Warren, children of John E. Warren, enter into an agreement with their mother Nancy Warren, widow. 15 Dec 1877. (Pp. 539-542)

DEED BOOK M

James Skerlock and wife, Adaline, formerly Rich, to W. B. Rich her interest of a child's part in the tract of land known as the Obediah Rich tract. 19 Dec 1876. (Pp. 542-543)

J. C. Stipe and wife, Nancy L., to James R. Chisom 300 acres in the 6th District. 27 Dec 1877. (Pp. 543-544)

John Hallum and wife, Frances, to Stith Lane 111 acres in the 9th District known as the E. L. McGinnis tract. 2 Mar 1877. (Pp. 544-545)

Clerk & Master to Joseph Thomas, colored, 15 acres belonging to the estate of W. L. Hathaway. 3 Jan 1878. (Pp. 545-546)

County Court Clerk to F. W. Hobson a tract of land belonging to the heirs of Nancy Jackson. 1 Jan 1878. (Pp. 547-548)

J. S. Dunlap and wife, Emma, to John V. Crowder one acre in the 9th District. 15 Mar 1876. (Pp. 548-549)

James Anderson and wife, M. J., to Perry Adcock 147 acres. 30 Apr 1877. (Pp. 549-551)

Wilson Sellars and wife, Mary, to Allen Wilson one and one half acres in the 13th District. 28 Dec 1877. (Pp. 551-552)

Clerk & Master to G. W. Hathaway 11 acres belonging to T. H. Berry. 8 Jan 1878. (Pp. 552-553)

Clerk & Master to J. D. Phillips 97 acres belonging to D. B. Davis and others. 3 Jan 1878. (Pp. 553-555)

W. T. Hoskins and wife, M. J., to R. B. Noland 142 acres in the 1st District on the road from Alexandria to Lancaster. 30 Mar 1872. (Pp. 555-556)

P. C. Pack and wife, B. F., to W. M. Pack their one seventh interest in 140 acres in the 9th District, it being the place where W. M. Pack now lives and deeded to Mariah Pack. 11 Jan 1878. (Pp. 556-557)

W. J. Green to Isaac D. Tittsworth 32 acres in the 9th District. 29 Dec 1877. (Pp. 557-558)

Joseph Starnes to William Holley 14 acres in the 15th District. 15 Jan 1875. (Pp. 558-559)

Thomas E. Bratton to Elijah J. Bratton a title bond. 17 Jan 1878. (Pp. 560-561)

Sheriff to J. D. Bond a tract of land belonging to A. Bone deceased. 7 Jan 1878. (Pp. 561-562)

John Chapman and wife, Roxany, to C. A. Bailiff their interest in the land of Thomas Bailiff deceased. 7 Nov 1872. (Pp. 563-564)

William A. McClellan and wife, Nancy, to John H. Tramel 175 acres in the 10th District. 25 Jan 1878. (Pp. 564-565)

John H. Tramel and wife, Martha J., to James W. Foutch 68 acres in the 10th District. 25 Jan 1878. (Pp. 565-566)

G. W. Hathaway and wife, Salina J., to William A. McClellan two acres in the 4th District. 25 Jan 1878. (P. 567)

E. J. Evans and wife, Eugenia, to (Isiah) White a lot adjoining the town of Smithville. 26 Jan 1878. (P. 568)

Christopher Wright and wife, Anna, for love and affection to their daughter, Texas Sanders a tract of land in the 6th District containing 50 acres. 10 Jan 1877. (P. 569)

E. J. Evans and wife, Eugenia, to John V. Crowder 150 acres in the 9th District. 2 Feb 1878. (P. 570)

P. L. Adamson to W. G. Brien 40 acres in the 3rd District. 4 Feb 1878. (P. 571)

William Eaton and wife, F. C., to William E. Foutch 50 acres in the 11th District. 30 Sep 1877. (Pp. 571-572)

J. M. Walker to W. B. Bridges 50 acres in the 1st District. 2 Feb 1878. (Pp. 572-573)

Emeline Pitman to Ira W. King 20 acres. Said Emeline has a life estate as one of the heirs of Yancy Malone. 17 Oct 1870. (Pp. 573-574)

John Crowder and wife, Sophronia, to W. W. Maxwell one and one half acres in the 9th District. 11 Sep 1877. (Pp. 574-575)

J. D. Baird and wife, Mary J., to J. M. Baird a house and lot in the town of Alexandria. 5 Dec 1877. (Pp. 576-577)

J. M. Baird to P. L. Wood three rods in the 1st District. 6 Feb 1878. (P. 577)

J. L. Robinson to W. B. Herman a one fourth interest in a tract of land in the 7th District. 4 Sep 1876. (P. 578)

Mathew Wilson and wife, Mary, to T. M. Hooper ten acres near Smithville on the east side of the old graveyard. 7 Feb 1878. (Pp. 579-580)

Martha Foster to her father, W. W. Foster, 50 acres in the 9th District. 11 May 1877. (P. 580)

G. W. McCarty and wife, Mary, to W. R. Foster 30 acres in the 7th District. 17 Jan 1877. (P. 581)

Asa Monroe Cantrell to John Green of Warren County a title bond. 3 Oct 1877. (Pp. 581-582)

Lucy Cantrell to John Green a title bond. 15 Oct 1877. (Pp. 582-583)

James W. Foutch and wife, Sarah J., to J. B. Robinson 100 acres on the Lebanon & Sparta Pike on top of Snow's Hill and known as the Wroe Place. 12 Feb 1878. (Pp. 583-584)

John B. Robinson and wife, Julie M., to J. B. Butler a title bond. 12 Feb 1878. (Pp. 584-585)

William R. Durham to David Durham 40 acres in the 7th District. 19 May 1877. (Pp. 585-586)

DEED BOOK M

J. F. Wood to James H. Blackburn all my interest in 107 acres in the 1st District. 30 Aug 1871. (P. 587)

Leonard H. Fite and wife, Malcena H., to James H. Blackburn and Robert Cantrell their interest in a tract of land in the 1st District. The land is encumbered by the life estate of Fannie Bowers, widow of Hezekiah Bowers. 21 Jul 1871. (Pp. 588-590)

George M. Bowers and wife, Tennessee, to James H. Blackburn and Robert Cantrell their interest which is one eighth in the land descended to us from Hezekiah Bowers. 21 Nov 1877. (Pp. 590-591)

Martin L. Green and wife, Margaret J., to James H. Blackburn their interest in a tract of land whereon Hezekiah Bowers lived at the time of his death. 15 Jun 1871. (Pp. 592-593)

Sarah Carroll, formerly Bowers, to W. A. Hayes her interest in a tract of land belonging to the estate of her father Hezekiah Bowers. 20 Sep 1876. (Pp. 593-594)

Peter Adams and wife, Rachel, to Alfred L. Hancock the west tract of land where the said Peter now lives and lying in the counties of Wilson and DeKalb. 12 Feb 1877. (Pp. 594-595)

Robert Cantrell of Wilson County to J. J. Ford his interest in the Hezekiah Bowers tract of land about one half mile south east of Alexandria. 10 Jan 1877. (Pp. 596-597)

T. L. Seawel and wife, P. A., to J. Q. Seawel a lot in the town of Smithville. 23 Feb 1878. (P. 597)

J. P. Whorton to Whorton J. Green a title bond. 20 Nov 1865. (P. 598)

J. D. Roland and wife, Susan A., to L. W. Neal their interest in 82 acres in the 1st District known as the dower of Andrew Pickett's wife. 2 Jan 1874. (Pp. 598-599)

Henry H. Pistole and wife, Mahulda; Joseph Pistole and wife, Eliza; W. L. Evans and wife Sarah A. had a division of the lands that James Pistole died seized and possessed of. Joseph Pistole to Henry H. Pistole his interest in the estate. 28 Feb 1878. (Pp. 599-601)

Eli Lafever and wife, Mary, to Mary A. Johnson 15 acres in the 8th District. 1 Mar 1878. (Pp. 601-602)

P. W. Presley for love and affection to John J. Presley 110 acres in the 16th District. 12 Feb 1878. (Pp. 602-603)

Clerk & Master to J. D. Phillips 80 acres. 4 Mar 1878. (Pp. 603-605)

James H. Blackburn to J. J. Ford 115 acres in the 1st District. 5 Jan 1874. (Pp. 605-606)

Samuel F. Patterson to W. W. Patterson one half interest in 127 acres located in the 1st District. 21 Jan 1876. (Pp. 606-607)

DEED BOOK M

Sanford Man and wife, Matilda, to L. Burger 19 acres in the 2nd District. 24 Dec 1877. (Pp. 607-608)

M. R. Smith and wife, M. A., to R. F. Hicks 77 acres in the 5th District. 8 Mar 1878. (Pp. 608-609)

Rebecca Garrison to Samuel H. Smith five acres in the 16th District. 25 Sep 1871. (Pp. 609-610)

John H. Savage to Josiah W. Dinges 300 acres on Dry Creek. 11 Mar 1878. (Pp. 610-611)

DEED BOOK N

W. B. Bridges and wife, Nancy C., to Rial Jennings 51 acres in the 1st District. 20 Oct 1877. (Pp. 1-2)

William Watters to McAdo Vanatta and Sanford Mann seven acres in the town of Liberty. Bounded: town spring. 30 Jun 1877. (Pp. 2-3)

Henry Pistole and wife Malinda; William Evans and wife Sarah; Joseph Pistole and wife Eliza have had a division of the lands of James Pistole. William Evans and others to Joseph Pistole a tract of land in the 12th District. 28 Feb 1878. (Pp. 3-5)

James W. Denney and wife, Martha J., to James A. Walker seven and one half acres in the 12th District. 3 Nov 1877. (Pp. 5-6)

John M. Walker and wife, Louisa, to Martha J. Walker 27½ acres in the 1st District. 1 Feb 1876. (Pp. 7-8)

John M. Allen of Thorpe County, Arkansas to Frances Allen 18 acres in DeKalb County. 12 Sep 1873. (Pp. 8-9)

John F. Luckey and wife, Martha, to Daniel Williams a town lot in the town of Alexandria. 1 Feb 1878. (Pp. 9-10)

James Truett and wife Julie, to John Vanatta 60 acres in the 13th District. 24 Dec 1875. (Pp. 11-12)

John M. Walker to James A. Walker three and one fourth acres in the 1st District. 6 Feb 1878. (P. 13)

William C. Jennings and wife, America F., to George A. Allen their one eighth part of all the lands belonging to the estate of John Allen. 11 Mar 1878. (P. 14)

Augustine S. Redman and wife Mary Jane, formerly Robinson, to Elbert Robinson five and one fourth acres in the 15th District so as to include the dwelling house in which A. M. Robinson formerly lived except the upper story which is reserved for the use of Sons of Temperance. 8 Apr 1873. (Pp. 15-16)

George Measles to William H. Magness a title bond. 2 Jul 1870. (Pp. 16-17)

Asberry Hayes and wife, Tennessee, to Jesse W. Scott 37 acres in the 2nd District. 23 Sep 1875. (Pp. 18-19)

S. S. Craddock and wife, Harriet M., to Jesse W. Scott a tract of land in the 2nd District. 2 Feb 1878. (Pp. 19-20)

C. W. L. Hale to the trustees of Searcey's Chapel in the 2nd District eighteen and one half poles to be used as a public highway. 1 Mar 1878. (P. 21)

Jasper Ruyle and wife, Matilda, to Bluford Mathis 70 acres in the 3rd District. 12 Jan 1877. (Pp. 22-23)

W. G. Bransford and others to J. M. Conditt and others a division of a tract of land. 24 Sep 1877. (Pp. 23-28)

W. H. Hayes and wife, R. H., to B. J. Bethel a tract of land in the 1st District. 12 Mar 1878. (Pp. 28-30)

W. T. Hoskins and wife, M. J., to J. L. Ayers a tract of land in the 12th District. 17 Feb 1877. (Pp. 31-32)

Charter of Corporation of Dowell Town. 19 Mar 1875. (Pp. 33-36)

G. M. Bowers and wife, Gennie, to W. F. Turner 35 acres in the 1st District. 24 Sep 1877. (Pp. 36-37)

John B. Walker to C. A. Cantrell 50 acres in the 6th District. 19 Mar 1855. (Pp. 37-38)

John C. Halcum, Malinda Halcum, Malvina Halcum, and Thomas H. Halcum to James C. Williams 100 acres in the 4th and 5th Districts. 29 Aug 1876. (Pp. 38-40)

John E. Warren to William Steel a tract of land in the 14th District, the number of acres are unknown. Bounded: the school house. 13 Oct 1870. (Pp. 40-41)

Louis Tippit or Webb to Elizabeth Sanders acknowledgement that John Tippit in his life time gave title to a tract of land in the 6th District to the said Elizabeth Sanders. 17 Aug 1839. (Pp. 41-42)

Nancy Webb to Wiley Sanders a quit claim to the land covered by Grant No. 1554, it being about three fourth's of an acre. 25 Oct 1877. (Pp. 42-43)

The heirs of John E. Warren agree to partition certain lands. 1 Apr 1878. (Pp. 43-54)

Thomas J. McClellan to E. A. Coggin a one fourth interest in the land allotted to the heirs of Lafayette McClellan. 6 Apr 1878. (Pp. 54-55)

William Foutch died intestate some time before the 9th of Feb 1874. County Court Clerk to John V. Crowder a tract of land belonging to the said Foutch. 26 Mar 1877. (Pp. 55-57)

Clerk & Master to Josiah White four acres belonging to the estate of David Fite. 10 Apr 1875. (Pp. 57-48)

Levi R. Taylor and wife, Rebecca, to John C. Taylor 17½ acres in the 10th District. 20 Mar 1878. (Pp. 59-60)

R. B. Nolen and wife, M. C., to D. W. Dinges 142 acres in the 1st District. 3 Feb 1878. (Pp. 60-62)

Mariah L. Hayes to Harry Allen a tract of land in the narrows of the Caney Fork River in the 9th District. 11 Apr 1878. (Pp. 62-63)

County Court Clerk to Perry Adcock a tract of land belonging to the estate of J. S. Kerby. The widow received her dower. 11 Apr 1878. (Pp. 63-65)

County Court Clerk to J. B. Farley 150 acres known as the Mathew Hunt Farm in the 4th District. 10 Apr 1875. (Pp. 65-66)

Aaron Durham to N. L. Wood 24 acres in the 7th District. 9 Oct 1877. (Pp. 67-68)

DEED BOOK N

Monroe Blair to Sarah Parsley 200 acres in the 4th District. 11 Mar 1878. (Pp. 68-70)

John C. Cannady and wife, Margaret A., to Rebecca F. Mullican and her children at her death ten acres in the 9th District. 17 May 1878. (Pp. 70-71)

Susan Bullard to John Miller 94 acres, it being one of the lots in the partition of the lands of Henry Bullard deceased. 17 May 1878. (Pp. 71-72)

Sheriff to Robert Cantrell and J. J. Ford a tract of land belonging to William Adamson. 6 Sep 1877. (Pp. 72-74)

William Adamson and wife, Parthenia, to J. J. Ford their interest a lot in the 1st District. 24 Sep 1877. (Pp. 75-76)

W. F. Foster and wife, Juda, to J. L. Colvert and others a town lot in the town of Smithville. Bounded: Walnut Street. 12 Apr 1878. (Pp. 76-78)

N. L. Wood and wife, Margaret, to John P. Tittsworth part of the Patsy Durham lands in the 7th District. 5 Apr 1878. (Pp. 78-79)

Sheriff to B. A. Cantrell a tract of land belonging to E. D. Pite. 6 Mar 1877. (Pp. 80-81)

Peter J. Turney and wife, Eliza, to George Turney 175 acres in the 3rd District. (Pp. 81-82)

John P. Tittsworth to James (Peatee) 67 acres in the 9th District. 21 May 1878. (Pp. 83-84)

The heirs of William and Jane McMillan deceased, to wit, Ran Scott, Jane Scott, Sam McMillan, Tom McMillan, J. W. Roberts, and Tennessee Roberts to J. D. Wheeler their interest in the estate of the said William and Jane McMillan. 5 Jun 1875. (Pp. 84-85)

J. W. Inge to W. M. and D. H. Hill 50 acres in the 2nd District. 22 Jan 1878. (Pp. 85-87)

Helen Schurer, Josie Hill and husband O. P., J. H. Schurer and wife M. O., C. M. Schurer, and F. M. Schurer, a minor, to J. V. Crowder and Martin Foutch five acres in the 9th District. Excluded is one acre deeded to J. C. Cannady so as to enclose the graveyard. 5 Apr 1877. (Pp. 87-89)

Charter for Temperance Hall Male and Female Academy. 1 Jun 1878. (PP. 90-93)

Martin Foutch to L. B. Avant a one half interest in a tract of land in the 9th District. 11 May 1878. (Pp. 93-95)

John A. Wright and wife, Mary, to Samuel Oakley 30 acres in the 17th District. 27 Aug 1873. (Pp. 95-97)

John Read and wife, Sarah, to Robert Nixon seven acres in the 15th District. 9 Dec 1876. (P7-98)

David Brock to John H. Savage a deed of trust. 9 Jul 1878. (Pp. 99-102)

W. C. Avant and wife, Nancy, to James Oakley and W. A. Turner 69 acres in the 12th District. 9 Jul 1878. (Pp. 102-103)

John T. Stokes and wife, Perlina, to L. and D. Driver 100 acres on Smith Fork in the 15th District. 4 Mar 1878. (Pp. 103-104)

John Starnes and wife, Amanda; A. D. Starnes and wife, Susan to G. M. McGee 11 acres in the 16th District. 13 Mar 1876. (Pp. 105-106)

Clerk & Master to T. W. Goodner a tract of land belonging to L. R. Lucas. 17 Jul 1878. (Pp. 106-107)

C. G. Bates and wife, Jane, to William Bates 95 acres in the 11th District. 18 Jul 1878. (Pp. 108-109)

William Bates to John B. Robinson and others a tract of land in the 11th District. 19 Jul 1878. (Pp. 109-111)

Thomas Frisby and wife, Juley, to James M. Bozarth five acres in the 14th District. 16 Sep 1876. (Pp. 111-112)

Isaac Tittsworth and wife, Caroline, to John P. Tittsworth round about 50 or 60 acres in the 5th District. 15 May 1878. (Pp. 113-114)

Mary Keel to Paralee Haney 40 acres in the 7th District. 21 Oct 1874. (Pp. 114-115)

G. W. Eastham and H. C. Eastham to William Goodman 40 acres in the 14th District. 15 Aug 1873. (Pp. 115-116)

F. C. White and wife, Lizzie, to William Hendrixson their interest in one fourth of an acre in the 2nd District. 17 Jun 1878. (Pp. 116-117)

W. C. Avant and wife, Nancy, to C. C. Avant a tract of land on the south side of Smith Fork. 24 Jan 1878. (Pp. 117-118)

W. J. Green to B. M. Hicks 103 acres near J. J. Summers new house on the McMinnville Road. 29 Dec 1877. (Pp. 119-120)

G. A. Bing to Spencer Bing one acre in the 9th District. 12 Dec 1876. (Pp. 120-121)

C. W. L. Hale to the trustees of the Methodist Episcopal Church 105 poles in the 2nd District. 6 Aug 1877. (Pp. 121-122)

William Underwood and wife Sarah J; Levi L. Johnson and wife Lucy A. E. to R. J. Montgomery six acres. 3 Aug 1878. (Pp. 123-124)

Elizabeth Fuson to John Fuson her one sixth interest in a tract of land in the 9th District. 5 May 1877. (Pp. 124-125)

L. J. Bing to G. W. (Keeley) a tract of land. 5 Aug 1878. (Pp. 125-131)

Yancy Pinegar and wife, Elizabeth to M. C. Green 90 acres in the 5th District. 12 Sep 1871. (Pp. 132-133)

J. B. Blye and wife R. D. to R. B. Hale and wife S. C. 50 acres in the 4th District. 16 Mar 1878. (Pp. 133-135)

Carrol Johnson and wife, Elizabeth, to Nancy Johnson their interest in a tract of land in the 9th District conveyed to us by our father William Johnson and containing 215 acres. Our interest is one tenth part. 10 Jun 1878. (Pp. 135-136)

Jesse R. Cantrell and wife, Elizabeth, to John V. Crowder 26 acres in the 9th District. 23 Jan 1877. (Pp. 136-137)

J. A. Winchester, G. A. Winchester, W. V. Winchester, E. E. Winchester, and G. W. Null, heirs of Jacob and Jane Null deceased, to V. M. and M. F. Williams 89 acres in the 16th District. 24 Aug 1876. (Pp. 138-139)

County Court Clerk to James H. Blackburn a town lot in the town of Alexandria owned by E. Tubb for tax purposes. 4 Mar 1876. (Pp. 140-141)

F. C. White and wife, Eliza, to T. Johnson three fifth's of an acre in the 4th District. 15 Nov 1875. (Pp. 141-142)

Watson Cantrell and wife Perlina; Isaac Cantrell and wife Samantha; P. G. Cantrell and wife Mourning; E. J. Lassiter and wife Rutha Jane; and Hannah Cantrell to A. M. Cantrell and wife Martha Jane their interest in 37 acres in the 5th District, it being the lot that Lucy Cantrell drawed from her father Watson Cantrell deceased. Watson Cantrell and wife Perlina are residents of Warren County. 31 Mar 1877. (Pp. 142-147)

P. G. Magness, Jr. to P. G. Magness, Sr. 67 acres in the 5th District. 30 Nov 1875. (Pp. 147-148)

Watson Cantrell and wife, Perlina, of Warren County and others to P. G. Cantrell a tract of land in the 5th District, it being the Jefferson Cantrell deceased land. 31 Mar 1877. (Pp. 148-150)

Isaac Cantrell and wife, Samantha, P. G. Cantrell and others to Hannah Cantrell their interest in 42 acres. 31 Mar 1877. (Pp. 150-152)

Samuel Henley and wife, M. J., to A. B. Hicks two small lots in the 13th District. 12 Feb 1878. (Pp. 152-153)

O. B. Wright and W. H. Magness to Calvin C. Garrison a tract of land in the 1st District. 18 Dec 1876. (Pp. 153-154)

Anna Wright to W. T. Wright two acres. 20 May 1878. (Pp. 154-155)

John R. Lawrence and wife, Gracy, to Morgan Lawrence a title bond. 21 Dec 1877. (Pp. 156-157)

Nancy Vicker died intestate prior to the 1st day of Jan 1871. There was no administrator of her personal estate. County Court Clerk to Joshua Vickers 50 acres belonging to the said Nancy Vickers. 8 Aug 1878. (Pp. 158-159)

Samuel Williams to Simeon Williams 90 acres in the 4th District. 31 Mar 1874. (Pp. 159-161)

W. W. Wade and wife, Bettie, to Harriet Tubb a house and lot in the town of Smithville. Bounded: Widow Dunlap. 23 Aug 1875. (Pp. 161-162)

Caroline V. Wade to W. W. Wade a title bond on a house and lot in the town of Smithville. 3 Nov 1877. (Pp. 162-163)

W. G. Foster and wife, Juda A., to Mary J. Dozier, Lucy Dozier, Isaac Dozier, and Honor Dozier a part of a town lot in the town of Smithville. 9 Aug 1878. (Pp. 163-165)

County Court Clerk to W. L. Cantrell 52 acres belonging to the estate of Green Cantrell. 9 Aug 1878. (Pp. 165-166)

County Court Clerk to John H. Savage three tracts of land. 27 May 1878. (Pp. 167-170)

John Elrod and wife, W. E.; E. Warren and wife, S. E.; F. D. Warren and wife, M. A.; A. M. Warren and wife, R. A.; R. J. Montgomery and wife, A.; W. T. Warren; and Nancy Warren to Lou Durham three acres in the 14th District. 28 Feb 1878. (Pp. 170-172)

Henry Bess and wife, M. E., to Harden Vick 50 acres in the 4th District. 18 Oct 1877. (Pp. 172-173)

T. M. Hooper and wife, M. D., to J. W. Gilbert a part of the T. S. Bennett old home tract conveyed by deed of gift by T. S. Bennett to his daughter, Frances Culwell, and then to J. H. Dodd by Filly Culwell and wife, Frances, and then to T. M. Hooper by J. H. Dodd. 31 Aug 1876. (Pp. 174-175)

W. H. Magness to W. H. Magness and others a trust deed. 13 Aug 1878. (Pp. 175-176)

R. Marler and wife, E. J., to T. J. Estes 23 acres in the 1st District. 21 Oct 1876. (Pp. 177-178)

M. H. Pack and wife, Martha, to Jessie R. Cantrell a tract of land in the 9th District. 19 Oct 1876. (Pp. 178-179)

W. L. Driver and wife, Nancy W., to J. S. Dunlap five acres in the 9th District. 4 Mar 1877. (Pp. 179-180)

Levi Haney and wife, Elender, to William Marsh 125 acres in the 9th District. 22 Mar 1878. (Pp. 180-182)

John W. Bullen and wife, Nancy A., to E. R. Northcutt a tract of land in the 5th District. 23 Jun 1877. (Pp. 182-184)

Clerk & Master to Isaac Turney a tract of land belonging to the estate of Isaac Turney. 1 Apr 1878. (Pp. 184-185)

Nancy J. Fuson to John Fuson a trust deed. 5 May 1877. (Pp. 185-186)

W. H. Hendrixson and wife, Frances, to Thomas Page and wife a tract of land. 29 Aug 1877. (Pp. 187-188)

Mathew Wilson and wife, Mary, to L. D. Crowder and R. D. Crowder a tract of land near Smithville. 19 Feb 1875. (Pp. 188-189)

DEED BOOK N

W. E. Durham and wife, Sophronia, to Chesley Turner and wife 24 acres near Mount View Church in the 7th District. 12 Feb 1876. (Pp. 189-190)

H. H. Overall to Wills Barrett 57 acres. 1 Jan 1875. (Pp. 191-192)

Noah Adcock to J. W. Adcock and wife, Mary, two tracts of land in the 7th District. 10 Jan 1876. (Pp. 192-193)

C. J. Britton and wife, Hannah, to A. M. Cantrell 42 acres in the 5th District. 28 Sep 1877. (Pp. 194-195)

L. F. Moore and wife, Elizabeth, to David Dunham a tract of land in the 4th District. Bounded: the dower of Nancy Alexander. 14 Feb 1876. (Pp. 195-196)

P. G. Magness to M. N. Smith 100 acres in the 5th District between Sink and Pine Creeks. 11 Feb 1878. (Pp. 196-197)

Dempsey Braswell and wife, Paralee, to Aaron Braswell all their interest in the lands of Nathan Braswell deceased. 29 Jul 1876. (Pp. 197-198)

Margaret L. Garrison to Jeff Herd, colored, one acre in the 1st District. 3 Jul 1877. (Pp. 198-199)

Jacob Adams and Peter Adams to J. R. King 30 acres in the 3rd District. 30 Jan 1878. (P. 200)

H. S. Hathaway and wife, Kizzie Ann, to Josey Harding 261 acres in the 5th District, it being my wife's interest in the estate of her father, Washington Parish deceased. 16 Aug 1877. (P. 201)

M. M. Brien to J. A. Wilson the tract of land in the 9th District whereon James C. Brien now lives, formerly the Parsley tract. 8 Feb 1878. (P. 202)

Sarah M. Fuson to John M. Fuson her one sixth interest in 100 acres in the 9th District, it being the same land that our father, John Fuson, died seized and possessed of. 27 Dec 1877. (Pp. 203-204)

Martin Foutch to A. M. Robinson a trust deed. 19 Sep 1877. (Pp. 204-205)

George L. Hearn to William and Joseph Rich three acres in the town of Alexandria. 9 Jan 1877. (Pp. 205-206)

Sheriff to Isaac Whaley 80 acres. 18 Mar 1878. (Pp. 206-208)

Samuel Casey and wife, Eliza, to the Directors of the Lebanon & Sparta Turnpike one half acre in the 4th District. 14 Sep 1877. (Pp. 208-209)

John Curtis and wife, Mary B., to Mathew Curtis 154 acres in the 4th District. 9 Nov 1877. (Pp. 209-211)

John Hallem to Solomon R. Lowrey a title bond. 19 Jul 1877. (Pp. 211-212)

DEED BOOK N

Harriet Tubb to W. W. Wade a tract of land in the 9th District on Fall Creek near the town of Smithville. 23 Aug 1875. (Pp. 213-214)

John V. Crowder and wife, Rachel S., to Rufus Johnson 54 acres on Helton's Creek in the 11th District. 25 Feb 1875. (Pp. 214-216)

G. W. Eastham to James H. Jones a tract of land in the 9th District. 23 Oct 1876. (Pp. 216-217)

John J. Callicott to John Jackson 11¼ acres in the 17th District. 19 Feb 1877. (Pp. 217-218)

William Rich to James Obediah Rich nine acres in the 3rd District. 19 Sep 1874. (Pp. 218-219)

Peter Adams and wife, Rachel, to J. C. Adamson, E. M. Adamson, P. L. Adamson, A. Elizabeth (Destiny), Rachel Jane Adamson, and W. B. Adamson 20 acres. Bounded: Nancy Adamson. 20 May 1878. (Pp. 219-221)

John B. Walker and wife, Mary, to Thomas W. Jones and wife, Frances E., for the love and affection we entertain for Frances E. Jones a tract of land in the 6th District. 30 Dec 1876. (Pp. 221-223)

W. C. Cantrell to J. C. (Savage) 50 acres in the 5th District. 11 Jun 1877. (Pp. 223-225)

Adam Tittle to G. W. Martin 35 acres in the 4th District. 2 Apr 1877. (Pp. 225-226)

W. H. Brown to Isaac C. and John L. Brown a tract of land in the 8th District. 7 Feb 1874. (Pp. 226-227)

David Dunham, Jr. to T. J. and J. L. Banks 44 acres in the 4th District. Bounded: the heirs of James Beckwith. 23 Nov 1876. (Pp. 227-228)

Samuel T. Mottley to Morgan Lawrence 156 acres in the 1st District. 20 Dec 1875. (Pp. 228-229)

James H. White to John Jones 56 acres in the 17th District that James Jones was seized and possessed of. 11 Feb 1865. (P. 230)

W. D. Petty and wife, Sarah, to Johnathan Johnson 50 acres in the 9th District. 2 Apr 1877. (P. 231)

Edward Lisk and wife, Synthia, to W. M. Jones 80 acres in the 9th District. 20 Apr 1876. (Pp. 232-233)

William and Nancy Hensley to John Lamberson a tract of land in the 17th District. 20 Aug 1873. (Pp. 233-234)

Leonard Cantrell to John Davis and wife 50 acres on Sink Creek. 20 May 1874. (P. 235)

Monroe Green and wife, Martha, to Tennessee W. Green a tract of land in the 9th District containing 30 acres. 3 Feb 1877. (P. 236)

DEED BOOK N

S. S. Redman to A. L. Jones a tract of land in the 5th District. 4 Mar 1877. (P. 237)

Martha J. Robinson to William Seawell a tract of land in the 4th District. 15 Oct 1877. (P. 238)

Isiah Pugh and wife, Ellen, to Jeremiah Keel 24 acres in the 4th District. 4 Sep 1874. (Pp. 239-240)

W. H. Magness to C. C. Murphy and wife, Bettie, a tract of land in the 9th District. 8 Dec 1877. (Pp. 240-241)

G. W. Eastham to Nelson Bradford 150 acres in the 9th District. 22 Nov 1875. (Pp. 241-242)

G. W. Purser and wife, M. H., to John W. Bain a tract of land in the 9th District. 9 Nov 1876. (Pp. 242-243)

S. W. Medley to Benjamin Glover 39 acres in the 8th District. 15 Nov 1875. (Pp. 243-244)

W. H. Hays and wife, R. S., to E. R. Trail 190 acres on the south side of Sink Creek. 16 May 1878. (Pp. 244-246)

Sarah Jane Adamson to A. J. Pugh 29 acres in the 3rd District. 10 Oct 1876. (Pp. 246-247)

Anna West to Jackson West a one half interest in 204 acres where I now live. 24 May 1877. (Pp. 247-248)

G. W. McCarty and wife, Mary, to G. J. Foster and wife, Nancy, about 75 acres in the 9th District. 6 Jan 1877. (P. 249)

William C. Gilbert and wife, T. A., to Abraham Cantrell and wife, Rebecca, 200 acres belonging to the estate of Thomas Reeves and lying in the 5th District. 28 Jan 1878. (P. 250)

M. H. Pack and wife, Martha, to Priscilla Pack a tract of land in the 9th District. 10 Jan 1876. (P. 251)

J. H. Mangrum and wife, Martha J., to H. L. Haney about 400 acres in the 5th District known as the John Parsley land. 16 Aug 1877. (P. 252)

John Maynard died intestate before the Oct Term of County Court 1869. County Court Clerk to B. M. Cantrell a tract of land belonging to the said John Maynard. 22 Aug 1878. (Pp. 253-255)

James Willis to J. M. Tinsley a tract of land in the 14th District. Bounded: the old July Steel place now belonging to John E. Warren's heirs. 21 Mar 1875. (P. 255)

James L. Robinson to E. L. Hutchings 85 acres known as the (Jonas) Robinson land. Bounded: Ambrose Robinson. 29 Jul 1873. (Pp. 256-257)

Esaw Pack died intestate several years before the 31st day of Aug 1875. County Court Clerk to Isaac Cantrell as tract of land belonging to the estate. 26 Aug 1878. (Pp. 257-258)

W. L. Wall and wife, Martha E., to G. W. Hathaway a lot in the 2nd District. 1 May 1878. (Pp. 258-259)

Edward Lish and wife, Synthia, to John P. Buckner 50 acres in the 9th District. 10 Aug 1878. (Pp. 260-261)

Franklin McDowell and wife, Malletta, to Wiley Sanders a tract of land in the 6th District formerly owned by William Fisher and sold by Chancery Court. 14 Jun 1878. (Pp. 261-263)

John W. Campbell and wife, Mary H., to John K. Turner a title bond to a tract of land in the 2nd District. 20 Dec 1877. (Pp. 263-264)

John W. Bain to Wilson E. Taylor a tract of land on Hurricane Creek in the 9th District. 4 Sep 1878. (Pp. 264-265)

Hiram Childress died about the year 1872 intestate. William Childress was appointed administrator. Said William Childress filed a petition against Luella Childress to sell a tract of land. County Court Clerk to Hanner Robinson, trustee for Susan Robinson a tract of land in the 14th District. 5 Sep 1878. (Pp. 265-266)

James W. Foutch and wife, Sarah J., to E. A. Coggin a tract of land in the 10th District. 5 Sep 1878. (Pp. 266-267)

J. J. Ford, Mary E. Ford, M. F. Doss, Martha E. Doss, W. H. Botts, A. B. Botts, R. L. Wright, and Harriet J. Wright for the love and affection we have for our brother, John W. Botts, to the said John W. Botts their interest in a tract of land formerly owned by our father, Aaron Botts. 15 Sep 1874. (Pp. 267-268)

Clerk & Master to W. C. Potter and G. R. Smith a tract of land belonging to John Linder. 11 Sep 1878. (Pp. 268-269)

Edmond League and J. R. League have each reserved by deed from our father and mother, D. M. League and Sarah League, a tract of land. Edmond League to D. M. League a title bond. 11 Sep 1878. (Pp. 269-270)

D. M. League and wife, Sarah, for love and affection to Edmond League 276 acres in the 8th District. 11 Sep 1878. (Pp. 270-271)

D. M. League and wife, Sarah, for love and affection to James R. League 249 acres in the 8th District. 4 Sep 1878. (Pp. 271-272)

D. M. League and wife, Sarah, for love and affection to their daughter, Mary Ann McGinnis, during her life and then to her children 195 acres in the 8th District. 11 Sep 1878. (Pp. 272-273)

John W. Bain to the Methodist Episcopal Church a deed of gift a tract of land in the 9th District for a church and a school house known as the Hurricane School House. 3 Aug 1878. (P. 274)

William Johnson to his daughter, Nancy Johnson, a deed of gift of 163 acres. 21 Sep 1878. (Pp. 274-275)

DEED BOOK N

William H. Magness to M. D. (Smallman) and wife, C. A., a tract of land in the 9th District. 13 Jun 1872. (Pp. 275-276)

Edmond League and wife, Caldonia; D. M. League and wife, Sarah to Sarah E. League, Sarah E. League, and Naomi Myerson to Pleasant Watts 200 acres in the 8th District. 26 Sep 1878. (Pp. 276-277)

John Groom to J. H. David a trust deed on a tract of land in the 13th District. 1 Sep 1875. (Pp. 278-279)

J. H. David and wife, Mary E., to Leonard F. David 12 acres in the 13th District. 28 Sep 1878. (Pp. 279-280)

Simeon L. Williams to Samuel Braswell one half acre in the 2nd District. 11 Sep 1878. (Pp. 280-281)

J. W. Campbell to Sanford Mann a tract of land in the 2nd District. 4 Oct 1878. (P. 281)

Joseph Pistole and wife, Eliza, to John Caplinger 16½ acres. 11 Apr 1878. (Pp. 282-283)

V. H. Williams and wife, H. F., to G. W. Null three acres in the 16th District. 13 Aug 1878. (Pp. 283-284)

Jason A. Foutch to George W. Greyston a trust deed. 17 Aug 1878. (P. 284)

E. T. Foster to Z. P. Lee a tract of land in the town of Smithville known as the school house lot. 9 Oct 1878. (Pp. 285-286)

Perry Adcock to his wife, Mary N. Adcock, and their children, Buregard Adcock, William Adcock, Caladona Adcock, and J. T. Adcock a tract of land in the 7th District. 10 Oct 1878. (Pp. 286-287)

S. W. (Bryan) and wife, Tennessee, to L. G. Bing a tract of land in the 5th District. 8 Sep 1875. (Pp. 287-288)

Lucien B. Avant to James W. Foutch 230 acres in the 9th District. 15 Oct 1878. (Pp. 288-289)

L. D. Crowder and R. D. Crowder to T. M. Hooper one acre near Smithville. 23 Sep 1878. (P. 290)

James L. Colvert and others enter into an agreement concerning a grant of land. 7 Mar 1878. (Pp. 290-291)

J. C. Jones and wife, S. A., to W. G. Pendleton a tract of land. 21 Oct 1878. (P. 292)

Horace Parker and wife, Kizney, to Thomas Chapman one acre in the 2nd District. 28 Sep 1878. (Pp. 292-293)

Sanford Mann to Thomas Chapman 40 acres in the 2nd District. 9 Oct 1878. (Pp. 293-294)

C. W. L. Hale to W. C. Youngblood a lot in the town of Liberty containing one fourth of an acre. Bounded: T. R. Huggins old wood shop. 3 Jan 1873. (Pp. 294-295)

John W. Lamberson and wife, E. H., to C. H. L. Hale a tract of land in the 2nd District. 4 Sep 1876. (Pp. 295-297)

John Whaley and wife, Mary A., formerly Hurney, M. A. C. Whaley, and S. M. Hurney to A. B. Cheatham 67 acres in the 9th District. 4 Nov 1878. (Pp. 297-298)

J. A. Moss to Green Moss 164 acres in the 16th District. 9 Mar 1878. (P. 299)

Calaway Neal to Henry H. Jones 110 acres in the 9th District. 1 Aug 1870. (Pp. 299-300)

C. H. Yergen and wife, Sarah, to G. W. Grayston a lot in the 17th District. 23 Apr 1878. (Pp. 301-302)

Thomas Crips and wife, Darthula, to Abraham Blair and George McAdo 75 acres in the 4th District. 12 Dec 1877. (Pp. 302-304)

Isaac Whaley and wife, Nancy D., to Robert F. Jones and Eliza M. Jones a lot in the 2nd District. 30 Oct 1878. (Pp. 304-305)

H. L. Haney and wife, Mary E., to John Haney and wife, Elizabeth, a tract of land in the 5th District. 19 Nov 1878. (P. 305)

John Miller and wife, Emeline, to Susan Bullard 50 acres in the 4th District. 25 Apr 1878. (Pp. 306-307)

Barney Johnson and wife, Nancy, to N. B. Hobs 50 acres in the 4th District. 2 Oct 1878. (P. 307)

George H. Foutch and wife, Clay, to D. W. Dinges a lot in the town of Alexandria. 20 Dec 1877. (P. 308)

Henry H. Jones and wife, S. F., to D. W. Dinges a lot about one mile east of Alexandria. 31 Oct 1878. (P. 309)

J. N. Brown and wife, Elizabeth, to R. B. Floid a house and lot in the town of Alexandria. 15 Aug 1878. (P. 310)

Christopher Owen and wife, Mary, to Sarah Jane Adamson 29 acres in the 3rd District. 8 Mar 1876. (Pp. 310-311)

T. W. Eason and wife, Emma, to G. M. Bowers a house and lot on the corner of Main and Church Streets in the town of Alexandria. 20 Mar 1878. (P. 312)

T. W. Goodner and wife, Angeline, to G. M. Bowers a house and lot on Church Street in Alexandria. 31 May 1878. (Pp. 312-313)

John M. Love to William Turner 35 acres. 21 Jan 1878. (Pp. 313-314)

Henry Adcock and wife, Marcy F., for love and affection for the Cumberland Presbyterian Church to the trustees about one acre in the 7th District. 22 Oct 1878. (Pp. 314-315)

William Bates to James Oakley 40 acres in the 11th District. 15 Dec 1876. (Pp. 315-316)

John V. Crowder and wife, R. S.; and L. B. Avant to John Lyles a tract of land in the 9th District. 18 May 1878. (Pp. 316-318)

William R. Dunham to Charity Neal during her natural life a tract of land in the 7th District. 20 Feb 1877. (Pp. 318-319)

C. Coffee, trustee, a quit claim deed to L. Adcock on 314 acres in the 15th District. 17 Oct 1878. (Pp. 319-320)

Leonard Adcock and wife, Sarah R., to Harvey Ridder and wife 40 acres in the 6th District. 7 Oct 1878. (Pp. 320-322)

Eligha Carr and wife, Mithursa J., to H. W. Frazier 180 acres in the 14th District. 8 Dec 1878. (Pp. 322-324)

James L. Colvert to Eligha Carr 40 acres. 8 Aug 1871. (Pp. 324-325)

James N. Roy for love and affection to Julia Hayes, wife of F. H. Hayes, a tract of land in the 13th District. 14 Dec 1878. (Pp. 325-327)

John Haney to Levi Haney 45 acres in the 5th District. 20 Dec 1878. (Pp. 327-328)

James Willis to Mary Sherald his interest in 300 acres in the 14th District. 16 Dec 1878. (Pp. 328-329)

R. D. Exum to Bird S. Sexton 60 acres in the 16th District. 28 Dec 1878. (Pp. 329-330)

Jefferson Rowland died, leaving a will which was probated in Mar 1869. Benjamin Rowland and David Rowland were named executors. David Rowland to Bird S. Sexton a tract of land belonging to the estate. 31 Dec 1878. (Pp. 330-335)

L. D. Hollandsworth and wife, Elizabeth, to Mary Angeline Hendrixson 55 acres in the 5th District. 13 Nov 1878. (Pp. 335-336)

Gallan Tucker and wife, Liza, to F. W. Garner 15 acres in the 16th District. 16 Aug 1878. (pp. 336-338)

Thomas J. Gill to L. P. and H. S. Gill his interest in 30 acres in the 16th District. 8 Jan 1879. (Pp. 339-340)

H. C. Eastham and wife, Helen J., to Colvert & Blankenship a tract of land known as the Eastham Porter land. 6 Jul 1878. (Pp. 340-342)

Fred Starnes and wife, Polly, to William Holley five acres in the 15th District. 4 Feb 1878. (Pp. 342-344)

Y. L. Herrington and wife, Margaret, to J. A. Moore ten acres in the 4th District. 13 Jan 1879. (Pp. 344-346)

John Willoughby to William E. Foutch one and one half acres in the 11th District. 2 Dec 1878. (Pp. 346-347)

Jasper Ruyle and wife, Matilda, to Isaac C. Turney and John T. Turney a title bond. 7 Nov 1873. (Pp. 347-349)

John P. Tittsworth and wife, Elizabeth, to R. H. Tittsworth a lien. 24 Jan 1879. (Pp. 349-350)

Eli Vick and wife, Amanda, to S. B. Sellars 240 acres in the 3rd District. 25 Jan 1879. (Pp. 351-353)

John H. Savage to B. Y. Cantrell about 150 acres on Holmes Creek. 1 Jan 1879. (Pp. 353-355)

Eli Vick and wife, Amanda, to William Vick for Eli Vick 240 acres in the 3rd District. 29 Jan 1879. (Pp. 355-357)

C. L. Barton to J. M. Baird a tract of land in the town of Alexandria. 1 Feb 1879. (Pp. 358-360)

Edmon Palmer to John C. Garrison a tract of land in the 1st District. Bounded: Liewsinda Palmer's dower. 17 Jan 1879. (Pp. 360-361)

Levi Nixon and wife, Riller, to Ira Lamberson a tract of land in the 17th District. 20 Oct 1876. (Pp. 361-364)

James Redman to Larkin H. Bain ten acres in the 9th District. 21 Jan 1876. (Pp. 364-365)

James Redman and wife, Easter, to Larkin H. Bain ten acres in the 9th District. 5 Mar 1878. (Pp. 365-366)

W. D. Marler and wife, A. J., to G. E. Henely 54 acres. 28 Aug 1877. (Pp. 366-368)

W. C. Cantrell and wife, Martha J., to John L. Hays a tract of land in the 9th District. 23 Sep 1878. (Pp. 368-370)

j. V. Crowder and wife, Rachel; J. W. Foutch and wife, S. J. to W. H. Magness a tract of land in the 9th District. 3 Feb 1879. (Pp. 370-373)

Bethel Parsley and wife, Selina, to Elizabeth J. Parsley 75 acres in the 9th District. 1 Feb 1879. (Pp. 373-374)

William C. Martin to W. P. Martin 32 acres in the 5th District. 5 Feb 1879. (Pp. 374-375)

John P. Tittsworth to Nancy Jones 25 acres in the 7th District. 3 Feb 1879. (Pp. 376-377)

Elizabeth J. Dunlap to Bethel Parsley a town lot and house in Smithville. Bounded: the lot where Harriet Tubb now lives. 1 Feb 1879. (Pp. 377-378)

Charles F. Cameron to Z. Camerson 85 acres. Said Camerons are residents of White County. 15 Feb 1879. (Pp. 378-379)

J. C. Cannady to Barnabus Johnson 90 acres. 14 Feb 1879. (P. 380)

Letha McRay to David Rowland and B. S. Sexton 60 acres in the 16th District. 22 Jan 1879. (Pp. 381-382)

G. R. West to James P. Barry 100 acres in the 13th District. 7 Jan 1879. (Pp. 382-383)

G. R. West to J. R. West 40 acres in the 13th District. 2 Jan 1879. (Pp. 383-384)

J. M. Baird and wife, Amanda R., to E. Turner three lots in the town of Alexandria. Lot three is bounded by the graveyard alley. 12 Feb 1879. (Pp. 384-386)

Frederick Starnes to Frances A. Wright 100 acres in the 15th District. 7 Jan 1875. (PP. 386-388)

F. A. Wright and wife, Annis E., to William Holly ten acres in the 16th District. 24 Feb 1879. (PP. 388-390)

John Turner and wife, Virginia A., to Evaline Fuson two and one half acres in the town of Liberty. 5 Feb 1879. (Pp. 390-392)

T. W. Goodner and wife, Angelia, to R. A. Lawrence a house and lot in the town of Alexandria. 18 Feb 1879. (Pp. 392-393)

G. R. West to Burges Dowel, colored, about 21½ acres in the 13th District. 1 Jan 1874. (Pp. 393-395)

G. R. West to Samuel McMillan about 45 acres in the 13th District. 1 Jan 1874. (Pp. 395-397)

Sebastian Williams to W. R. Bryant ten and one half acres in the 3rd District. 27 Feb 1879. (Pp. 397-398)

Luise E. Buckner; Sarah T. James and husband Hartwell; Catherine H. Lefever and husband Jesse F.; Robert H. Buckner; Mary E. Pedigo and husband Richard; James D. Buckner; and John P. Buckner to Edmond League 40 acres in the 9th District. 18 Oct 1875. (Pp. 398-401)

John C. Cannady to Hiram Hildreth a cash note on Alexander Hildreth. 1 Mar 1869. (Pp. 401-402)

J. J. Ford and wife, Mary E., to William A. Hayes about 130 or 135 acres in the 1st District. 15 Jan 1877. (Pp. 402-404)

W. G. Rowland and wife, E. J., to B. A. Adamson 13 acres in the 1st District. 10 Dec 1878. (Pp. 404-406)

W. T. Robinson and wife, Lucy J., to J. H. Stevens 79 acres in the 12th District. 6 Mar 1879. (Pp. 406-408)

D. P. Searcy to W. C. Youngblood one tenth of an acre in the 2nd District. 1 Sep 1874. (Pp. 408-409)

W. C. Youngblood and wife, Mary S., to C. W. L. Hall and William Vick one third of an acre in the 2nd District. 11 May 1878. (Pp. 409-411)

James T. Garner to Pinkney Medley 60 acres in the 16th District. 17 Feb 1879. (Pp. 411-412)

T. L. D. Ferrell to A. G. Mullican eight acres in the 5th District. 14 Mar 1879. (Pp. 412-413)

W. R. Phillips to James R. Adcock and wife, Sarah, 110 acres in the 7th District. 27 Jul 1878. (Pp. 413-415)

Tilman Adcock and wife, Sarah A., to W. C. Cantrell 81¼ acres in the 7th District. 28 Nov 1878. (Pp. 415-417)

Isaac Brown; J. L. Brown and wife, Mary, to W. H. Brown 61 acres in the 8th District. 10 Jul 1878. (Pp. 417-418)

Chancery Court to J. S. Palmer 149 acres in the 8th District belonging to Abraham Ditty deceased. 23 Feb 1877. (Pp. 419-420)

Adam Tittle and wife, Charlotta, to D. L. Mitchell and wife, Elizabeth, of Warren County 125 acres in the 4th District. 18 Mar 1879. (Pp. 420-422)

J. T. Armstrong and wife, L. A., to John B. Robinson Lot No. 46 in the town of Liberty. 19 Mar 1879. (Pp. 422-423)

P. L. Adamson and wife, M. F., to Richard Mathis 30 acres in the 3rd District. 12 Oct 1877. (Pp. 423-424)

R. H. Lee to Nicholas Chambers Lot No. 44 in the town of Smithville. 1 Mar 1879. (Pp. 424-425)

Kinchen D. Exum and wife, Elizabeth, to James T. Exum 15 acres in the 16th District. 24 Feb 1879. (Pp. 425-427)

Jackson Malone and wife, Harriet E., to Yancy Malone 160 acres in the 17th District. 24 Nov 1871. (Pp. 427-428)

Yancy Malone and wife, Elizabeth, to William F. Askue 65 acres in the 17th District. 20 Jul 1878. (Pp. 428-430)

Yancy Malone and wife, Elizabeth, to J. A. Foutch 70 acres in the 17th District. 20 Jul 1878. (Pp. 430-432)

Clabron Vaughn and wife, Margret, to L. F. Vaughn 50 acres in the 16th District. 27 Nov 1877. (Pp. 432-434)

Jason A. Foutch and wife, Caldonia, to G. W. Gregston their interest in a tract of land. 11 Mar 1879. (Pp. 434-436)

James Ford and wife, Isabella, to W. W. Wade 15 acres in the 9th District. 27 Jan 1879. (Pp. 436-438)

John L. Brown, W. H. Brown, and Isaac C. Brown enter into an agreement to rescind a contract on a tract of land. 1 Mar 1877. (P. 438)

C. C. Murphy and wife, Betty, to John Harrison a lot on the south west side of Smithville. 17 Apr 1879. (Pp. 439-440)

By descent from Anna Rhody deceased, Henry Rhody, John Rhody, Columbus Rhody, Nancy Shehane, Mary Pistole were entitled to equal and undivided interest in 175 acres in the 3rd District. County Court Clerk to Thomas Groom the 175 acres. 19 Apr 1879. (Pp. 440-442)

Clerk & Master to Thomas J. Swift a house and lot in the town of Alexandria belonging to W. B. Lawrence. 10 Apr 1879. (Pp. 442-444)

Henry Schurer and others to Thomas B. Potter a lot in the 9th District adjoining Smithville. 16 Oct 1878. (Pp. 444-446)

Thomas J. Swift and wife, Martha, to D. W. Dinges a house and lot in Alexandria. 25 Apr 1879. (Pp. 446-448)

William G. Rowland and wife, E. J., to A. J. C. Marler a tract of land in the 1st District. 18 Sep 1878. (Pp. 448-449)

Jasper Ruyle and wife, Matilda, to James Allen a town lot in the town of Liberty. 2 May 1879. (Pp. 449-450)

Lafayette Kerly and wife, Margaret, to William Young 45 acres. 16 Dec 1876. (Pp. 450-451)

G. W. Cameron and wife, Prudence, to E. J. Evans two town lots in the town of Smithville. Bounded: south of the lot on which the said G. W. Cameron now lives, and south by a lot formerly claimed by the Methodist Episcopal Church. 22 Apr 1879. (Pp. 451-453)

Telitha C. Turner to Mary Eledge 16 acres in the 4th District. 12 May 1879. (Pp. 454-454)

J. T. Turner and wife, S. C., to James E. Drury a lot in the 2nd District. 24 Feb 1879. (Pp. 454-455)

Helen Schurer to C. M. Schurer 150 acres in the 12th District. Bounded: Caroline Fite. 10 Mar 1879. (Pp. 455-459)

Calvin C. Garrison and wife, Mary A., to John D. Bone a town lot in the town of Alexandria. 29 Mar 1879. (Pp. 459-460)

Clerk & Master to P. T. Shores a tract of land belonging to John Linder. 17 May 1879. (Pp. 461-462)

P. T. Shores and wife, Maggie, to James Dearman a lot in the town of Smithville. 17 May 1879. (Pp. 462-463)

Thomas Fisher to J. J. Ford of DeKalb County, M. M. Brien of Davidson County, and Robert Cantrell of Wilson County his interest in a tract of land. 22 May 1879. (Pp. 464-465)

Hezekiah Calhoon to N. D. Eason a house and lot in the town of Alexandria. 22 Dec 1876. (Pp. 465-466)

T. N. Christian to James Dearman a title bond. 2 Jun 1879. (Pp. 466-467)

Thomas Fisher to James Sampson 40 acres. 22 Feb 1879. (Pp. 468-469)

Hardin Vickers and wife, Sarah A., to W. H. Vaughn a tract of land. 2 Jun 1879. (Pp. 469-470)

Frederic Starnes to John A. Moss a tract of land in the 16th District. 5 Mar 1879. (Pp. 470-471)

Isaac Whaley and wife, Nancy D., to W. J. Gossett one acre in the 2nd District. 20 Apr 1867. (Pp. 471-473)

P. J. Lee and wife, Barthena, to H. C. Eastham two tracts of land in the 9th District. 26 Jun 1879. (Pp. 473-474)

Sheriff to Potter & Smith a tract of land belonging to T. L. Seawel. 19 Jun 1879. (Pp. 474-477)

Sanford Mann and wife, Matilda, to Paterick Geraty a lot

in the 2nd District. 29 Mar 1879. (Pp. 477-478)

County Court Clerk to F. W. Hobson 52 acres in the 11th District. 3 Jul 1879. (Pp. 478-480)

E. I. Wright and wife, Lo, to M. D. Russell a tract of land. 1 Mar 1879. (Pp. 480-481)

Benjamin Cantrell to W. A. Adcock a tract of land in the 7th District. 25 Oct 1878. (Pp. 482-483)

W. N. Adcock and wife, Lavenia, to James H. Parish a tract of land in the 7th District. 10 Jul 1879. (Pp. 483-484)

James Hollinsworth and wife, Sarah A., to Eli Vick one half acre in the 2nd District. 7 Jul 1879. (Pp. 484-485)

Thomas D. Bass and wife, V. N., to W. H. Hays a tract of land in the 12th District. 26 Nov 1878. (Pp. 486-487)

J. C. Fisher to Yancy Malone 40 acres in the 17th District. 23 Dec 1868. (Pp. 487-488)

Yancy Malone and wife, Dora Ann, to I. B. Tubb and R. M. Tubb 143½ acres in the 17th District. 16 Aug 1871. (Pp. 489-490)

John M. Foster to Charles T. Burton 80 acres in the 16th District. 26 Apr 1870. (Pp. 491-492)

William Griffith and wife, Eliza Jane, to Jonathan F. Griffin 20½ acres in the 13th District. 10 Apr 1879. (Pp. 492-494)

Frederick Starnes to Tandy W. Fitts 100 acres in the 15th District. 14 Apr 1877. (Pp. 494-495)

E. D. Hutchins and wife, Melissa, to T. W. Fitts a tract of land in the 15th District. 11 Sep 1877. (Pp. 495-496)

John Sullivan and wife, Martha, to John E. Robinson their interest in the estate of their grandfather, John Robinson. 13 Oct 1877. (Pp. 496-498)

A. F. McConnell and wife, Martha Elizabeth, to Aaron Cantrell 30 acres in the 7th District. 13 Oct 1875. (Pp. 498-499)

Leroy Braswell and wife, Lucinda, to James Snow nine acres in the 4th District. 19 Oct 1875. (Pp. 500-501)

G. W. Hathaway and wife, Selina, to W. B. Rippetoe one acre in the 2nd District. 21 Jul 1877. (Pp. 501-502)

T. N. Christian to J. L. Hollinsworth a title bond. 22 Jul 1879. (Pp. 502-503)

John Stoner and wife, Sarah, to Emeline Freeman 73 acres in the 5th District. 8 Aug 1872. (Pp. 504-505)

T. N. Christian and others to James McDaniel a tract of land in the 9th District known as the Gay heirs' land. 10 Dec 1877. (Pp. 505-506)

P. T. Shores to James McDaniel a tract of land in the 9th District. 16 Jun 1879. (Pp. 506-507)

William Bates and wife, Cynthia, to T. P. Lawrence one half acre in the 11th District. 6 Dec 1876. (Pp. 507-509)

John P. Haney and wife, Elizabeth to Nathan T. Wall 40 acres in the 6th District. 14 May 1879. (Pp. 509-510)

Aaron Braswell to W. B. Barnes his one half interest in the Nathaniel Braswell tract in the 4th District. 29 Nov 1878. (Pp. 510-511)

William T. Jones and wife, Martha E., to Z. T. Judd about 86 acres in the 16th District, it being their interest in the estate of Carline Haley deceased. 25 Jun 1878. (Pp. 542-543)

J. H. Holley and wife, Charlotta, to Z. T. Judd their interest in the estate of Carline Holley deceased. 25 Jun 1878. (Pp. 514-515)

Pallas Smith for love and affection to his wife, Elizabeth, and her children, now living or hereafter to be born to me (but should I die and the said Elizabeth marry again and bare by her second marriage other children, they are not to be embraced inthe deed of gift) 150 acres in the 12th District. 13 Aug 1879. (Pp. 515-516)

James H. Lamberson and wife, Mary, to E. M. Whaley 14 acres in the 2nd District. 6 Feb 1879. (Pp. 516-518)

Isaac N. Fite and wife, Madora M., to E. M. Whaley 305 square poles in the 2nd District. 6 Feb 1879. (Pp. 518-519)

Andrew Robinson to Harriet Melvina Hildreth 125 acres in the 4th District. 18 Aug 1873. (Pp. 519-520)

James George and wife, Mary, to Hiram Hildreth a tract of land in the 4th District. 6 Oct 1877. (Pp. 521-522)

Clerk & Master to C. G. Cobler and A. I. Fanning a tract of land belonging to A. L. Davis. 26 Aug 1879. (Pp. 522-525)

Clerk & Master to William H. Hays a tract of land belonging to Douglas B. Davis. 26 Aug 1879. (Pp. 525-528)

B. C. Wilkerson to W. R. Parrish three undivided shares of the Washington Parrish tract of land in the 5th District. 21 Aug 1879. (Pp. 528-529)

W. I. Shields to T. W. Shields one acre near Smithville. 21 Jul 1879. (Pp. 529-530)

T. M. Hooper to Samuel Hooper a tract of land near Smithville on the east side of A. B. Hooper's lots. 28 Aug 1879. (Pp. 530-531)

John C. Loving and wife, Mary, to J. P. Tittsworth a tract of land in the 5th District. 18 Feb 1879. (Pp. 531-532)

A. E. Frazier and Thomas Pack to the commissioners of the 9th District a tract of land for a school. 22 Aug 1879. (Pp. 533-534)

Samuel Braswell et als to William Braswell et als a tract of land. 27 Aug 1879. (Pp. 534-535)

John C. Cannady and wife, M. A., to William Moor Collard 14 acres in the 9th District. 18 Aug 1879. (Pp. 535-536)

N. T. Stewart to T. I. Hass a tract of land in the 4th District. Bounded: Widow Jones. 10 Sep 1878. (P. 537)

T. J. Lee and wife, E. J., to R. A. Smith 23 acres in the 16th District. 4 Jun 1879. (Pp. 538-539)

George McGee and wife, Nicey C., to W. E. Bartlett their interest in the Jerry Coggins land in the 1st District. 5 Aug 1879. (Pp. 539-542)

John Hays died sometime about the year 1865. County Court Clerk to D. S. Boyd a tract of land belonging to the deceased. The widow, Elizabeth Hays, received her dower. 20 Sep 1879. (Pp. 542-543)

Phila A. Seawell to T. N. Christian about four acres in the town of Smithville. 30 Jul 1879. (Pp. 544-545)

John M. Gilbert and wife, Malinda, to T. N. Christian five acres in the 9th District. 25 Aug 1879. (Pp. 545-546)

Virginia T. Givan, one of the heirs of Robert Givan, to William M. Fite her interest, consisting of one third, in the dower of Elizh, widow of said Robert Givan. 5 Sep 1872. (Pp. 547-548)

W. M. Fite and wife, Sarah C. to C. W. L. Hale 138 acres in the 3rd District. 30 Sep 1879. (Pp. 548-550)

W. T. Robinson and wife, Lucy J., to Benjamin Anderson a lot in Doweltown in the 2nd District. 1 Feb 1879. (Pp. 550-552)

C. W. L. Hale to James Givan about 35 acres in the 3rd District. 30 Sep 1879. (Pp. 552-553)

C. W. L. Hale to Thomas Givan 103 acres in the 3rd District. 1 Oct 1879. (Pp. 553-554)

S. H. Gray and wife, Matildy, to W. H. Magness 92½ acres in the 9th District. 4 Sep 1879. (Pp. 555-556)

James T. Exum to Kinchen D. Exum 15 acres in the 16th District. 7 Oct 1879. (Pp. 556-557)

J. C. and wife, Nancy, to J. C. Taylor, Jr. we suppose, 25 acres on Indian Creek in the 10th District. 3 Feb 1879. (Pp. 557-559)

Thomas Frisby and wife, Julia, to Robert Montgomery a tract of land in the 14th District. 15 Oct 1879. (Pp. 559-560)

Phila A. Seawell, J. Q. Seawell, and Alice Seawell to T. N. Christian a house and lot in Smithville. Bounded: Mountain Street. 16 Sep 1879. (Pp. 560-562)

DEED BOOK N

Mary Patterson to John P. Tittsworth her interest in the land of her deceased father, Jackey Davis, on Pine Creek in the 5th District. 29 Sep 1879. (Pp. 562-563)

John P. Tittsworth and wife, Elizabeth, to E. Berry 50 acres in the 5th District. 22 Oct 1879. (Pp. 563-564)

M. D. Bussel and wife, Nancy, to Margaret M. E. Colvert and John H. Colvert four acres in the 9th District. 1 Sep 1879. (Pp. 564-565)

Sheriff to T. W. Wade 60 acres belonging to Thomas Lancaster. 2 Oct 1879. (Pp. 566-567)

Sanford Mann to McAdoo Vannatta and A. B. Hicks a tract of land in the 2nd District. 27 Oct 1879. (Pp. 567-568)

James George and wife, Mary, to William Bess about 50 acres in the 4th District. 20 Oct 1879. (Pp. 569-570)

Y. M. Malone and wife, Phebia, to J. M. Sandlin the dower land held by my mother, Elizabeth Malone, in the 11th District. 17 Jul 1878. (Pp. 570-571)

W. G. Bransford and wife Fannie P.; D. M. Bradford and wife M. C.; I. B. Ward and wife T. P.; G. W. Stephens; and Emmer Stephens, all of Smith County, to John P. Tittsworth five lots of the Stephens lots. 22 Oct 1879. (Pp. 572-574)

E. M. Whaley and wife, Elizabeth, to I. N. Fite three acres in the 2nd District. 6 Jan 1879. (Pp. 574-575)

John H. Allen and wife, Eliz., to Isaac N. Fite and wife, Dora, 11 acres in the 2nd District. 12 Feb 1879. (Pp. 576-577)

Wyatt Rollins and wife, Rhoda, to Samuel Williams 102 poles near the corporate limits of Alexandria. 10 Sep 1879. (Pp. 577-578)

Levi Haney and wife, Ellen, to John P. Haney 45 acres in the 5th District. 18 Oct 1879. (Pp. 579-580)

Sanford Mann and wife, Matilda, to Patric Geraty a tract of land in Dowell Town. 24 Sep 1879. (Pp. 580-581)

Henry B. McDonald in his last will and testament left to Julia M. Robinson, wife of John B. Robinson, left the said Julia M. about 85 acres. The land has been sold to John C. Sanders. 4 Aug 1879. (Pp. 582-585)

Sheriff to Berry and Demoville a tract of land belonging to Vickers and Crips. 6 Sep 1879. (Pp. 585-587)

Amanda E. Davis to T. W. Wade one acre on the north side of Smithville. 25 Nov 1879. (Pp. 587-588)

Clerk & Master to Mrs. M. A. Staley a tract of land. 29 NOv 1879. (Pp. 588-590)

L. G. Bing and wife, M. A., to Harden Cantrell and wife, Jane, 75 acres on Sink Creek. 18 Nov 1879. (Pp. 591-593)

William Capshaw to A. B. Hathaway 50 acres in the 6th District. 1 Dec 1879. (Pp. 593-594)

W. G. Foster and wife, J. A., to J. C. Jones 20 acres in the 9th District. 3 Dec 1879. (Pp. 594-595)

Mrs. Polly Brien and M. M. Brien, Jr., trustee for the benefit of Mrs. Pollie Brien, wife of M. M. Brien, Sr., are in possession of a tract of land. Said Polly Brien to her children, to wit, M. M. Brien, Jr., W. A. Brien, Robert C. Brien, and Mrs. A. G. Kercheval 260 acres on Purtle's Creek. 26 Nov 1879. (Pp. 595-597)

M. M. Brien, Jr., trustee, to F. Miller Schurer a tract of land. 28 Nov 1879. (Pp. 597-599)

Luisa J. Davis to the Elders of the Cumberland Presbyterian Church two acres in the 14th District. 12 Nov 1879. (Pp. 599-600)

T. W. Fitts and B. F. Winfree agree to an exchange of land in the 15th District. 19 Nov 1879. (Pp. 601-602)

John W. Groom to Joseph B. West and others near one half an acre in the 13th District for school purposes. 5 Aug 1879. (Pp. 603-604)

D. A. Parker to W. B. Farler 50 acres in the 4th District. 8 Mar 1873. (Pp. 604-605)

Eli Vick and wife, Amanda, to William G. Bratten 35 acres in the 3rd District. 5 Sep 1878. (Pp. 605-607)

M. M. Brien, Sr. to M. M. Brien, Jr., trustee, a tract of 268½ acres on Pirtle's Creek. 28 Nov 1879. (Pp. 607-611)

J. G. Squires and wife, S. E., to David Gordon, colored, the Robert Dale lot in the town of Liberty. 25 Dec 1874. (Pp. 611-612)

Allen Wilson and wife, Elizabeth, to William H. Hays one and one half acres in the 13th District. 6 Aug 1879. (Pp. 612-613)

A. E. Frazier and wife, Nancy Ann, to D. J. Taylor 90 acres in the 9th District. 30 Dec 1879. (Pp. 614-616)

Thomas Groom and John W. Truett, Administrators of William Measles, to H. B. Groom 11 acres. 26 Dec 1879. (Pp. 616-617)

C. C. Avant and wife E. J.; J. H. Stephens and wife M. T.; J. P. Barry and wife J. S. filed suit against James Grooms and wife M. L.; Julia Barry; Zora Barry; Willie Barry; Alonzo Barry; and G. R. West, Administrator of P. S. Barry, to have the lands of the said P. S. Barry partitioned or sold. County Court Clerk to John Grooms a tract of land belonging to the said P. S. Barry. 2 Jan 1880. (Pp. 617-620)

Emeline Fuston filed a petition in Circuit Court against Martha Fuston and the other heirs of James Fuston asking for the sale of lands belonging to the deceased including six and one fourth acres of hill land, known as ni__er hill near the town of Liberty. The land was sold to Arthusa Matilda Ruyle. 3 Jan 1880. (Pp. 620-622)

James Truett and wife, Julia, to James Gibbs four acres in the 13th District. 27 Dec 1879. (Pp. 622-624)

D. M. Dinges and wife, Nora, to S. W. McClellan one third of an acre in the 1st District. 21 Nov 1879. (Pp. 624-624)

R. C. Bone and wife, Anna F., to the trustees of Alexandria Masonic Academy Lot No. 11 on what is known as Bone's addition to the town of Alexandria 28 feet off of the side of their lot to be used as a public street leading from West Main to Locust Street. 1 Sep 1879. (Pp. 625-626)

John P. Tittsworth and wife, Elizabeth, to John C. Loring 175 acres in the 5th District. 7 Oct 1879. (Pp. 627-628)

Joseph Clark, trustee, to James F. Youngblood a tract of land in the 2nd District. Bounded: Liberty Methodist Church. 15 Jan 1872. (Pp. 628-630)

James H. Fite to W. C. Potter the Martha Hunt lot in Smithville for tax purposes. 15 Oct 1879. (Pp. 630-631)

G. W. Hathaway and wife, Selina Jane, to J. W. Griffith one acre in the 2nd District. 5 Nov 1877. (Pp. 631-633)

William Adamson and wife, Parthena C., to Lafayette Garrison about one acre in the 1st District. 2 Sep 1878. (Pp. 633-634)

L. W. Neal and wife, M. Q., to Lafayette Garrison a tract of land in the 1st District. 16 Sep 1878. (Pp. 634-636)

J. B. Locke and wife Hannah N. to William H. Magness, Jr. their interest in the personal estate of P. G. Magness, Jr. 9 Dec 1879. (Pp. 636-637)

Martin M. Phillips and wife, Fatima, to William H. Magness, Jr. their interest in the personal estate of P. G. Magness, Jr. including the home tract and subject to the homestead and dower of M. J. Magness, widow of said deceased. 25 Jan 1879. (Pp. 637-639)

Clerk & Master to I. C. Jones a tract of land belonging to S. B. Whaley. 12 Jan 1880. (Pp. 639-640)

M. S. West to the trustees elect for school purposes of the 13th District a tract in the southeast corner of a tract of land on which I now live on the west side of the Lebanon & Sparta Pike near one half acre. 25 Jul 1879. (Pp. 641-642)

Moses A. Stark and wife, Sarah E., to John C. Johnson 36 acres in the 3rd District. 26 Jan 1880. (Pp. 642-643)

David Gordon and wife, Anlizey, colored, to John Thomas, colored, a lot in the town of Liberty known as the Robert Dale lot. 25 Jan 1880. Bounded: east by the old school house lot; west by College Street. 25 Jan 1880. (Pp. 643-644)

John A. Cantrell and wife, Nancy, for love and affection to their grandchildren, to wit, Mary J. Adcock, wife of M. E. Adcock; Nancy Arnold, wife of Eli Arnold; Loudoria Webb, wife of Daniel Webb; and John Redman, they being the heirs of our daughter, Eliza Redman deceased who was the wife of Archabald Redman deceased, a tract of land in the 7th District. 29 Sep 1879. (Pp. 644-646)

T. W. Eason, Administrator of N. D. Eason, to W. M. Bradford a house and lot in the town of Alexandria. 29 May 1879. (Pp. 646-647)

L. W. Neal and wife, M. J. to J. P. Barry their interest in 65 acres in the 1st District. 15 Oct 1875. (Pp. 647-648)

Leander Hays to Moses H. Fite eight acres in the 3rd District. 16 Apr 1877. (Pp. 648-649)

Arthusa Matilda Ruyle, wife of Jasper Ruyle, to James Allen and C. J. Allen a tract of land in the 2nd District. 5 Jan 1880. (Pp. 649-650)

Eli Vick and wife, Amanda, to William Vick 39¼ acres in the 2nd District. 6 Feb 1880. (Pp. 651-652)

A. S. Redman and wife, M. J., to James H. Starn one half acre in the 2nd District. 10 Jan 1877. (Pp. 652-653)

Edward V. Polland to his son, William Z. Polland and wife, Nancy, a deed of gift of the tract of land where they now live in the 11th District and containing 50 acres. 4 Jan 1853. (Pp. 653-654)

Barley Miller to Joseph Hibdon 41 acres in the 5th District. 13 Feb 1875. (Pp. 654-655)

T. G. Squires and wife, Sarah C., to Eli and Thomas Vick one eighth of an acre in the 2nd District. 6 Feb 1880. (Pp. 656-657)

W. M. Hill and wife, Mary C.; and D. H. Hill to I. W. Inge 51 acres in the 2nd District. 11 Feb 1880. (Pp. 657-658)

John R. Lyles and wife Polly; Wiley Snow and wife Catherine to Tilman Crook 40 acres in the 4th District. 7 Aug 1871. (Pp. 658-660)

William M. Fite and wife, Sarah C., to Jacob Young and W. T. Fite one half acre in the 13th District. 17 Feb 1880. (Pp. 660-661)

W. H. Hays and wife, R. S., to T. D. Bass, Jr. 47½ acres in the 12th District. 28 Oct 1879. (Pp. 662-663)

William C. Davis and wife, Thena A., to A. J. Caplinger 42 acres in the 4th District. 12 Feb 1880. (Pp. 661-662)

W. R. Parrish and wife, Aseneth, to P. H. Hankins 75 acres in the 5th District. 21 Aug 1879. (Pp. 665-666)

James R. Fuston and wife, Paralee, to Isaac Alexander and wife, Helen, their interest in the Sampson Braswell old tract.

27 Aug 1879. (Pp. 667-668)

Isaac Jones and wife, Jane, to William W. Foutch 47 acres in the 11th District. 1 Feb 1876. (Pp. 668-669)

Isaac Alexander and wife, Helen, to Martha Frazier, widow of A. L. Frazier, a tract of land in the 4th District. 24 Feb 1880. (Pp. 669-670)

James Snow and wife, Elizabeth G., to James M. Snow 50 acres in the 4th District. 15 Jul 1879. (Pp. 671-672)

J. C. McDaniel and wife, F. A., to Elizabeth R. Floyd about five acres in the 9th District. 20 Jun 1879. (Pp. 672-673)

W. A. McClellan and wife, Nancy, to Pat Garity the Riley Taylor lot in Doweltown. 6 Jan 1880. (Pp. 673-674)

James H. Lamberson and wife, Mary, to Thomas H. Stark one half acre in the 2nd District. 20 Mar 1875. (Pp. 674-676)

F. M. Close and wife, Malinda, to Benjamin Ellis ten acres. Bounded: Helen Close. 1 Oct 1879. (Pp. 676-677)

James A. Hathaway and wife, Dora A., to C. C. Robinson one half acre in the 2nd District. 1 May 1878. (Pp. 677-679)

Ader Curtis to her sister, Cansada, her interest in the lands of Ben Curtis deceased and her interest in the widow's dower. 11 Mar 1880. (P. 679)

Revenue Collector to Allen Johnson a tract of land in the 9th District containing about 100 acres belonging to Caruthers and McClain. The transfer was made to the said Allen Johnson by request in writing by his father William Johnson. 15 Aug 1879. (Pp. 680-681)

William Holly and wife, Catherine, to H. J. Winchester five acres in the 16th District. 9 Feb 1880. (Pp. 681-682)

Thomas Fuson and wife, Mary, to James A. Yeargin a house and lot in Doweltown, being a part of the land that I purchased of J. H. Fuson. 29 Apr 1878. (Pp. 682-684)

David Fisher and wife, Harriet, to A. H. McDowell, Maletta McDowell, and Robert E. McDowell 25 acres in the 6th District. 16 Nov 1874. (Pp. 684-685)

Sampson Yeargin and wife, Becky, to Smith Hendrixson ten acres in the 4th District. 8 Oct 1877.. (Pp. 685-687)

John W. Jacobs and wife, S. T., to C. Jacobs a tract of land in the 12th District. 21 Feb 1877. (Pp. 687-688)

William Goodman and wife, Sarah, to Maregan McGuire 13 acres. 29 May 1875. (Pp. 688-690)

John C. Cannady for love and affection for the town of Smithville to the County Judge and others a piece of property known as the south end of College Street. Bounded: Lot No. 85. 30 Mar 1880. (Pp. 690-691)

DEED BOOK N

L. G. Bing and wife, Martha, to G. W. Sanders her interest in 97 acres that her father, Harden Cantrell, in 1868 made as a deed of gift to his children. The children were Talitha Sanders, H. P. Cantrell, W. C. Cantrell, F. M. Cantrell, and Martha Bing. 14 Apr 1880. (Pp. 691-693)

R. C. Bone and wife, Anna F., to D. W. Dinges Lots 10 and 12 in what is known as Bone's addition to Alexandria. 1 Dec 1879. (Pp. 693-694)

James M. Baird and wife, Amanda R., to Byron F. Bell their one half interest in a tract of land on the road leading from Alexandria to Carthage. 13 Apr 1880. (Pp. 695-696)

Sheriff to S. W. McClellan three acres in the 1st District. 23 Apr 1880. (Pp. 696-700)

Morgan Lawrence and wife, Louisa, to S. W. McClellan a title bond. 1 Jan 1876. (Pp. 700-701)

F. A. Wright and wife, Annis E., to William Holley one half acre in the 15th District. 19 Apr 1880. (Pp. 701-703)

Thomas S. Bennett for love and affection to his daughter, Elizabeth E. Hendrickson 50 acres in the 9th District. 2 Jan 1871. (Pp. 703-704)

David Kelley to A. D. Driver and wife, Isabel, 25 acres in the 12th District. 24 Apr 1880. (Pp. 704-706)

Nelson Sneed, colored, and wife, Frances A., colored, to John D. Bone a tract of land in the 1st District, it being the lot upon which Fanny Brazel, colored, now lives. 4 Mar 1880. (Pp. 706-707)

Mary A. McGuire to Susan Robinson several tracts of land in the 14th District. 24 May 1880. (Pp. 707-708)

Clerk & Master to Mary A. McGuire a tract of land belonging to H. McGuire. Said Mary A. McGuire and H. McGuire were husband and wife. Said Mary A. was entitled to a divorce. 24 May 1880. (Pp. 708-710)

William James and wife, Jane, to E. Lisk 40 acres in the 9th District. 13 May 1880. (Pp. 710-711)

W. C. Cantrell and wife, Martha J., to T. M. Reynolds five and one half acres in the 6th District. 5 Jan 1880. (Pp. 711-712)

Nicholas Chambers to S. D. Blankenship and wife, M. C., a town lot in the town of Smithville, it being the lot whereon I now live and is known as Lot No. 17 in the old town plan. Bounded: Water Street. 10 Jun 1880. (Pp. 712-714)

Clerk & Master to W. S. Wester a tract of land belonging to Jesse Farley deceased and located in DeKalb and Putnam Counties. 3 Jun 1880. (Pp. 714-716)

James D. Robinson for love and affection for my wife, Nancy, and my three children, to wit, Eliza, Olla, and Charley a deed of gift of all the personal property that my wife had when we were married or that was given to her by her mother. The condition of this is that this is not to be used against me or to my prejudice in any suit that may be brought against me in any of the courts of this State for damages or divorce. My wife is to relinquish all claims on me or my property at any time during my life. I do further more agree that my wife is to keep the children as long as she can keep them in respectability and she is to allow me the provilege to go to her house to see the children by bring any of the Parker boys with me or the children is to be sent to the house of Dr. Drake so that I can see them. 23 Mar 1880. (Pp. 1-2)

Mary Alexander, Malissa C. Alexander, Samuel H. Alexander, Aniza F. Alexander, Easter A. Alexander, and William B. Alexander to John W. Moore 50 acres in the 9th District. 7 Nov 1874. (Pp. 3-4)

John W. Moore to the Lebanon & Sparta Turnpike Company 150 acres on which I now live. 25 Jun 1880. (Pp. 4-6)

John T. Stokes to his wife, Elizabeth, and his son, Thomas Benton Stokes, and his other children, to wit, Robert Lee Stokes, John Morgan Stokes, Jefferson Davis Stokes, and Isabell Stokes 300 acres in the 15th District. (Pp. 6-7)

Z. T. Richardson, R. Richardson, H. I. Tubb, M. L. Blankenship, and V. Hayes to James R. Tubb their interest in a town lot in the town of Smithville. 16 Feb 1874. (Pp. 7-8)

James M. Baker, trustee, to John P. Tittsworth a tract of land in the 7th District. 5 Jun 1880. (Pp. 8-10)

J. J. Ford and wife, Mary E., to Benjamin Parsley about ten acres on the Caney Fork. 2 Jul 1880. (Pp. 10-11)

Solomon Davis to T. J. Davis three acres in the 12th District. 12 Jul 1880. (Pp. 11-12)

J. D. Griffith, Administrator of W. T. Griffith, to J. M. Wood a tract of land belonging to the estate of W. T. Griffith. Mentions Josephine Moss, formerly Josephine Griffith. 5 Jul 1880. (Pp. 12-114)

E. J. Robinson to C. C. Prichard 43 acres in the 2nd District. 12 Jun 1880. (Pp. 14-15)

J. L. Ayers and wife, Delila, to Yancy Malone 70 acres in the 17th District. 12 Aug 1879. (Pp. 15-17)

W. A. Turner to James Oakley 69 acres in the 12th District. 1 Jan 1880. (Pp. 18-19)

James Hale to Josiah Spurlock 70 acres in the 3rd District. 30 Oct 1879. (Pp. 19-20)

Jonathan Dedman to John Pitman one acre in the 17th District. 3 Apr 1879. (Pp. 20-21)

DEED BOOK O

James H. Fite, Trustee, to Mary J. Herron a tract of land belonging to William and David Herron for tax purposes. 15 Jul 1880. (Pp. 21-22)

Yancy Malone and wife, Amanda E., to P. L. Reynolds 70 acres in the 17th District. 15 Jul 1880. (Pp. 23-25)

J. W. Groom and A. F. Groom to John C. Johnson 42 acres in the 3rd District. 26 Dec 1879. (Pp. 25-26)

J. V. Crowder to W. F. Foutch 16 acres in the 11th District. 16 Jul 1880. (Pp. 26-27)

Thomas N. Christian and wife, Rebecca J., to the Trustees of the Assembly of the Cumberland Presbyterian Church a lot in the town of Smithville for $45. Bounded: College Street. 20 Jan 1880. (Pp. 27-28)

John Trapp for love and affection for the public school interest a lot in the 10th District and School District No. 3 at the gap of the ridge. A building is to be built for a school house for that purpose and none other. Whenever it ceases to be used for school purposes, it is to be mine again or fall back to my estate. 10 Jul 1877. (P. 29)

Letha T. McGee to W. E. Bartlett the Jeremiah Coggins land in the 16th District. 23 Aug 1879. (Pp. 30-31)

John Meritt and wife, Nancy, for love and affection to Nancy J. Wester 53½ acres in the 16th District. Bounded: the school house. 22 Jul 1880. (Pp. 31-32)

William Adcock to Jacob Adcock a tract of land on the bluff of Sink Creek in the 6th District. 25 Dec 1858. (Pp. 32-33)

Jacob Adcock to Sarah Adcock a tract of land in the 6th District. Bounded: Henry Adcock. 27 Dec 1858. (Pp. 33-34)

John Meritt and wife, Nancy, for love and affection to Eliza J. Johnson 35 acres in the 16th District. 22 Jul 1880. (Pp. 34-36)

Jasper A. Hayes and wife, Sarah E., to S. S. Craddock two tracts of land on Dismal Creek in the 2nd District. 4 Sep 1875. (Pp. 36-37)

Isaiah White to John Parker a tract of land in the 4th District. 28 Feb 1880. (Pp. 38-39)

W. T. Hoskins and wife, M. J., to P. L. Reynolds 50 acres in the 12th District. 8 Mar 1879. (Pp. 39-40)

Thomas E. Bratten and wife Sallie; E. J. Bratten and wife, Matilda to Evans, Fite, & Porter 130 acres in the 13th District. 10 Jul 1880. (Pp. 40-42)

John Meritt to W. E. Bartlett 46 acres in the 11th District. 4 Jun 1880. (Pp. 42-43)

T. B. New to W. E. Bartlett his interest in the personal property of Nelson New deceased. 31 Jan 1880. (Pp. 43-44)

DEED BOOK O

Elias Lane and wife, Paralee, to John J. Summers 150 acres in the 9th District. 16 Feb 1880. (Pp. 45-46)

James N. Cartwright to J. L. Bowen his one half interest in 901 acres. 22 Apr 1880. (Pp. 46-47)

D. M. Garrison died seized and possessed of a tract of land in the 13th District. E. J. Bratten and other heirs filed suit against Sanford Bratten and other heirs asking that a tract of land be sold. County Court Clerk to Thomas E. Bratten a tract of land belonging to the estate of D. M. Garrison. 10 Jul 1880. (Pp. 47-48)

James C. Fisher to William C. Malone 85 acres in the 17th District. 29 Aug 1872. (Pp. 49-50)

J. F. Holley to Z. T. Judd his interest in the land of Carline Holley deceased. 16 Aug 1880. (Pp. 50-51)

A. P. Adcock, Eveline Adcock, Elender Adcock, William Love and wife Jane, W. J. Adcock, Mary Ann Adcock, J. R. Adcock, and Sarah Adcock to James K. Adcock their interest in a tract of land owned by Isaac Adcock deceased. 30 Mar 1874. (Pp. 51-53)

James K. Adcock and wife, Sarah, to John C. Adcock and James Tittsworth 100 acres in the 7th District. 16 Aug 1880. (Pp. 53-55)

County Court Clerk to Johnathan Deadman a tract of land belonging to the heirs of M. B. Foutch, to wit, J. M. Foutch, Thomas Foutch, Elizabeth Foutch, Adeline Foutch, William B. Foutch, and Martin L. Foutch. 16 Jul 1880. (Pp. 55-57)

William Young and wife, Sofrona, to J. W. Certen 45 acres. 21 Aug 1880. (Pp. 57-58)

Aaron Cantrell and wife, Sarah, to Fannie Allen 67 acres in the 9th District. 14 Aug 1880. (Pp. 58-60)

C. Starnes and wife, Nancy, to M. W. Starnes 20 acres in the 16th District. 1 Jul 1880. (Pp. 60-62)

S. E. Burger and wife, Hannah, to Mary Ann Barnes 177 acres in the 5th District. 24 Feb 1876. (Pp. 62-63)

Mary Ann Barnes for love and affection to her children, to wit, Willis M. Barnes, Mary J. Barnes, and Stephen C. Barnes about 177 acres in the 5th District. 7 Sep 1880. (Pp. 63-65)

Whig Garrison and wife, Lizabeth, to Murges Wroling two acres in the 7th District. 24 Nov 1877. (Pp. 65-67)

R. C. Bone and wife, Anna F., to Alva Bryant their interest in Lots 17 and 19 in what is known as Bone's Addition to the town of Alexandria. 12 Apr 1879. (Pp. 67-68)

Thomas Driver to George W. Gregston five acres in the 17th District. 5 Feb 1880. (P. 69)

C. G. Bates and wife, Jane, to J. T. Jones four acres in the 11th District. 16 Jul 1878. (Pp. 70-71)

DEED BOOK O

Nancy Webb to Harriet Webb a tract of land in the 6th District for the love and affection I have for the said Harriet. 5 Feb 1879. (Pp. 71-72)

John D. Givan and wife, Elizabeth J., to U. E. Jones 43 acres in the 5th District. 14 Sep 1880. (Pp. 72-73)

I. N. Johnson to Eliza Hunt 100 acres in the 5th District. 6 Nov 1878. (Pp. 73-74)

John A. Cantrell and wife, Nancy, for the love and affection we have four our son and daughter, to wit, Irena Judkins, wife of H. T. Judkins; and J. D. Cantrell the Gibb land in the 7th District. 29 Sep 1879. (Pp. 74-76)

W. T. Robinson and wife, Lucy J., to Elijah J. Robinson, trustee for Sarah C. Fite, she being the wife of W. M. Fite, 66 acres in the 4th District. 5 Oct 1880. (Pp. 76-78)

W. S. Wester and wife, N. J., to William D. Prichard 19 acres in the 16th District. 29 Jul 1880. (Pp. 78-80)

Milus Northcut, colored, to W. T. Robinson one half acre in the 4th District. Bounded: north by my mill tract. 28 May 1875. (Pp. 80-81)

Josiah Griffith and wife, Susanna, to O. D. Griffith 28 acres in the 2nd District. 24 Nov 1869. (Pp. 81-83)

J. T. Turner and wife, Sophronia, to Milus Northcut about three fourth's of an acre near Dowell Town. 13 Dec 1877. (Pp. 83-84)

B. M. Cantrell to Luther Love the John Maynard tract of 50 acres in the 9th District. 5 Oct 1880. (Pp. 84-85)

G. B. Pedigo and wife, Virginia, to L. G. Love 33 acres in the 9th District. 21 Sep 1880. (Pp. 85-87)

Hezekiah Puckett and wife, Mary, to L. G. Love their interest in a tract of land belonging to the heirs of Robert Love deceased, it being one third of one eighth part. 13 Mar 1876. (Pp. 87-88)

Benjamin Anderson and wife, M. A., to W. G. Robinson 66 acres in the 4th District. 6 Oct 1879. (Pp. 88-90)

E. A. Coggin and wife, F. M., to E. C. Martin their two fourth's interest in a tract of land in the 10th District. There is a right of way from Lot No. 4 to Indian Creek. 14 Oct 1880. (Pp. 90-91)

Louis Parker to Samuel Williams 15½ acres in the 4th District. 29 Aug 1847. (Pp. 91-92)

Clerk & Master to F. M. Parkerson and wife a tract of land known as the Stanford lands. I. J. Stanford is a party to the suit. 22 Sep 1879. (Pp. 92-95)

F. M. Parkerson and wife, Elizabeth, to John V. Crowder ten acres in the 4th Districg. Bounded: Widow Stanford's dower. 22 Sep 1879. (Pp. 95-97)

J. V. Crowder to Elizabeth Parkerson, wife of F. M. Parkerson, 90 square poles in the 9th District. 22 Sep 1879. (Pp. 97-98)

Rufus Johnson and wife, Rachel S., to Isaac Sandlin their interest in the dower land held by their mother, Elizabeth Malone, and located in the 11th District. 19 Apr 1880. (Pp. 98-99)

David Brock to J. M. Luna 57½ acres in the 7th District. 21 Sep 1880. (Pp. 99-100)

W. C. Gilbert and wife, F. A., and Obedience Stanley to Miles Tittsworth 23 acres. 7 Oct 1878. (Pp. 100-102)

J. W. Fowler and wife, Parlee, to L. D. Moore their interest in 50 acres in the 9th District. 20 Oct 1880. (Pp. 102-103)

W. G. Crowley to Elijah Whitely and the other trustees for the benefit of the African Methodist Church a lot in the 9th District on Allen's Ferry Road to be used for a church and school house. 13 Oct 1880. (Pp. 103-104)

Seth M. Whaley and wife, Mary E., to James E. Beckwith their two seventh's interest in a tract of land. 28 Apr 1880. (Pp. 104-106)

John W. Bullen and wife, Nancy A., to S. D. Blankenship and wife, M. E., one acre in the 9th District. 30 Oct 1880. (Pp. 106-107)

B. M. Webb and wife, M. H., to Isiah White the house and lot occupied by us which we purchased from L. J. Potter and wife located near the old corporation limits of the town of Smithville. 16 Aug 1880. (Pp. 107-109)

Sarah Hutchins, wife of James B. Hutchins, to F. F. Rigsby 15 acres. 1 Mar 1879. (Pp. 109-110)

Bird S. Sexton to H. D. Exum 12 acres in the 16th District. 12 Nov 1880. (Pp. 111-112)

James Dearman and wife, Harriet C., to T. N. Christian their interest in a lot in Smithville. Bounded: north by South Street. 9 Sep 1880. (Pp. 112-113)

James Hollandsworth and wife, Sarah A., to L. J. Potter a title bond. 3 Dec 1880. (Pp. 113-114)

John A. Cantrell and wife, Nancy, for love and affection to their son, Julias A. Cantrell, a tract of land in the 9th District. 29 Sep 1879. (Pp. 114-116)

C. A. Allen to G. A. Smith and wife, M. A., a lot in the town of Liberty. Bounded: south by Lebanon & Sparta Turnpike. 10 Nov 1880. (Pp. 116-117)

George A. Smith and wife, M. A., to C. A. Allen one acre in the town of Liberty. 10 Nov 1880. (Pp. 117-119)

W. H. Hayes and wife, R. S., to Samuel Grindstaff 16 acres

in the 2nd District, it being my interest in my father's land. 30 Nov 1880. (Pp. 119-120)

John R. Lawrence and wife, Gracy, to D. W. Dinges a tract of land in the 12th District. 14 Sep 1880. (Pp. 121-122)

Berry Y. Cantrell and wife, E. J., to M. L. Bonham 150 acres in the 9th District. 13 Dec 1880. (Pp. 123-124)

Eli Vick to J. W. Goggin 15½ acres in the 3rd District. 29 Dec 1870. (Pp. 124-125)

Isiah White and wife, L. A., to B. M. Meritt a house and lot on the west of the town of Smithville. 10 Nov 1880. (Pp. 126-127)

S. D. Blankenship and wife, M. E., to John W. Bullen and wife, Nancy A., a tract of land in the town of Smithville. Bounded: on the west by the original street on the west side of the old town plan. 30 Oct 1880. (Pp. 127-128)

T. W. Wade to Nelson Bradford all my interest, it being one fourth, in 75 acres in the 9th District. 26 Jun 1880. (Pp. 128-129)

Suriah Blair, alias Sarah Tredwell, of Searcy County, Arkansas to Mary C. Turney her interest in the dower of Mrs. Mary Turney, widow of Joseph Turney and located in the 3rd District. 25 Nov 1880. (Pp. 129-130)

R. C. Bone and wife, Anna F., to D. O. Williams Lots 7 and 8 in what is known as Bone's addition to the town of Alexandria. 1 Aug 1878. (Pp. 131-132)

Harrison Bayne died intestate in the year 1863. County Court Clerk to Thomas Bayne a tract of land belonging to the estate of the said Harrison Bayne. M. F. Bayne filed suit against Charity Bayne asking that the land be sold. 4 Jan 1881. (Pp. 132-134)

John B. Robinson and wife, Julia M., to James W. Foutch 100 acres in the 9th District. 6 Oct 1880. (Pp. 134-135)

C. A. Bailiff and wife, Mary F., to James A. Walker one half acre in the 1st District. 24 Dec 1879. (Pp. 136-137)

Jacob Measles and wife, E. J., to James A. Walker 24 acres in the 1st District. 19 Mar 1880. (Pp. 137-139)

William W. Foster and wife, Rebecca, to Edmon League 65 acres in the 9th District. 2 Feb 1880. (Pp. 139-141)

Cynthia Cantrell to John A. Cantrell full charge of a farm north of my house, this farm being the farm upon which said John Cantrell did clear land in the year 1879 and 1880. 1 Feb 1881. (Pp. 141-142)

John A. Cantrell to J. B. Parish his interest in a tract of land in the 6th District. 1 Feb 1881. (Pp. 142-144)

Davey Calicot and wife, Lotty, to J. and J. W. Clark the land on which we now live. 2 Jul 1881. (Pp. 144-145)

DEED BOOK O

L. J. Bratten and wife, M. T., to G. M. Starks 35 acres in the 3rd District. 1 Mar 1879. (Pp. 145-147)

H. L. W. Capshaw and wife, Elizabeth, to E. A. Green about 50 acres in the 6th District. 29 Dec 1871. (Pp. 147-149)

John D. Givan and wife, Elizabeth, to J. M. Martin three tracts of land in the 5th District. Bounded: south by the Poor House tract of land. 30 Sep 1880. (Pp. 149-151)

W. H. Evans of the firm of Evans, Fite, & Porter to L. H. Davis 130 acres. 3 Feb 1881. (Pp. 151-152)

Thomas Groom and wife, Mary, to James Groom 57 acres in the 3rd District. 28 Jan 1881. (Pp. 152-154)

Thomas Groom to Nancy B. Shehane 33 acres in the 3rd District. 28 Jan 1881. (Pp. 154-156)

Thomas Groom to N. H. Craddock 38 acres in the 3rd District. 28 Jan 1881. (Pp. 156-158)

Thomas Groom to John Craddock 50 acres in the 3rd District. 28 Jan 1881. (Pp. 158-160)

Moses H. Fite, Administrator of Thomas C. Fite, to W. J. Fite about 24½ acres in the 3rd District. 17 Jul 1880. (Pp. 160-161)

George G. Dillard and wife, H., to T. N. Christian their one half interest in a store house and lot in the town of Smithville on the west side of the Square. 9 Feb 1881. (Pp. 161-162)

Moses H. Fite, Administrator of Thomas C. Fite, to S. W. Keaton 18 acres in the 3rd District. 18 Dec 1877. (Pp. 162-164)

Nancy Adcock, formerly Webb, to Harriet Webb the lands in the 6th District willed to Louis Webb (alias Louis Tipet) which I inherited from said Louis Webb, my father who is now dead. 5 Feb 1881. (Pp. 164-166)

J. P. Tittsworth and wife, T. C., to America Patterson about 50 acres in the 5th District. 3 Feb 1879. (Pp. 166-167)

America Patterson to Jasper Fowler 50 acres in the 5th District. 16 Feb 1881. (Pp. 168-169)

John M. Haley and wife, J. T., to Jacob M. Haley 40 acres in Clear Fork. 26 Jan 1881. (Pp. 169-170)

The heirs of James Bozarth, to wit, R. T. Frisby and wife, Julia; Nathaniel Parker and wife, Helen, to J. M. Bozarth about 75 acres. Bounded: Sally Bozarth. 9 Feb 1881. (Pp. 171-172)

W. T. Hoskins and wife, Malissa J.; W. T. Robinson and wife, Lucy J., to John Corley, Sr. 268½ acres in the 12th District. 23 Jun 1876. (Pp. 172-175)

Elizabeth Corley, Mary Corley, John R. Corley, James J.

Corley and wife, Martha F., William B. Corley and wife, Eter, to N. L. Corley their interest in a tract of land that John Corley deceased bought of W. T. Hoskins containing 268½ acres and lying in the 12th District. 23 Jun 1876. (Pp. 175-178)

T. J. Hass and wife, Martha A., to William C. Davis 50 acres in the 4th District. 28 Oct 1879. (Pp. 178-180)

County Court Clerk to John V. Crowder 31 acres in the 9th District belonging to Judson Dale deceased. Suit was filed against Laura Dale for the purpose of selling the land. 24 Nov 1880. (Pp. 180-181)

John V. Crowder to W. E. Davis a swap of 31 acres in the 9th District. 21 Feb 1881. (Pp. 181-182)

Clerk & Master to R. W. Nesmith a tract of land belonging to Thomas Reeves deceased. 14 Feb 1881. (Pp. 182-185)

William H. Magness and wife, E. J., to W. R. Smith and wife, Connie, the David Fite house and lot adjoining the town of Smithville containing two and one half acres. Bounded: on the road leading to the Fulton Academy. 27 Jan 1881. (Pp. 185-186)

John B. Tubb, J. R. Tubb, L. B. Tubb, and M. M. Tubb to Thomas E. Winnard and Richard Winnard about 50 acres in the 9th District. 4 Mar 1881. (Pp. 186-188)

Isaiah White and wife, Lucy A., to W. H. H. Bond about four acres in the 9th District. 8 Mar 1881. (Pp. 188-189)

W. J. Malone and wife, Elizabeth, to Elizabeth Hendrickson 55 acres in the 5th District. 4 Mar 1881. (Pp. 189-191)

John Barger and wife, Martha C., to Thomas Bayne three acres in the 2nd District. 23 Aug 1877. (Pp. 191-192)

Leonard Fite of Wilson County for love and affection to his daughter, Nancy Davis, three lots in the town of Alexandria. 14 Mar 1881. (Pp. 192-193)

Alexander Blanton and wife, Lucinda, to Jeremiah Bain their interest in the dowery of Sinah Bain out of the lands of Peter Bain. 8 Sep 1856. (Pp. 193-195)

J. R. Taylor and wife, Elizabeth, to Pat Garity about two and one half acres in the 2nd District. 25 Feb 1881. (Pp. 195-196)

T. J. Hass and wife, M. A., to W. T. Robinson a tract of land in the 4th District near a house where said Hass now lives. 24 Nov 1880. (Pp. 196-198)

A. T. Fisher and wife, Mary, to John Fisher a tract of land in the 6th District. 15 Dec 1879. (Pp. 199-200)

Joseph A. Starnes and wife, Mourning A., to James Robinson 53½ acres in the 15th District. 15 Nov 1875. (Pp. 200-201)

G. B. Atwell; T. White and wife Lacy A.; W. H. Atwell; James A. Atwell; E. K. Atwell and wife Sue; and Virginia F.

(Loe) to T. M. Hooper their interest in the li estate of R. G. Smith, it being the land that the said Smith bought of L. J. Bratten. 17 Mar 1881. (Pp. 202-203)

James H. Stark and wife, Mary P., to Thomas H. Stark and James P. Stark 480 feet in the 2nd District. 25 Jan 1881. (Pp. 203-205)

William C. Davis and wife, Thena A., to J. V. Crowder 40 acres in the 4th District. 21 Feb 1881. (Pp. 205-206)

W. C. Gilbert and wife, T. A., to S. F. Hale and S. J. Hale 100 acres in the 5th District. 26 Mar 1881. (Pp. 207-208)

Elizabeth Trammel to John R. Baine her interest in a tract of land in the 6th District. Bounded: the dower lands laid off to Sinah Bain deceased of the lands of Peter Bain deceased. 12 Mar 1881. (Pp. 208-209)

John R. Baine and wife, Sarah Lu, to W. T. Wright 245½ acres in the 6th District including and excluding the graveyard and church lot on said land. Bounded: the dower of Sinah Bain. 14 Mar 1881. (Pp. 209-211)

B. F. Winfrey and wife, Judah, to Arwine Page a tract of land in the 15th District. 1 Feb 1881. (Pp. 211-213)

A. J. Lockheart and wife, T. A., to John Lockheart a tract of land on Eagle Creek. 17 Jan 1881. (Pp. 213-214)

E. M. Whaley and wife, Eliza J., to M. A. Cumbell 105 acres in the 2nd District. 2 Oct 1880. (Pp. 214-216)

John H. Clemmons to C. T. Burton 100 acres on the east side of the Caney Fork in the 16th District. 9 Aug 1874. (Pp. 216-217)

William Steel and wife, Elizabeth, to James Steel 80 acres in the 8th District. 5 Apr 1881. (Pp. 217-219)

Miles Tittsworth and wife, Mary, to Elizabeth M. Allen 23 acres in the 5th District. 5 Apr 1881. (Pp. 219-221)

John W. Bullen and wife, Nancy, to J. D. Phillips a town lot in the town of Smithville. Bounded: Walnut Street. 7 Apr 1881. (Pp. 221-222)

N. L. Corley and wife, M. J., to James Ellis the upper end of the Morgan Lawrence farm in the 12th District. 12 Mar 1881. (Pp. 222-224)

E. J. Evans and wife, Eugenia, to S. L. Williams and wife a lot in the 9th District. 7 Apr 1881. (Pp. 224-226)

M. H. Pack and wife, Martha, to Mary E. Cantrell, wife of G. W. Cantrell 40 acres in the 9th District. 11 Apr 1881. (Pp. 226-227)

Lucinda Capshaw to W. R. and J. J. Smith the Capshaw Yellow Store House in the town of Smithville. Bounded: west side of the Public Square where North Street comes to the said Square on the south side of said street. 13 Apr 1881. (Pp. 227-229)

M. N. Smith and wife, Sarah, to J. R. Smith 50 acres in the 5th District. Bounded: McMinnville Road. 16 Apr 1881. (Pp. 229-231)

Isiah White and wife, Lucy A., to M. H. Webb a house and lot in the 9th District now occupied by Joshua Hollinsworth. 16 Aug 1880. (Pp. 231-232)

A. J. Bond and wife, M. E., to W. H. H. Bond their one half interest in a tract of land on Holmes Creek in the 18th District. 11 Apr 1881. (Pp. 232-234)

A. L. Foster and wife Mary E.; and Prudence Cameron to E. T. Foster their interest in several lots of land. 25 Apr 1881. (Pp. 234-236)

Henry Bass and wife, Elizabeth, to S. B. Harriman 165 acres in the 4th District. 4 Mar 1875. (Pp. 236-237)

E. T. Foster, A. L. Foster, and Mary E. Foster, and Prudence Cameron to G. W. Cameron their interest in a tract of land south of Smithville on Short Mountain. 25 Apr 1881. (Pp. 237-239)

John W. Sandlin, Sarah Sandlin, Isaac M. Sandlin, Robert H. Sandlin, Monroe Malone and wife Pheba C., Carrol Bennett and wife Louiza M. filed suit in County Court against Albert Sandlin for the purpose of selling or partitioning the land of Rudolf Sandlin deceased. County Court Clerk to J. W. Sandlin 93 acres. States that Martha Sandlin is the wife of John W. Sandlin. 24 Nov 1880. (Pp. 239-243)

Edmon League and wife, Caldonia, to Elizabeth Rackley 40 acres in the 8th District. 29 Mar 1880. (Pp. 244-246)

John Griffith and wife, Sarah, to Jonathan F. Griffith two acres in the 13th District. 10 Mar 1880. (Pp. 246-248)

Mary Satterfield to Martha A. Cantrell and A. M. Cantrell a tract of land in the 13th District of Warren County. 11 May 1881. (Pp. 248-249)

W. W. Morgan and wife, Mary Jane; J. T. Driver and wife F. Q. to T. M. Hooper their interest, it being one fourth, in the land of Isiah Driver deceased. 16 Apr 1881. (Pp. 249-251)

John P. Tittsworth and wife, Elizabeth, to J. M. Anderson the Hardy Cantrell land in the 5th District. 14 Oct 1880. (Pp. 251-253)

Allas M. Martin and husband W. H.; A. Redman and husband Thomas E.; S. S. Redman; A. L. Jones and wife Res; John D. Givins and wife Elizabeth to Mary J. Wooldridge their interest in 25 acres in the 5th District. 1 Oct 1880. (Pp. 253-256)

John C. Cannady and wife, M. A., to Barnabus Johnson about 90 acres in the 3rd District. 14 Feb 1879. (Pp. 256-258)

Survey of Peter Adams land. 18 May 1881. (Pp. 258-259)

DEED BOOK O

John M. Foster to Isaac R. Conger a tract of land. 26 Feb 1872. (Pp. 259-260)

Nancy P. Tittsworth to Calvin Anderson a tract of land in the 5th District. 14 Oct 1878. (Pp. 261-262)

America Polland to Calvin W. Anderson 29 acres on Sink Creek, it being the land conveyed by Watson Cantrell deceased to the said America Polland. 12 Aug 1879. (Pp. 262-263)

Clerk & Master to J. C. Watson a tract of land. 30 May 1881. (Pp. 263-265)

J. W. Scott and wife, Jane, to J. W. Scott, Jr. and the other trustees of the Methodist Episcopal Church a tract of land. 5 Feb 1880. (Pp. 266-268)

John A. Moss to J. K. Starnes 200 acres in the 16th District. 6 Jun 1881. (Pp. 268-269)

J. T. Youngblood and wife, Elizabeth, to William C. Youngblood the Jane Caroline Youngblood land in Liberty. 20 May 1878. (Pp. 270-273)

T. H. Richardson and W. C. Youngblood to T. B. Potter three acres in the 9th District. Bounded: M. E. Richardson and her former husband Richard Richardson. 18 Sep 1880. (Pp. 273-274)

C. T. Burton and wife, S. B., to William E. Foster 180 acres in the 18th District. 4 Apr 1881. (Pp. 275-277)

John M. Foster to Joel Foster 80 acres in the 16th District. 2 Jan 1875. (Pp. 277-278)

John Meritt to Mary A. Foster 17 acres in the 16th District. 30 Dec 1879. (Pp. 278-279)

G. P. M. Williams and wife Sarah; and Elizabeth F. Williams to Joseph Turney 11½ acres in the 2nd District. 8 Sep 1879. (Pp. 280-281)

J. W. Walker to Jane Walker, widow of A. W. Walker, a promissory note. 25 Feb 1878. (P. 282)

Thomas E. Vick to William L. Vick one eighth of an acre in the 2nd District. 28 Jun 1881. (Pp. 283-284)

C. W. L. Hale to Pat Garity 158 poles in the 2nd District. 4 Sep 1881. (Pp. 284-285)

John W. Shaw to M. T. Cooper a tract of land. 13 Sep 1872. (Pp. 285-286)

M. N. Smith for love and affection to his wife, Sarah Smith, all his household property. 5 Jul 1881. (Pp. 286-287)

Alford L. Hancock to John Dirting during his natural life and then to William H. Dirting, John A. Dirting, and Sarah Dirting about 80 acres in the 3rd District. 30 Jul 1881. (P. 288)

John V. Crowder and wife, R. H., to E. J. Evans three tracts of land in the 9th District. 2 Feb 1878. (Pp. 289-291)

DEED BOOK O

Jane Petris to John Bray 124½ acres in the 14th District. 1 Nov 1878. (Pp. 291-292)

John Bray and wife, Candish, of Simpson County, Kentucky to Jonathan Bray their power of attorney to sell 150 acres on Falling Water in DeKalb County. 10 May 1881. (Pp. 292-294)

E. J. Evans and wife, Eugenia, to James W. Fite several tracts of land in the 9th District. 10 Aug 1881. (Pp. 294-296)

Jonathan Johnson and wife, Lucinda, to P. T. Shores 87 acres in the 9th District. 17 Aug 1881. (Pp. 296-298)

George H. Siemon of Brooklyn, New York to Frederick L. Siemon of the same place 4000 acres in DeKalb County. 16 Aug 1881. (Pp. 298-300)

George H. Siemon of Brooklyn, New York to George H. Young of the same place 4000 acres. 16 Aug 1881. (Pp. 300-302)

Clerk & Master to B. M. Cantrell and others a tract of land containing 40,234 acres. 23 Aug 1881. (Pp. 302-304)

William Bates to J. W. Reynolds a quit claim to 250 acres in the 11th District. 30 Aug 1881. (P. 305)

L. Eveline Fuson for love and affection to Susan Evans, wife of George Evans, during her life and then to her children 100 acres in the 9th District. 21 Aug 1881. (P. 306)

Henry Bains to John K. Bains his interest in 245½ acres in the 6th District. 30 Jul 1881. (Pp. 307-308)

Smallman & Carnes to M. H. Webb one half of the law office known as the Cantrell & Ford Law Office in the town of Smithville. Bounded: the north side of the Public Square between the Methodist Church and the Dunlap lot. 31 Dec 1880. (Pp. 308-309)

T. B. Potter and wife Samantha D., to M. D. Smallman, President of Pure Fountain College, and the trustees ten acres in the 9th District. 1 Sep 1881. (Pp. 310-311)

John C. Cannady and wife, Margaret A., to J. C. Crouch a tract of land in the 9th District. 10 Sep 1881. (Pp. 311-312)

L. Evaline Fuson for love and affection to her daughter, Mary B. Hunt, wife of W. M. Hunt, during her natural life and then to her children a house and lot in the town of Liberty containing too and one half acres. 21 Aug 1881. (Pp. 312-313)

James H. Lamberson and wife, Mary, to J. P. Starks one half acre in the 2nd District. 25 Oct 1879. (Pp. 313-314)

County Court Clerk to T. H. W. Richardson a tract of land belonging to the estate of J. H. Reeves when died about 1862. 2 Jan 1881. (Pp. 315-318)

I. N. Murphy and wife, Rachel, to Israel Long 75 acres.

6 Nov 1875. (Pp. 318-320)

L. H. Davis and wife, Connie, to Jacob P. Taylor 130 acres. 30 Sep 1881. (Pp. 321-322)

T. J. Finley and wife, E. F., of Collin County, Texas to Stephen S. (Kur) their interest in the estate of N. W. New. 19 Sep 1881. (Pp. 322-323)

John Reed and wife, Sarah, to William E. Jones 20 acres in the 15th District. 6 Oct 1881. (Pp. 323-325)

J. L. Lawrence and wife, Mary, to S. W. McClellan 156 acres in the 1st District. 1 Jan 1876. (Pp. 325-327)

John P. Tittsworth, Elizabeth Tittsworth, J. D. Tittsworth, T. C. Tittsworth, C. Goodson and wife Lietta, Martha Cantrell, T. B. Cantrell, T. M. Reynolds, M. J. Reynolds, Miles Tittsworth for love and affection to John Tittsworth and William Tittsworth, sons of our deceased brother, Elisha Tittsworth, a tract of land in the 5th District. 10 May 1879. (Pp. 327-329)

Thomas Grooms versus William Fite and wife Caroline, Jordan W. Goggin and wife Virginia, Shelah Robinson, Wingate Robinson, Robert Robinson, L. Robinson, and Linsley Robinson. Said parties are the children and heirs of R. J. Givens deceased who are residents of Cannon County. 29 Aug 1881. (Pp. 330-338)

Calvin W. Anderson and wife, M. A., to Alford Allen 29 acres on Sink Creek. 10 Oct 1881. (Pp. 338-339)

J. W. Anderson and wife, Missoury, to Alford Allen a tract of land in the 5th District. 10 Oct 1881. (Pp. 340-341)

Jasper Williams to Pearson Evans 50 acres in the 5th District. 8 Feb 1879. (Pp. 341-342)

J. B. Taylor and wife, Martha, to P. G. Taylor 35 acres in Indian Creek in the 10th District. 24 Sep 1881. (Pp. 343-344)

Clerk & Master to Ed League a tract of land. 19 Oct 1881. (Pp. 344-346)

Mary J. Robinson to Elom Edge a tract of land in the 4th District. 17 Dec 1879. (Pp. 346-347)

Clerk & Master to Edmond League a tract of land. 25 Oct 1881. (Pp. 347-349)

Coleman Helem for love and affection to his wife, Mary, all of his household furniture. 31 Oct 1881. (Pp. 349-350)

A. B. Hicks to T. H. Stark and J. P. Stark his one half interest in a tract of land in the 2nd District. 1 Sep 1881. (Pp. 350-351)

D. S. Mitchell and wife, Elizabeth, to W. M. Barrett 126 acres in the 4th District. 8 Oct 1881. (Pp. 351-353)

C. W. L. Hale to Thomas H. Fite a tract of land in the 3rd District. 13 Dec 1880. (Pp. 353-355)

DEED BOOK O

Jerry Fisher and wife, M. H., to William Davis for the consideration of a tract of land swaped to us in the 12th District a tract of land in the 4th District. 4 Nov 1881. (Pp. 355-356)

P. G. Magness to L. P. Potter a tract of land in the 5th District. 7 Nov 1881. (P. 357)

William M. Hale and wife, Mildred, to John L. Hale 94¼ acres in the 18th District. 8 Nov 1881. (Pp. 357-359)

Sarah Shaw, wife of John W. Shaw and formerly wife of W. R. Billings, for love and affection to her children, to wit, I. N. Billings, J. J. Billings, W. F. Billings, and G. W. Billings her right of dower in two tracts of land in the 14th District. 13 Oct 1881. (Pp. 359-361)

B. M. Meritt and wife, Margaret to T. W. Wade a town lot in the town of Smithville. Bounded: Fulton Academy lot. 12 Nov 1881. (Pp. 361-362)

J. L. Colvert to Susan (Dewese) 120 acres in the 14th District. 8 Aug 1871. (Pp. 363-364)

James Oakley and wife, Sarah F., 114 acres in the 16th District. 17 May 1881. (Pp. 364-366)

G. E. Henley and wife, Lucy, to James M. Foutch a tract of land in the 11th District. 18 Nov 1881. (Pp. 366-367)

County Court Clerk to James M. Foutch a tract of land belonging to the estate of John Hale deceased. 26 Mar 1881. (Pp. 368-370)

A. J. (Toney) Snow and wife, S. H.; R. R. Slack and wife, W. M.; Jeremiah Davidson; and John (Kiton) to T. M. Hooper their eleven fourteenth's interest in 143 acres in the 9th District. 8 Nov 1881. (Pp. 370-373)

John W. Sandlin to I. M. Sandlin 21 acres in the 1st District. 5 May 1880. (Pp. 373-374)

William Bates and wife, Jane, to C. G. Bates 95 acres in the 11th District. 12 Oct 1880. (Pp. 374-375)

W. L. Robinson and wife, Lucy J., to John A. Robinson 81 acres in the 2nd District. 17 Dec 1881. (Pp. 376-377)

William Robinson, Executor of T. J. Williams, to J. E. Williams 25 acres in the 4th District. 24 Nov 1881. (Pp. 377-378)

J. J. Ford and wife, Mary E., of DeKalb County; Robert Cantrell and wife, Martha, of Wilson County; M. M. Brien and wife, Mary A., Thomas D. Fite and wife, Laura G., of Davidson County to J. W. Reynolds a tract of land in the 11th District. 31 Aug 1881. (Pp. 378-380)

Elizabeth (Torbet) to J. H. Savage a tract of land one and one half miles south of Smithville. 20 Dec 1881. (Pp. 381-382)

C. G. Bates and wife, Jane, to G. W. Reynolds 95 acres in the 11th District. 20 Dec 1881. (Pp. 382-383)

John F. Fuson to M. M. Allen the interest of Margaret Fuson, now Margaret Allen, in the lands of our father, John Fuson. 24 Dec 1881. (P. 384)

John Trapp and wife, Elizabeth, to J. T. Trapp seven and one half acres in the 18th District. 11 Jan 1881. (Pp. 385-386)

W. G. Crowley to C. G. Bates a title bond. 26 Dec 1881. (Pp. 386-387)

Alford Allen to his son, T. C. Allen, 35 acres in the 5th District. Mentions W. J. Allen, my deceased son. 15 Oct 1881. (Pp. 387-389)

Wilson H. Hendrixson and wife, Frances, to James W. Foutch a tract of land in the 10th District. 23 Mar 1881. (Pp. 389-391)

P. T. Shores and wife, Maggie, and W. M. Shores to E. J. Evans a tract of land in the town of Smithville. 6 Aug 1881. (Pp. 391-392)

Spencer Bing and wife, Mary, to E. J. Evans a town lot in the town of Smithville, it being Lot No. 38. 24 Sep 1881. (Pp. 392-393)

S. Page and wife, Samandy; R. M. Trapp and wife, Mary E., to M. L. Bondham and wife, Rebecca, their interest in the estate of John Trapp. 21 Nov 1881. (Pp. 394-395)

M. L. Bondham and wife, Rebecca, to J. T. Trapp 50 acres in the 18th District. 19 Dec 1881. (Pp. 396-397)

John B. Robinson, T. W. Wade, and Lilard Thompson to J. W. Reynolds a quit claim to a tract of land. 16 Dec 1881. (Pp. 397-399)

W. T. Robinson and wife, L. J., to J. W. McNeal 15 acres in the 2nd District. 24 Mar 1881. (Pp. 399-400)

William Goodman and wife, Sarah, to I. N. Billings 40 acres in the 14th District. 9 Feb 1881. (P. 401)

B. M. Cantrell to John D. Rigsby a quit claim to three parcels of land in the 9th District. 10 Jan 1882. (Pp. 402-403)

William H. Hayes to Robert Yeargin 37 acres in the 14th District. 31 Dec 1881. (Pp. 403-404)

William H. Hayes to John M. Hayes a tract of land in the 14th District. 31 Dec 1881. (P. 405)

William Bullard to B. M. Cantrell and T. W. Wade, attornies, 84 acres in the 5th District. 15 Dec 1881. (P. 406)

A. Smith and wife, Mary J., to Jacob Adams their interest in the estate of Mathew Sellars, it being one third of one third of one share. 10 Dec 1881. (P. 407)

John P. Tittsworth and wife, Elizabeth, to F. Turner a tract of land in the 7th District. 2 Dec 1880. (Pp. 408-409)

J. Bailey Peyton to I. D. Tittsworth 40 acres three miles south of Smithville. 5 Feb 1880. (Pp. 409-410)

B. F. Hale to J. T. Hale 205 acres, it being land on which my mother, C. S. Hale, now lives and claims as her dower. 1 Feb 1882. (Pp. 410-411)

Edmond League and wife, Caldonia, to Nancy Burton 200 acres in the 9th District. 11 Feb 1882. (Pp. 411-413)

Levi Foutch and wife, Mahaley, to J. R. Hern a lot in the 1st District. 9 Dec 1881. (Pp. 413-415)

Johnathan Dearman and wife to J. M. Foutch 16½ acres in the 17th District. 22 Feb 1882. (Pp. 415-416)

Wiley Snow and wife, Catherine, to A. E. (Blakemore) 75 acres in the 4th District. 3 Oct 1881. (Pp. 416-417)

Amanda R. Baird, widow of J. M. Baird; Carrie Baird, and Ophelia Bell, the only heirs of said deceased, in connection with Byron Bell, husband to said Ophelia, filed suit to sell a tract of land. County Court Clerk to J. L. (Bonner) the said tract of land. 28 Jan 1882. (Pp. 418-420)

John R. Lyles and wife, Mary, to W. H. Rhody and wife 40 acres in the 9th District. 27 Feb 1882. (Pp. 420-421)

Samuel Snow to Savage & Davis a horse as a trust deed. 20 Mar 1882. (Pp. 421-422)

J. T. Jones to W. S. Parker four acres in the 11th District. 13 Apr 1880. (Pp. 422-423)

H. A. Hill and wife, Martha C., to W. T. Robinson a tract of land in the 2nd District. 16 Sep 1881. (Pp. 423-425)

J. T. Trapp for love and affection for the old Two Seed Predestination Baptist Church of Christ and the advancement of the Church of Christ a tract of land on Holmes Creek. When the land ceases to be used as a church of this faith and order, then the land is to return to me. 21 Jan 1882. (Pp. 425-426)

John P. Tittsworth and wife, Elizabeth, to L. G. Bing a swap of land. 30 Dec 1879. (Pp. 426-428)

H. W. Boatwright and wife, Mary E., to David C. Taylor five and one half acres in the 10th District. 31 Mar 1882. (Pp. 428-429)

L. E. Simpson; W. W. Patterson and wife, I. J., to D. W. Dinges 27 acres. 17 Dec 1881. (Pp. 429-431)

Alford P. Smith and wife Allice; and P. J. Smith to J. L. Turner a tract of land in the 15th District. 2 Feb 1882. (Pp. 431-433)

Josiah J. Jones, R. D. Jones, and Ezra M. Jones to John C.

Taylor their interest in the estate of Joseph Jones. 7 Dec 1881. (Pp. 433-434)

J. L. Ayers and wife, Delia J., to J. C. Bass 59 acres in the 12th District. 17 Oct 1876. (Pp. 434-436)

Sarah Cantrell to A. W. J. Cantrell in consideration of the said A. W. Cantrell boarding, lodging, and seeing after and taking care of me a tract of land in the 5th District. 7 Mar 1882. (Pp. 436-438)

Clerk & Master to J. M. Baker, trustee, a tract of land belonging to the estate of Alexander Martin in the 14th District. 5 Apr 1882. (Pp. 438-441)

T. W. Fitts and wife, Isabel, to W. G. Fitts 100 acres in the 15th District. 6 Dec 1880. (Pp. 442-443)

Edmond League and wife, Caldonia, to H. F. Love 240 acres known as the Eli tract of the Davis lands and located in the 9th District. 7 Apr 1882. (Pp. 444-445)

T. N. Christian for love and affection to his wife, Rebecca J., and children a house and lot in Smithville. 14 Feb 1882. (Pp. 446-449)

John K. Starnes and wife, Amanda, to Luther Starnes their interest in 70 acres in the 16th District. 15 Apr 1882. (Pp. 450-451)

William Robinson, Executor of T. J. Williams, to J. S. Barry 63 acres in the 4th District. 24 Nov 1881. (Pp. 452-453)

W. T. Robinson and wife, Lucy J., to J. W. McNeal a tract of land in Dowelltown. 17 Apr 1882. (Pp. 453-454)

Mariah L. Hayes for love and affection to her grandson, James M. Hayes, Jr., and his father, my son, James M. Hayes, Sr., 200 acres to take effect at the death of his father. 27 Jul 1874. (Pp. 454-456)

William Seawell and wife, Caroline, to Martha J. Robinson 50 acres in the 4th District. 10 Dec 1879. (Pp. 456-457)

John Burton and S. E. Burton agree to a division of land in the 8th District. 21 Mar 1881. (Pp. 458-460)

A. P. Adcock, Eveline Adcock, Elender Adcock, William Love and wife Jane, W. J. Adcock, Mary Ann Adcock, J. K. Adcock, and Sarah Adcock, heirs of Isaac Adcock, to W. J. Adcock their interest in 100 acres in the 7th District. 30 Mar 1874. (Pp. 461-463)

Jonathan Delong and wife, Malinda, to W. J. Adcock 70 acres in the 7th District. 17 Apr 1875. (Pp. 463-464)

Sanford Mann and wife, Matilda, to J. R. Taylor one fifth of an acre at Dowelltown. 11 Jan 1881. (Pp. 465-466)

J. R. Taylor and wife, Elizabeth, to Connell Morrow & Company one half acre. 17 May 1882. (Pp. 466-468)

W. G. Foster and wife, Juda, and C. C. Murphy to W. C. Crowley a tract of land about one half mile south of Smithville. 10 Apr 1882. (Pp. 469-470)

John J. Burton and wife, Mary, to Edmond League and wife 150 acres in the 8th District. 11 Feb 1882. (Pp. 470-472)

Edmond League and wife, Caldonia, to B. B. West and J. S. Harrison a mortgage. 14 Mar 1882. (Pp. 472-474)

S. D. Blankenship and wife, M. E., to R. A. Youngblood a lot in the town of Smithville. 12 Oct 1881. (Pp. 475-476)

William Haney and wife, Parlee, to Lucinda Capshaw Lots 3, 6, and 7 in the town of Smithville. 11 Apr 1882. (Pp. 476-477)

James M. Conditt to John Ferrell 50 acres in the 5th District. 2 Aug 1880. (Pp. 477-478)

John H. Fuson, trustee, to James Willis a tract of land in the 14th District for taxes. 2 Apr 1878. (Pp. 478-480)

Jacob Adams to P. C. Adams 114 acres in the 3rd District. 6 May 1882. (Pp. 480-481)

The heirs of J. H. Dodd to M. H. Webb a tract of land. The heirs include T. S. Bennett and wife Sarah, Anna Smith, James A. Smith and wife Nancy M. 29 May 1882. (Pp. 481-483)

D. W. Dinges to B. A. Adamson Lots 10 and 12 in the town of Alexandria. 5 May 1882. (Pp. 483-484)

Thomas Grooms to John Rhody a tract of land in the 3rd District. 15 Apr 1880. (P. 485)

B. M. Webb and wife, M. H., agree to exchange with James A. Smith for the Daniel Smith Mills the house and lot in Smithville on which we now live. 25 May 1882. (P. 486)

J. A. Rhody and wife, Mary, to W. L. Waters 74 acres in the 3rd District. 10 Jun 1882. (Pp. 487-488)

J. B. Crouch and wife, Elizabeth, to W. W. Wade 53 acres in the 9th District, it being the place where we nowlive. 19 Jun 1882. (Pp. 488-489)

Amanda E. Davis to B. M. Meritt a tract of land near the town of Smithville. 20 May 1882. (P. 490)

John P. Tittsworth and wife for the consideration of the entire interest of E. J. Dunlap in the land of her father, John Davis, to the said Elizabeth J. Dunlap a tract of land in the 9th District. 23 Jun 1882. (P. 491)

J. D. Tittsworth to B. W. Hicks six acres about three miles from Smithville. 24 Jan 1882. (P. 492)

L. J. Magness to Fannie Allen 75 acres in the 7th District. 23 Jun 1882. (Pp. 492-494)

Henry Wooden and wife, Elizabeth, and Mary Wooden to Levi Foutch ten acres. 1 Apr 1881. (Pp. 495-496)

J. M. Sandlin and wife, Jane, to William J. Robinson a tract of land in the 11th District. 14 Dec 1880. (Pp. 496-497)

T. W. Fitts and wife, Isabel, to W. G. Fitts 18 acres in the 15th District. 1 Jun 1882. (Pp. 498-499)

John E. Atnip to J. T. Trapp and the other school directors of the 18th District one half acre to be used for a school house. When it ceases to be used as a school site, then the land with improvements is to belong to me. Bounded: in my field on the east side of Holmes Creek near a spring. 1 Nov 1881. (P. 499)

W. B. Tramel and wife, Sarah Elizabeth Tramel, and Elizabeth Tramel about four acres in the 10th District. 11 Jul 1882. (Pp. 500-501)

T. W. Green and wife, Mary C., to R. C. Pedigo 58 acres in the 9th District. 19 Jul 1882. (Pp. 501-504)

James C. Jones and wife, M. J., to W. G. Crowley a tract of land about one mile south of Smithville on both sides of what is known as the Morgan Branch. 17 Jan 1882. (Pp. 504-505)

Thomas Mason died intestate on 14 Oct 1864. John Linder was appointed administrator. Nancy Mason, widow of the said Thomas Mason, filed suit to receive her dower. The dower was sold by decree for the purpose of paying debts. County Court Clerk to N. E. Cantrell said land. 6 Jun 1881. (Pp. 505-507)

H. A. Overall to T. G. Wood 28 acres in the 3rd District. 8 May 1877. (Pp. 507-508)

B. C. Wilkinson to J. A. Cantrell about five acres in the 5th District. 1 Dec 1880. (Pp. 508-509)

John Pinegar and wife, Mary J., to Yancey Pinegar during his life and then to Harriet Pinegar the Elizabeth Pinegar tract of land in the 7th District. 4 Jul 1881. (P. 510)

Clerk & Master to John Lockheart a tract of land. Felix Robertson and wife filed suit asking for the sale. 31 Mar 1881. (Pp. 511-512)

James Ford and wife, Isabel, to W. C. and J. Lockheart 100 acres in the 9th District. 1 Mar 1882. (Pp. 512-513)

Thomas Turner and wife, Sophronia, to M. L. Turner and wife, Elizabeth, an oblong square so as to include three fourth's of an acre in the 2nd District. 23 May 1881. (Pp. 514-516)

W. L. Driver and wife, Nancy W., to G. R. Smith a tract of land in the 9th District. 18 Mar 1882. (Pp. 516-517)

William James, John James, Margaret James, Nancy James, Andrew Lafever and wife Eller, T. S. Johnson, and Hamilton James, each being of full age and the only persons interested in the estate of Elizabeth James in the 8th District on the Caney Fork River where Hampton James now lives agree to an equal division of the land. 17 Feb 1881. (Pp. 517-523)

T. J. Allen to L. J. Magness, trustee for Malissa Magness, his wife, a tract of land in the 9th District. 8 Jul 1881. (Pp. 523-524)

W. L. Judkins and wife, America A., to Aaron Cantrell half of a tract of land that contains 190 acres in the 7th District. 18 Aug 1882. (Pp. 525-526)

Isaiah White to Frances C. White 40 acres in the 2nd District. 6 Jul 1880. (Pp. 526-527)

W. D. Carnes and T. N. Christian to J. M. Snow 73 acres in the 4th District. (Page 527 and continued to Page 539)

The heirs of (Houston) James, to wit, Nancy James, Martha Murry, William James, Eliza James, Margrett James, A. J. Lafever, and Ella Lafever enter into an agreement. 5 May 1882. (Pp. 528-533)

Clerk & Master to B. L. Estes a tract of land. Mentions Mary Estes. 11 Sep 1878. (Pp. 534-535)

William James et als to Margrett James Lot No. 3. 5 May 1882. (Pp. 536-537)

James H. Fite and wife, C. E., to G. R. Smith several tracts of land in the 9th District. 25 Aug 1882. (Pp. 537-539)

Sebastian Williams for love and affection to Parallee Williams to take effect at my death 77 acres in the 3rd District. 3 Feb 1881. (P. 540)

Clerk & Master to James A. Moore a tract of land belonging to the estate of John Parsley. Mentions Thomas Parsley, Nancy Parsley, and Tennessee Smith. 6 Dec 1880. (Pp. 541-543)

Malindy Redman died intestate prior to the May Term of County Court. County Court Clerk to Aaron Cantrell a tract of land belonging to the deceased. Matildy Driver and others filed suit asking for the sale. 5 Jul 1881. (Pp. 543-544)

James Ray to Anderson Davis three and one half acres in the 6th District. 16 Mar 1881. (P. 545)

Robert Tramel to Anderson Davis 40 acres in the 6th District. 30 Sep 1880. (Pp. 546-548)

W. R. Bryant and W. G. Bryant to C. J. Allen a promissory note. 21 Aug 1880. (Pp. 548-549)

E. W. Cantrell and T. C. Cantrell to S. K. Cantrell a tract of land in the 5th District. 18 Jan 1882. (P. 550)

Columbus Scott and wife, Mary C., to Elam Edge 450 acres in the 4th District. 1 Oct 1878. (P. 551)

Betsy Ann Chumley, formerly Edge, to Elam Edge all her interest in 450 acres. 4 Sep 1882. (P. 552)

John S. Close to John R. Corder a tract of land in the 12th District. 20 Nov 1875. (Pp. 553-554)

DEED BOOK O

John S. Close to T. A. Close my old homestead in the 12th District. 3 Apr 1880. (P. 555)

Lucindy Capshaw to James Dearman a part of the Capshaw house and lot in the 9th District. 3 Aug 1882. (Pp. 556-557)

E. Berry and wife, M. C., to S. S. Young 50 acres in the 5th District. 5 Oct 1881. (Pp. 557-558)

James Dearman and wife, Harriet C. to Lucindy Capshaw a house and lot in the town of Smithville. 30 Aug 1882. (Pp. 559-560)

James Oakley to W. E. Bartlett 25 acres in the 16th District. 1 Jun 1880. (Pp. 560-561)

T. N. Christian and W. D. Carnes to W. C. Lewis a tract of land one mile south of Smithville. 27 Feb 1877. (P. 562)

James Marler and wife, Sarah, to Dock Bates a tract of land in the 11th District, containing 32 acres. 30 Jan 1880. (Pp. 563-565)

William M. Bradford to J. H. Foutch 32 acres in the 11th District. 18 Jul 1878. (Pp. 565-566)

Richard Lamberson and wife, Tabitha, to M. A. Crowley one and one half acres on the west side of Holmes Creek. 22 Jan 1881. (Pp. 566-568)

J. J. Summers and wife, Rutha, to E. (Love) a tract of land in the 5th District. 16 Feb 1880. (Pp. 568-569)

DEED BOOK P

E. J. Evans and wife, Virginia, to W. W. Wade three acres in the 9th District near the corporation line of Smithville. 28 Aug 1882. (Pp. 1-2)

J. A. Moores and wife, Amanda, to A. C. Mullican three acres in the 5th District. 4 Sep 1882. (Pp. 2-3)

A. C. Mullican and wife, A. C., to T. W. Wade 60 acres in the 5th District. 4 Sep 1882. (Pp. 3-4)

T. W. Wade and wife, Jennie, to J. B. Wilson a town lot in Smithville on the west side of the town. 31 Aug 1882. (Pp. 4-5)

M. V. Smith and wife, Sarah, to Robert Trail a tract of land. 10 Apr 1881. (P. 6)

S. S. Craddock and wife, Harriet M., to Jasper N. Hayes 132 acres in the 8th District. 3 Sep 1875. (Pp. 7-8)

Sheriff to D. W. Dinges a house and lot in Alexandria. Bounded: north by the Lebanon & Sparta Pike; south by R. C. Bone. 20 Sep 1882. (Pp. 8-10)

William Sellars, Executor of Mathew Sellars, to G. W. Marks a tract of land belonging to the deceased. 11 Sep 1865. (Pp. 10-11)

Jesse T. Hollis and wife, H. B., to J. P. Tittsworth a tract of land in the 9th District. 27 Sep 1882. (P. 12)

Clerk & Master to William A. Moss a tract of land belonging to the estate of Hesekiah Love deceased. Suit was filed by J. H. Love against R. S. Love, Nancy Love, M. V. Love, W. E. Love, R. O. Love, and Ida J. Love, the widow, children, and grandchildren of said Hesekiah Love. 24 Nov 1881. (Pp. 13-14)

John Barger and wife, Martha, to Thomas Keeton and others a tract of land containing 113 acres. 25 Sep 1882. (Pp. 14-16)

P. G. Magness, Sr. to M. N. Smith 100 acres in the 5th District. 14 Aug 1876. (P. 17)

T. W. Robinson to D. A. West 50 acres in the 2nd District. 4 Oct 1882. (Pp. 18-19)

I. J. Driver to T. M. Hooper his one fourth interest in a tract of land belonging to Isiah Driver deceased. 3 Oct 1882. (P. 20)

T. N. Christian, trustee of his wife and children, to W. D. Carnes a one half interest in several parcels of land in the 3rd District. 6 Oct 1882. (Pp. 21-22)

W. D. G. Carnes and wife, Sarah E., to T. W. Wade and James T. Hayes a tract of land in the 9th District. 7 Oct 1882. (Pp. 22-24)

J. H. Veach and wife, Mary A., to J. H. Hooper a house and lot near the old corporate line of Smithville. 9 Oct 1882. (Pp. 24-25)

DEED BOOK P

J. J. Ford to C. C. Avant the Cantrell & Ford Law Office in the town of Smithville. Bounded: street running north and south from the north side of the Public Square. 16 Mar 1881. (Pp. 25-26)

John Barger and wife, Martha Caroline, to Cynthia J. Allen and others 40 acres in the 2nd District. 25 Sep 1882. (Pp. 26-28)

Mathew Wilson and wife, Mary, to A. B. Hooper one and one fourth acres in the town of Smithville. 24 Sep 1881. (Pp. 28-29)

Rial Jennings and wife, Margaret, to S. B. Adamson 51 acres. 6 Aug 1881. (Pp. 29-30)

Mary Goodson and Jane Goodson to J. R. P. Goodson 100 acres in the 6th District. 26 Sep 1872. (Pp. 30-32)

J. H. Bozarth to William Bozarth 75 acres in the 8th District. 21 Aug 1878. (Pp. 32-33)

Job Trapp to his sons, J. T. Trapp, M. V. Trapp, and John S. Trapp; and daughters Rebecca Judkins, S. J. Denton, Amanda Atnip, Eliza Crips, and Nancy O. Cantrell; and grandchildren Mary Medlin, Roland Pedigo, I. D. Pedigo, and S. J. Pedigo 320 acres in the 18th District. 14 Oct 1882. (Pp. 33-35)

T. N. Christian and wife, R. J., to R. B. Ware a house and lot in the town of Smithville. Bounded: east by the Public Square. 18 Oct 1882. (Pp. 36-37)

Asa Driver and wife, Tabytha, to Dempsey Driver 37 acres in the 12th District. 20 Oct 1882. (Pp. 37-38)

William Kelley to A. D. Driver 11 acres in the 12th District. 20 Oct 1882. (Pp. 38-39)

M. Brown and wife, M. A., to J. P. Tittsworth a house and lot in the town of Smithville. 21 Oct 1882. (Pp. 39-40)

J. P. Tittsworth and wife, Elizabeth, to M. Brown a house and lot in the town of Smithville. 21 Oct 1882. (Pp. 40-42)

Henry Adcock and wife, M. J., to Catherine Adcock a tract of land in the 7th District forever free from the liabilities of her present or any future husband. 31 Aug 1882. (Pp. 42-43)

Sheriff to T. J. Fisher a tract of land in the 2nd District. 5 Oct 1882. (Pp. 44-45)

Henry Adcock and wife, M. J., to Margaret Anderson, a daughter of the said Henry Adcock, a tract of land in the 7th District. 10 Apr 1882. (Pp. 45-46)

Peyton Gill of Pine Bluff, Arkansas appoints Houston Gill his power of attorney to sell his half interest in a tract of land in the 16th District. 29 Mar 1881. (Pp. 46-47)

Peyton Gill; Houston S. Gill; F. R. Gill, wife of Houston Gill; M. L. Gill, wife of T. J. Gill deceased, to H. L. Hardcastle a tract of land in the 16th District belonging to the estate of T. L. Gill containing 27 acres. 10 May 1881. (Pp. 47-49)

Hiram Hildreth to George Byford 50 acres in the 4th District. 10 Jul 1875. (Pp. 49-52)

W. G. Foster and wife, J. A., to J. H. Veach two acres in the 9th District about one half mile south of Smithville. Bounded: east of Pure Fountain College. 15 May 1882. (Pp. 52-53)

C. W. L. Hale to Pat Garity one acre in the 2nd District. 12 Oct 1881. (Pp. 53-54)

Allen Wilson and wife, Elizabeth, to A. R. Hicks a tract of land in the 13th District. 25 Aug 1882. (Pp. 55-56)

John C. Taylor and wife, Nancy, to John C. Taylor, Jr. three acres in the 10th District. 15 Jul 1882. (Pp. 56-57)

William M. Bradford to G. E. Henley 50 acres in the 11th District. 5 May 1882. (Pp. 57-58)

James M. Shehane to B. F. Hill 135 acres in the 3rd District. 20 Nov 1882. (Pp. 58-59)

J. J. Ford to W. B. Bridges 55 acres in the 1st District. 6 Aug 1881. (P. 60)

John P. Haney and wife, Elizabeth, to N. T. Hall a tract of land in the 6th District. 23 Nov 1882. (P. 61)

William H. Magness and wife, E. J., to P. B. (Blahn) one and three fourth's acres in the 9th District. 10 Aug 1878. (Pp. 62-63)

M. Brown and wife, Mary Ann, to Alvin Avant the place in Smithville where we have been living for several years. Bounded: the new Presbyterian Church and on the west by Mountain Street. 2 Dec 1882. (P. 63)

T. H. Wade and wife Jannie; and J. T. Hays to J. J. Smith and wife, Sallie, a lot on the south side of Main Street in the town of Smithville. 7 Dec 1882. (Pp. 63-66)

J. C. Turney and wife, M. E., to C. J. Dodd 30 acres in the 3rd District. 15 Sep 1879. (Pp. 66-67)

Thomas Ward and wife, Elizabeth, to C. J. Dodd 35 acres in the 3rd District. 15 Sep 1879. (Pp. 67-68)

George A. Evans and wife, Susie, to John A. Evans their one sixth interest in two third's of 150 acres in the 10th District. 5 Sep 1882. (Pp. 68-69)

W. J. Robinson and other heirs of David and Elizabeth Malone deceased filed suit against John Crook and wife and other heirs to sell the Elizabeth Malone dowery. County Court Clerk to John Willoughby said land. 1 Dec 1882. (Pp. 69-71)

B. S. Mitchell to J. B. Mitchell and G. W. Mitchell my interest in 150 acres in the 10th District. My interest is one seventh. 16 Sep 1880. (Pp. 71-72)

DEED BOOK P

J. D. Phillips to J. H. Hooper a house and lot in the town of Smithville. Bounded: Walnut Street. 20 Dec 1882. (P. 72)

J. H. Hooper to J. D. Phillips a tract of land near the corporate limits of Smithville. Bounded: the southeast corner of J. C. Cannady's widow's yard. 20 Dec 1882. (P. 72)

W. G. Foster and wife, J. A., to T. E. Winnard a tract of land in the 9th District on the Smithville & McMinnville Road. 22 Dec 1882. (P. 74)

J. A. Saunders and wife, Martha E.; and Kitty Monroe to W. M. Hale 100 acres in the 10th District. Said Kitty has a lifetime interest in said land. 19 Dec 1882. (Pp. 75-76)

Robert C. Bone and wife, Anna F., to B. A. Adamson a town lot in the town of Alexandria. 14 Dec 1882. Said Bones are residents of Cook County, Texas. (Pp. 76-77)

T. N. Christian to John Mason a lot in Smithville. Bounded: north by South Street. 19 Nov 1880. (Pp. 77-78)

James Truett and wife, Julia, to Dinges and Floyd a tract of land in the 13th District. 8 Jan 1885. (Pp. 78-79)

M. L. Bonham and wife, Rebecca; R. M. Trapp and wife Mary E.; and N. E. Trapp, all of full age and heirs of John Trapp deceased, to A. Page and wife, Amanda, a tract of land in the 15th District including the place where the said A. Page now lives. 21 Nov 1881. (Pp. 79-80)

A. J. Edwards and wife, Minnie, to D. W. Dinges a house and lot known as the O. D. Williams place, later the dower of Mrs. Williams. 1 Jan 1883. (Pp. 80-81)

T. N. Christian and wife to A. D. Pack and wife, Elizabeth, five acres in the 9th District. 22 Aug 1881. (P. 82)

James B. Blythe to R. B. Hale and wife, S. C., a compromise agreement. 27 Jan 1883. (Pp. 82-85)

Nancy Davis to S. F. and S. H. Davis of Davidson County the tract of land in Alexandria conveyed to me by my father Leonard Fite. 27 Jan 1883. (P. 85)

W. B. Corley and wife Etar; John R. Corley and wife Sarah; N. L. Corley and wife Martha J.; W. T. Robinson and wife Lucy J.; J. J. Calicott and wife Ann; and Elizabeth Corley to James Corley their interest in a tract of land in the 17th District. 3 Oct 1881. (Pp. 86-89)

A. T. Fisher to Henry Jonte a tract of land in the 6th District. 31 Oct 1883. (Pp. 89-90)

J. T. Hollis to J. C. Taylor his one half interest in a tract of land in the 10th District. 5 Feb 1883. (Pp. 90-91)

R. B. Hale to J. M. Martin 61 acres in the 4th District. 30 Jan 1883. (Pp. 91-92)

W. J. Monroe; Robert H. Monroe and wife Sally, of Montgomery County, Virginia to E. W. Monroe their interest in 100 acres in the 10th District. 26 Dec 1882. (Pp. 92-93)

Clerk & Master to J. M. Henley a tract of land belonging to William Fite. 19 Feb 1883. (Pp. 93-94)

E. J. Evans and wife, Eugenia, to G. R. Smith four and one half acres in the 9th District. 20 Feb 1883. (Pp. 94-95)

C. G. Bates and wife, F. J., to M. H. Webb 11 acres and the grist mill in the 9th District. 22 Feb 1883. (Pp. 95-96)

W. H. Garner and wife, Angeline; and W. F. Garner to John F. Stacy 35 acres in the 16th District. 5 Dec 1881. (Pp. 96-97)

Prettyman Jones, Administrator of Thomas Anderson, to James A. Alexander 80 acres. 17 Jul 1871. (Pp. 97-98)

Alfred Allen to Hugh Allen 85 acres in the 10th District. 22 Jan 1883. (P. 99)

A. B. Hooper and wife, E. E., to G. S. Davis and wife one and one fourth acres in the 9th District. 24 Feb 1882. (Pp. 99-100)

M. C. Green and wife, Eliza E., to O. D. Green 90 acres in the 5th District. 25 Aug 1882. (Pp. 100-102)

O. D. Green and wife, Sarah T., to R. Marler 90 acres in the 5th District. 3 Mar 1883. (Pp. 102-103)

John L. Horner and wife, Mary J., of Washington County, Virginia to E. W. Monroe their interest in 100 acres in the 10th District. 12 Feb 1883. (Pp. 103-104)

James Ellis and wife, Caroline, to L. J. Davis seven acres in the 12th District. 6 Apr 1881. (Pp. 105-106)

Edmond League and wife, Caldonia, to C. G. Walker 47½ acres in the 9th District. 9 Sep 1881. (P. 106)

Clerk & Master to J. M. Walker a tract of land belonging to James Davis deceased. 10 Mar 1883. (Pp. 107-108)

H. C. Eastham and wife, Helen, to I. N. Drake for the benefit of his wife and children a tract of land in the 9th District. 26 Sep 1881. (Pp. 108-109)

John S. Trapp and wife, Isabel, to Job Trapp 320 acres in the 18th District. 13 Mar 1883. (Pp. 109-111)

S. E. Simpson and wife, N. J., to T. W. Eason 29 acres in the 1st District. 17 Dec 1881. (Pp. 111-112)

M. V. Trapp to Job Trapp his interest in a tract of land deeded by gift to heirs of Jobe Trapp in the 18th District and containing 320 acres. 14 Mar 1883. (Pp. 112-113)

W. H. Magness to John W. Towles 500 acres in the 6th District. 10 Aug 1882. (Pp. 113-114)

Phila Seawell to W. C. Gilbert and wife, T. A., 100 acres in the 9th District. 16 Mar 1883. (Pp. 114-115)

DEED BOOK P

James A. Smith and wife, N. M., to W. H. Tyre a town lot in the town of Smithville. 14 Mar 1883. (Pp. 115-116)

Clerk & Master to Isaac Dunham 40 acres in the 6th District. 8 Oct 1881. (Pp. 116-117)

E. T. Foster; A. L. Foster and wife, M. E., to Smith Wade about one and one half acres southwest of Smithville. 25 Apr 1881. (Pp. 117-118)

T. W. Shields and wife, Susan E.; and R. E. Shields to T. M. Hooper three acres in the 9th District. 24 Feb 1883. (Pp. 118-119)

B. M. Cantrell and others to D. J. Taylor a trust deed on a tract of land in the 10th District. 26 Mar 1883. (Pp. 119-121)

W. J. Hollis and wife, Luella, to W. C. Potter one and three fourth acres in the 9th District on the north boundary line of the town of Smithville. 27 Mar 1883. (P. 121)

Bethel Parsley and wife, Salina, to L. T. Crowder 9632 square feet in the town of Smithville. 26 Mar 1883. (P. 122)

James L. Robinson and wife, Frances, to William Jones ten acres in the 15th District. 16 Apr 1881. (Pp. 123-124)

William H. Jones to W. E. Jones nine and one fourth acres in the 15th District. 1 Sep 1881. (Pp. 124-125)

T. W. Green and wife, M. E., to N. T. Wall a tract of land in the 6th District. 26 Mar 1883. (Pp. 125-126)

E. W. Monroe to W. M. Hale the share he purchased of John L. Horner and wife, Mary J., of Washington County, Virginia in 100 acres in the 10th District. 26 Feb 1883. (Pp. 126-128)

William P. Kelley, Permelia Kelley, and Talitha Kelley to P. L. Reynolds 86½ acres in the 17th District. 20 Oct 1877. (Pp. 128-131)

John Lamberson and wife, Nancy, to Peter L. Reynolds two tracts of land known as the land set a part to James Bates' heirs. 20 Aug 1873. (Pp. 131-132)

G. W. Hathaway and wife, S. J., to Gilford Allen a tract of land in the 2nd District, it being the same that we have heretofore deeded to A. L. Norton who has mislaid or lost the said deed. 30 Dec 1881. (Pp. 132-134)

Clerk & Master to W. L. Turney a tract of land belonging to C. H. Hale. 14 Apr 1883. (Pp. 134-135)

Asberry Hayes and wife, Tennie, to James A. Yeargin, William H. Yeargin, S. S. Yeargin, Caldonia Yeargin, Lulu Yeargin, and Osa Yeargin, children and heirs of H. J. Yeargin, one half acre in the 2nd District. 22 Jul 1882. (Pp. 135-136)

B. J. Starnes; and M. W. Starnes, wife of T. H. Starnes, to J. J. Hardcastle 20 acres in the 15th District. 2 Apr 1893. (Pp. 136-137)

DEED BOOK P

P. T. Shores and wife, Maggie, to Johnathan Johnson 87 acres in the 9th District. 29 Nov 1881. (Pp. 138-139)

William D. Evans and wife, Sarah J., to Thomas G. Bratten 40 acres in the 2nd District. 17 Sep 1873. (Pp. 139-140)

Isaac Cantrell and wife, M. L., to Horace G. Atnip the tract of land in the 9th District where we now live. 10 May 1883. (Pp. 140-142)

Clerk & Master to Sylvanus Pucket a tract of land. 8 May 1883. (Pp. 142-143)

Joseph Mitchell and wife, Sylvania, to the Methodist Episcopal Church one acre for church and school purposes. 5 May 1883. (Pp. 144-145)

T. W. Fitts and wife, Isabel, to Jasper N. Fitts 150 acres on the north side of Indian Creek in the 10th District. 28 Aug 1882. (Pp. 146-147)

Jasper N. Fitts to Samuel Walker 75 acres in the 10th District. 4 May 1883. (Pp. 147-148)

W. E. Bartlett to W. L. Hardcastle about one acre in the 16th District. 7 May 1883. (Pp. 148-149)

Thomas Shearl to Mary Shearl his interest in the land that his uncle, Isac Easy, will to him. 22 May 1883. (Pp. 149-150)

Bransford Bennett to William K. Bennett 11 acres in the 2nd District. 5 Nov 1870. (Pp. 150-151)

W. M. M. Bond to Charles Burton 200 acres known as the James Bond land in the 18th District. 21 Apr 1881. (P. 151)

John W. Pack and wife, Martha J., to William M. Pack 40 acres in the 9th District, it being the place whereon William M. Pack now lives. 12 Jun 1883. (Pp. 152-153)

Isaac Cantrell and wife, M. J., to B. H. Pack 100 acres in the 9th District. 10 May 1883. (P. 153)

A. P. Adcock to William Love and wife, Jane, their interest in the general plot of Isaac Adcock and containing 52½ acres. 30 Mar 1874. (Pp. 154-159)

Solomon Goodman and Elizabeth Johnson to J. A. Johnson 20 acres in the 9th District. 14 Feb 1882. (Pp. 159-160)

Clerk & Master to W. H. Magness one half acre belonging to W. M. Dewitt. 25 Jun 1883. (Pp. 160-161)

Sheriff to W. H. Magness a one half interest in Taylor's Mill. 23 Jun 1883. (Pp. 162-163)

R. C. Bone and wife, Anna F., of Cooke County, Texas to T. F. Bowman a town lot in the town of Alexandria. 9 Jun 1883. (P. 164)

C. W. L. Hale to Mary Ann Jenkins one acre in the 2nd District. 21 Aug 1879. (P. 165)

The trustees of the Methodist Episcopal Church to Margaret A. Turrentine a tract of land on Indian Creek in the 10th District, it being the tract of land of which William N. McNamara was seized and possessed at the time of his death and which was bequeathed by him to his widow, Margaret A. McNamara, now Margaret A. Turrentine, during her natural life and at her death to go to the Methodist Episcopal Church. 12 Jul 1883. (Pp. 166-167)

James L. Fuson and wife, Malissa, to A. J. Fuson their interest in a tract of land in the 9th District known as the lands of Jonathan Fuson deceased. 15 Jan 1883. (Pp. 167-168)

Mary Atnip to A. J. Fuson her one eleventh part of the lands of Jonathan Fuson. 13 Mar 1880. (Pp. 168-169)

Simeon Williams and wife, Manervy, formerly Fuson, to A. J. Fuson their interest in the lands of Jonathan Fuson deceased. 1 Mar 1879. (Pp. 169-170)

C. M. Schurer, being in bad health and and owing but a small amount and being desirous to put my wife in a comfortable situation, for love and affection to my said wife, Mollie A. Schurer a house and lot in Alexandria where I now reside and was conveyed to me by my mother, Helen Schurer, by deed on 11 Mar 1879. 26 Jul 1883. (Pp. 170-172)

Nancy E. Fuson to A. J. Fuson her interest in the lands of Jonathan Fuson. 13 Mar 1880. (Pp. 172-173)

John Fuson, Elias Fuson and wife A. J., Betty A. Fuson, Jane Fuson, Mathew Allen and wife Sarah M., all heirs of John Fuson deceased, to A. J. Fuson their one sixth of one twelfth interest in the lands of Jonathan Fuson. 5 Feb 1879. (Pp. 173-174)

John S. Close to F. M. Close 81 acres in the 12th District. 20 Apr 1880. (Pp. 175-176)

William W. Farmer to I. W. Reynolds a tract of land on the north side of Wolf Creek containing 23 acres. 28 Oct 1879. (P. 177)

William M. Farmer to L. P. Coggin 45 acres in the 16th District. 28 Oct 1879. (Pp. 177-178)

M. A. Wood to R. B. Hendrickson a tract of land in the 9th District. 9 Jul 1883. (Pp. 178-179)

W. C. Gilbert and wife, T. A., to Phila A. Sewel their interest in a portion of a town lot in the town of Smithville. Bounded: due north of the well situated on said lot running with line of Public Square west 49 feet. 19 Mar 1883. (Pp. 179-180)

Sanford Mann and wife, Matilda, to Thomas Chapman about 90 acres in the 2nd District. 31 Jul 1883. (Pp. 180-181)

Wilson Turrentine and wife, M. A., to J. H. Trammel the old McNamara Place in the 10th District, containing 100 acres. Said land was deeded by the Methodist Church. Aug 1883. (Pp. 182-183)

Phila A. Seawel to R. B. West a portion of a lot in Smithville on the south side of the Public Square known as the W. C. Gilbert lot. 1 Aug 1883. (P. 184)

T. W. Jones and wife, Frances E., to J. B. Parish a tract of land in the 6th District. 30 Jun 1883. (Pp. 184-186)

Isaac Cooper and wife, Talitha, to T. B. Malone and the other school directors a tract of land on Dismal Creek in the 19th District for school purposes. 10 May 1883. (P. 186)

M. A. Turrentine to the trustees of the Methodist Episcopal Church on Indian Creek in the 10th District. 8 Aug 1883. (P. 187)

A. J. Caplinger and wife, Isabel, to Samuel Caplinger a tract of land in the 12th District. 18 Apr 1883. (Pp. 188-189)

J. B. Parish to John A. Cantrell 80 acres in the 6th District. 8 Feb 1881. (Pp. 189-190)

Martha J. Robinson to Henry A. Taylor 100 acres in the 10th District. 9 Aug 1883. (Pp. 190-191)

Thomas J. Crips and wife, Darthuley, to Allen Watson 61 acres in the 4th District. 17 Aug 1883. (Pp. 191-192)

Thomas Smith and wife, A. V. Smith, to T. J. Taylor 55 acres in Indian Creek. 8 Sep 1883. (Pp. 192-193)

Clerk & Master to John Lockheart a tract of land. 8 Sep 1883. (Pp. 194-195)

Alexander M. Warren and wife, Ruth A., to William T. Warren a tract of land given to us as heirs of John E. Warren deceased. 20 Aug 1883. (Pp. 195-196)

John Hodge to John Haney and wife, Elizabeth, three acres in the 9th District. 5 Nov 1881. (Pp. 196-197)

C. S. Frazier, Sheriff, to Ailsey Lack a tract of land belonging to Riley Vaughn. 11 Sep 1883. (P. 197)

M. M. Brien to A. B. Cheatham a tract of land. 5 Sep 1883. (P. 198)

S. S. Quesenbury and wife, R. J., to J. C. Adamson 60 acres in the 3rd District. 23 Aug 1883. (P. 199)

S. L. Desting and wife, Mary F., to John Adamson and Rachel Jane Adamson 50 acres in the 3rd District. 23 Jan 1882. (Pp. 200-202)

R. A. Smith to L. J. Garner and A. V. Merritt 23 acres in the 16th District. 27 Sep 1879. (Pp. 202-203)

R. W. Goodner and wife, Angilia, to Eliza Baird, colored, two acres in the 1st District. 2 May 1883. (P. 204)

Clerk & Master to E. M. Whaley a tract of land. 7 Feb 1882. (Pp. 205-206)

DEED BOOK P

Clerk & Master to W. B. Farler 140 acres in the 4th District. 18 Sep 1883. (Pp. 207-208)

T. W. Wade and wife Fannie; and J. T. Hayes to J. J. Smith and wife, Sallie, the Parker lot in Smithville. 15 Sep 1883. (Pp. 208-209)

J. D. Koger and wife, Nannie, to J. A. Barnes their interest in a tract of land in the 14th District which they derived from Caroline Koger and her husband David Koger. The other heirs are J. A. Barnes and wife Maggie, Palestine Herd and husband Joseph, James Koger, and Caroline Koger. 12 Sep 1883. (Pp. 209-210)

N. E. Trapp, being of full age and heir of John Trapp, to R. M. Trapp 22¼ acres in the 15th District. Mentions sister Mary E. Trapp. 22 Nov 1881. (Pp. 210-211)

H. W. Boatwright and wife, M. E., to J. H. Hendrixson their one half interest in the John Trapp land in the 10th District. 22 Sep 1883. (Pp. 211-212)

A. S. McClellan and wife, Cinda, to David J. Taylor their one half interest in the land of William McClellan deceased allotted in the divide of lands to my mother, Paralee Curtis, formerly McClellan. 22 Sep 1883. (Pp. 212-213)

Clerk & Master to Andrew Lockheart a tract of land. 23 Apr 1883. (Pp. 213-215)

Clerk & Master to Mary Lockheart 53 acres. 24 Sep 1883. (Pp. 215-216)

William Griffith to Jacob Taylor one and one half acres in the 12th District. 31 Mar 1883. (Pp. 216-217)

Andrew Lockheart to Perry Stoglin a tract of land in the 9th District. 23 Apr 1883. (Pp. 217-218)

Jacob Taylor and wife, Polly, to William Griffith one and one half acres in the 18th District. 31 Mar 1883. (Pp. 218-219)

James E. Rodgers, Executor of John S. Rodgers, to N. B. Bozarth one half of the timber on 900 acres. 5 Nov 1880. (P. 219)

William Robinson, Executor of T. J. Williams, to John E. Williams 34 acres in the 4th District. 1 Oct 1883. (P. 220)

Nicholas Chambers and wife, Eran, to Zed Mulenax 100 acres in the 5th District. 3 Oct 1883. (Pp. 220-221)

John H. Savage to Thomas B. Keef 65 acres on Dry Creek. 16 Jul 1881. (Pp. 221-222)

John C. Holcomb to Isaac Johnson a tract of land in the 5th District. 13 Sep 1879. (Pp. 222-223)

Charles G. Pinegar and wife, Martha J., to Harvey A. Pinegar their interest in the land of Mary L. Pinegar and Charles G. Pinegar containing about 60 acres in the 7th District. 4 Nov

1882. (Pp. 223-224)

Jane Turner, Ava Mitchell, S. J. Stuart, H. Stuart, G. W. Mitchell, E. W. Mitchell, and W. J. Mitchell to W. E. Taylor and H. C. Taylor about 60 acres known as the E. D. Fish old tract in the 10th District. 1 Jan 1883. (Pp. 224-226)

R. W. Sanders and wife, Texas, to W. T. Wright 50 acres in the 6th District. 8 Mar 1883. (Pp. 226-227)

William Barnes and wife, Jane, to John R. Lyles eight and one half acres in the 9th District. 7 Sep 1883. (P. 227)

V. H. Hays to his wife, Luellie, and her children 160 acres in the 14th District. 27 Oct 1883. (Pp. 228-229)

Thomas Driver to G. W. Grayson 29 acres in the 17th District. 15 Sep 1883. (P. 229)

P. T. Shores and wife, Maggie, to I. N. Drake a house and lot on Mountain Street in Smithville. 27 Oct 1883. (P. 230)

B. M. Dodd and wife, C. J., to Nancy Spurlock 75 acres in the 3rd District. Bounded: W. L. Dodd deceased. 13 Oct 1883. (Pp. 230-232)

Henry H. Morris and wife, Fannie, to Rolan Butcher 92½ acres in the 3rd District. 11 Sep 1882. (Pp. 232-233)

W. H. Christian to James S. Rowland 53 acres in the 17th District. 19 Oct 1883. (Pp. 233-234)

M. M. Brien, Sr. for love and affection to his brother, James C. Brien, 150 acres in the 9th District, it being a part of my 500 acre tract. 11 Mar 1873. (Pp. 234-235)

J. J. Ford to W. B. Bridges 55 acres in the 1st District. 6 Aug 1881. (Pp. 235-236)

White Myers and wife, Marietta, to J. D. Wheeler a house and lot in the town of Alexandria. 22 Nov 1883. (Pp. 236-237)

J. D. Wheeler and wife, Drusilla B., to T. W. Eason a house and lot in the town of Alexandria. 12 Nov 1883. (P. 237)

H. C. Taylor and wife, C. J., to J. C. Taylor their interest in a tract of land in the 10th District. 3 Nov 1883. (P. 238)

A. M. Robinson and wife, Mary E., to Jackson Malone 25 poles in the 11th District. 1 Oct 1883. (P. 239)

John A. Fuson and Mary Fuson, Administrators of Thomas Fuson, to Thomas Fuson a town lot in Doweltown. 13 Nov 1883. (P. 239-240)

D. W. Dinges and R. B. Floyd to D. W. Dinges 125 acres in the 13th District. 25 Aug 1883. (Pp. 240-241)

Sheriff to J. T. Trapp and Isaac Denton 25 acres in the 18th District for a judgment against M. V. Trapp for $75 for an assault to kill. 10 Feb 1883. (Pp. 241-242)

T. W. Fitts and wife, Isabel, to Edmond C. Walker five acres in the 10th District. 26 Nov 1883. (Pp. 242-243)

W. W. Foster to W. A. Johnson 88 acres in the 9th District. 8 Sep 1882. (P. 243)

M. M. Brien and wife, Polly, to Miles Tittsworth a tract of land in the 9th District. 25 Oct 1883. (P. 244)

P. G. Cantrell and wife, Mourning, to Caroline McWhirter a tract of land in the 5th District. 20 Feb 1883. (Pp. 244-245)

John Griffith and wife, Sarah, to J. H. Vickers 24 acres in the 13th District. 21 Sep 1883. (Pp. 245-246)

W. L. Hardcastle, Administrator of B. F. Winfrey, to James M. Dulaney a tract of land in Cove Hollow. 1 Dec 1883. (Pp. 246-247)

Thomas E. Bratten and wife, Sarah W., to Joseph B. West 11 acres in the 13th District. 5 Oct 1880. (Pp. 247-248)

O. F. Young, Commissioner, to Elisha Luna 133 acres on the Caney Fork. 1 Jan 1883. (Pp. 248-249)

W. A. Johnson to G. W. McCarter 88 acres in the 9th District. 11 Sep 1883. (Pp. 249-250)

J. M. Malone and wife, Catherine, to S. J. Hale ten acres in the 11th District. 19 Nov 1883. (Pp. 250-251)

R. M. Dodd and wife, C. J., formerly Turney and daughter of Joseph Turney and Mary Turney, to George Turnery their interest in a tract of land in the 3rd District. 27 Nov 1883. (P. 251)

County Court Clerk to Z. T. Judd 86 acres in the 16th District. 5 Dec 1883. (Pp. 252-253)

George Turney and wife, M. A., to R. M. Todd a tract of land in the 3rd District. 27 Nov 1883. (P. 253)

I. N. Drake and wife, E. R., to P. T. Shores four acres in the 9th District. 27 Oct 1883. (Pp. 253-254)

W. B. Corley to his wife, Etta, his interest in 100 acres in the 17th District. 10 Dec 1883. (Pp. 254-255)

County Court Clerk to W. S. Burton a tract of land in the 16th District. 8 Nov 1883. (Pp. 255-256)

Thomas Chapman to Edward Gothard a lot in Doweltown. 6 Jan 1880. (Pp. 256-257)

A. B. Hooper to T. M. Hooper one acre in the town of Smithville. 18 Dec 1883. (P. 257)

A. D. Pack and wife, Elizabeth, to C. F. Puckett and wife, Nancy, five acres in the 9th District. 27 Jan 1883. (P. 258)

F. B. Nolner and wife, Martha, to E. J. Evans about 35 acres in the 9th District. 20 Dec 1883. (Pp. 258-259)

W. J. Givan to (Lutian). Preston a quit claim to a house in Alexandria that I now occupy. 1 Dec 1883. (P. 260)

F. P. Sanders and wife, E. J., to S. S. Young 72 acres on Pine Creek. 23 Jan 1883. (P. 261)

L. G. Bing and wife, M. A., to S. S. Young 50 acres in the 5th District. 23 Jan 1883. (P. 262)

Elizabeth Floyd to W. C. Lewis one half acre in the 9th District. 28 Nov 1883. (P. 263)

County Court Clerk to Joseph A. Rutland a house and lot in Alexandria belonging to H. C. Rutland. 9 Jan 1884. (Pp. 263-264)

Luman Allen of Cook County, Illinois to W. G. Wilson of the same place a tract of land belonging to James Dunlap and wife, Emma C. 7 Jan 1884. (Pp. 264-266)

Abraham Cantrell and wife, Rebecca, to William Cantrell 20 acres in the 9th District. 11 Dec 1883. (Pp. 266-267)

John C. Taylor, Sr. and wife, Nancy, to David C. Taylor two acres in the 10th District. 2 Sep 1882. (Pp. 267-268)

County Court Clerk to James Compton a tract of land belonging to the heirs of Jacob H. Vantrease. 14 Jan 1884. (Pp. 268-270)

James Plunkett et als versus John E. Clark et als. Complainant Rhoda Plunkett by her next friend recovers from the defendant. 10 Jan 1884. (Pp. 271-272)

F. B. Nollner and wife, M. H., to R. Black a tract of land in the 9th District. 10 Jul 1882. (Pp. 272-273)

Andrew Williams and wife, Mercilla, to L. C. Williams 34 acres in the 17th District. 4 Feb 1882. (Pp. 273-275)

County Court Clerk to J. J. Presley a tract of land. 28 Jan 1884. (Pp. 275-276)

J. W. Groom and wife, A. F., to H. B. Groom 200 acres in the 3rd District. 25 Nov 1882. (Pp. 277-278)

Jasper Ruyle and wife, Matilda, to Bluford Mathis a tract of land in the 3rd District. 29 Jan 1884. (Pp. 278-279)

B. J. Bethel to William Robinson Lot No. 5 in the 13th District which W. C. Bennett drew out of his father's land. 12 May 1875. (Pp. 279-280)

Clerk & Master to John L. Bond a tract of land that J. L. Bond died seized and possessed of and leaving to his children viz. Elizabeth Bond, Tennessee Hallum, M. L. Bond, J. D. Bond, J. C. Bond, John L. Bond, Hatton Bond, and Hartie Bond. 4 Feb 1884. (Pp. 280-281)

S. D. Moore and wife, C. A., to R. Black one acre in the 9th District. 14 Nov 1882. (P. 282)

S. S. Hooper to A. C. Hooper 75 acres in the 9th District. 12 Feb 1883. (P. 283)

Taylor Blythe, Eliza A. Blythe, H. M. Keaton, Mary J. Keaton,

DEED BOOK P

James Alexander, Amanda E. Alexander, Alex Hallum, and Sarah Hallum to J. C. Bennett 100 acres in the 4th District. 25 Feb 1881. (Pp. 283-285)

J. P. Tittsworth to J. S. Dunlap a town lot in the town of Smithville. 27 Sep 1883. (Pp. 285-286)

J. H. Hendrickson and wife, Sarah, to R. M. Trapp in consideration of an equal division of the home place of John Trapp their one half interest in said tract. 6 Feb 1884. (Pp. 286-287)

Sheriff to D. P. Rankin & Company the interest of James and Ruben Fisher in two tracts of land in the 17th District. 6 Feb 1884. (Pp. 288-289)

John H. Allen to William Vick three acres in the 13th District. 14 Dec 1883. (P. 290)

William R. Dunham and wife, Nancy, to Martha Dunham a tract of land in the 6th District. 7 Sep 1883. (Pp. 290-292)

Gribble, Webb, & Avant to Celean Hale their one sixth interest in a tract of land in the 3rd District. 1 Feb 1884. (P. 292)

Clerk & Master to W. W. Foster a tract of land subject to a lien. 28 Apr 1883. (Pp. 293-294)

W. H. Hendrickson and wife, L. F., to J. A. Roady one fourth of an acre on the Lebanon & Sparta Pike. 1 Mar 1883. (Pp. 294-295)

Nancy Johnson to Samuel Barks a title bond. 15 Feb 1884. (Pp. 295-296)

John A. Roady and wife, Mary, to H. M. Anderson 61 acres in the 3rd District. 20 Feb 1884. (Pp. 296-297)

T. W. Eason and wife, Emma H., to D. W. Dinges 29 acres in the 1st District. 21 Feb 1884. (P. 298)

B. M. Cantrell and others to John L. Pirtle 75 acres in the 9th District. 21 Aug 1883. (Pp. 298-299)

H. J. Winchester and wife, Lucy, to W. M. Holley five acres in the 16th District. 28 Feb 1884. (Pp. 299-300)

Clerk & Master to James Lockheart a tract of land subject to a lien. 10 Mar 1884. (Pp. 300-301)

W. C. Lockheart and John Lockheart to Robert Wagoner 24 acres in the 9th District. 8 Sep 1883. (Pp. 301-302)

John E. Robinson and wife, Margaret E., to G. W. Martin one acre in the 15th District. 15 Nov 1883. (Pp. 302-303)

Nancy Parsley and others petition in County Court against Tennessee Smith et als seeking among other things the assignment of the dower of Nancy Parsley, widow of John Parsley. 16 Jan 1884. (Pp. 304-305)

Clerk & Master to Ned Huddleston a tract of land subject to a lien. 10 Mar 1884. (Pp. 305-306)

The heirs of John Trapp deceased to J. T. Trapp and Isaac Denton a tract of land in the 18th District. 17 Mar 1883. (Pp. 306-309)

C. W. Hale and wife, Lizzie, to B. B. Taylor five acres in the 2nd District. 11 Feb 1882. (Pp. 309-310)

Survey of the lands of C. W. Hale. 6 Feb 1882. (P. 311)

Andrew Carr and wife, Kiddy, to E. S. Jones 25 acres in the 16th District. 29 Jul 1883. (Pp. 312-313)

Andrew Carr and wife to the trustees a tract of land in the 16th District for a school and church house. 14 Aug 1877. (P. 313)

Andrew Carr and wife, Kiddie, to T. C. Harper ten acres in the 16th District. 26 Dec 1882. (P. 314)

G. W. Walton to Mrs. Mary Halum 90 acres in the 10th District free from the liability of her husband. 3 Mar 1884. (Pp. 314-315)

County Court Clerk to J. J. Pedigo a tract of land belonging to the estate of Charles Ferrell. Mentions the widow, M. A. J. Ferrell. 25 Apr 1883. (Pp. 315-316)

J. H. Tittsworth to John P. Tittsworth the Arch Bane place in the 5th District. 13 Feb 1884. (P. 317)

James H. White for love and affection to his wife, Nancy P. White, my farm that we now live on in the 2nd District so that she may have a house to rear her children. This is owing to my feeble health and fear that she may have to make the further part of her life in a great measure alone or without me. 20 Mar 1884. (Pp. 318-319)

Joseph Clark versus John D. Bone, Administrator of Alfred Bone deceased. 27 Feb 1884. (Pp. 319-320)

W. H. H. Bond and wife, Fannie, to R. G. Williams their interest in the dower of Margaret Williams out of the lands of Richmond Williams deceased. 12 Mar 1884. (Pp. 320-321)

Mary Elizabeth Owen to T. D. Bass 62 acres in the 3rd District. 11 Mar 1880. (Pp. 321-322)

G. M. Stark and wife, Emily, to T. D. Bass five acres in the 3rd District. 31 Dec 1883. (Pp. 322-323)

Jasper Owen and wife, N. E., to T. D. Bass 60 acres in the 3rd District. 24 Mar 1884. (Pp. 323-324)

T. E. Winnard and wife, Mollie; Richard Winnard and wife Juda to M. A. Crawley a tract of land in the 9th District. Mentions where the road crosses from Webb's Mill (formerly Bennett's Mill) to Sligo Ferry. 3 Mar 1884. (Pp. 324-325)

William Bozarth to L. L. Bozarth 60 acres in the 8th District. 14 Dec 1883. (Pp. 325-326)

Pat Garity and wife, Sally M., to H. A. Hill 197 acres in the 4th District. 6 Oct 1882. (Pp. 326-327)

H. A. Hill and wife, M. C., to Nathan Driver eight acres in the 4th District. 20 Mar 1884. (Pp. 327-328)

R. L. Page and wife, Kisa M., to A. C. Mullican several tracts of land in the 10th District. These lands were willed to Mary Mullican, the wife of J. J. Mullican deceased, during her natural life and this deed is to take effect at or after her death. 27 Feb 1884. (Pp. 329-330)

Joseph A. Starnes and wife, M. S., to M. W. Starnes 130 acres in the 15th District. 28 Mar 1884. (Pp. 330-331)

Mary Ann Starnes versus J. M. Starnes et als. Final Decree. The complainant is entitled to have the deed amended. 3 Apr 1884. (Pp. 331-332)

Clerk & Master to W. H. Magness some 68 acres in the 1st District. 10 Jan 1884. (Pp. 332-333)

Samuel C. Johnson to W. S. Johnson 139 acres, it being the farm on which I now live on the Caney Fork. 16 Aug 1883. (Pp. 333-335)

Sarah Bethel, Harriet Wamack, J. B. Wamack, W. M. Hill, Mary Hill, and Delia Bethel to E. M. Whaley ten acres in the 2nd District. 20 Mar 1882. (Pp. 335-336)

Clerk & Master to Harden Vickers about 50 acres in the 4th District. 17 Apr 1884. (Pp. 336-337)

J. S. Dunlap and wife, Emma, to L. G. Batton a town lot in the town of Smithville. 17 Apr 1884. (Pp. 337-338)

W. H. Magness to W. C. Potter his interest in a tract of land in the 9th District. 4 Dec 1883. (P. 338)

Clerk & Master to M. Parker 148 acres. 4 Jan 1884. (Pp. 339-340)

Clerk & Master to N. Parker 42 acres. 19 Apr 1884. (Pp. 340-341)

J. H. Veach and wife, Mary, to Z. P. Lee a tract of land on the south side of Smithville. 16 Apr 1884. (Pp. 341-342)

Stephen Goodner and wife, Mary, to E. W. Walker about one third of an acre in the town of Alexandria. 29 Nov 1882. (Pp. 342-343)

Evans Walker and wife, Mary, to the Primitive Baptist Church, colored, a tract of land known now as the Walker's Chapel Primitive Baptist Church. 1 Mar 1884. (Pp. 343-344)

W, W. Foster to J. S. Foster 112 acres in the 9th District. 20 Dec 1881. (Pp. 344-345)

Sallie Bratten for love and affection to her daughter, Nancy H. Clark three fourth's of an acre in the 2nd District. 8 May

1884. (P. 345)

Horace McGuire to James Dearman two houses and lots in the town of Smithville. 17 May 1884. (Pp. 346-347)

J. P. Trail to Esquire Warren a tract of land on Pine Creek in the 5th District. 6 May 1883. (P. 347)

J. B. Cantrell and wife, Sarah E., to Isaac Bozarth their interest in the land that Joshua League died seized and possessed of in the 9th District. 1 Nov 1881. (Pp. 348-349)

W. D. Bartlett to John New, colored, 22 acres in the 16th District. 2 May 1883. (P. 349)

W. E. Bartlett to John New 25½ acres in the 16th District. 2 May 1883. (P. 350)

Clerk & Master to J. B. Williams a tract of land containing 78 acres in the 15th District. 9 May 1881. (Pp. 351-352)

S. S. Hooper to Charles Crowder a tract of land in the 7th District. 14 Nov 1879. (Pp. 353-354)

W. T. Hale for love and affection to his wife, Lula, and his children, Charley L. and Herbert L. a house and lot in Liberty. 24 Jun 1884. (Pp. 354-355)

W. G. Crawley and wife, R. M., to A. D. Pack a tract of land in the 9th District. 11 Aug 1883. (P. 355)

Clerk & Master to J. T. Phillips a tract of land. 30 Jun 1884. (Pp. 356-357)

J. H. White and wife, N. P., to A. E. Stanford the lot known as C. E. Pullen's store house lot in the 2nd District. 21 May 1884. (Pp. 357-358)

R. A. Botts and wife, Julie, to R. A. Lawrence a house and lot in the town of Alexandria. 5 Feb 1884. (Pp. 358-359)

James Neal and wife, Mary T., to John Neal and Jane R. Neal eight acres in the 2nd District. 10 Dec 1880. (Pp. 359-360)

S. W. McClellan to L. E. Thompson a tract of land near Hickman's Creek. 3 Jun 1884. (Pp. 360-361)

J. E. Groom and wife, M. C., to J. T. Craddock 20¼ acres in the 3rd District. 1 Sep 1883. (Pp. 361-362)

J. E. Groom and wife to N. H. Craddock 38½ acres in the 3rd District. 1 Sep 1883. (Pp. 363-364)

John Trusty and wife, Margaret Ann, to John Caplinger a tract of land in the 12th District. 19 Jan 1884. (Pp. 364-365)

F. M. Turner and wife, Sarah, to J. C. Bass 81 acres in the 12th District. 1 Jan 1884. (Pp. 365-366)

David C. Taylor and wife, Margaret, to John Caplinger their interest in the Allen Trusty estate. 21 Jan 1884. (Pp. 367-368)

R. C. Bone and wife, Anna F., to H. C. Flippin their interest in a lot in Alexandria. 31 Jan 1880. (P. 368)

DEED BOOK P

E. W. Bass and Susan Bass to J. L. Ayers nine acres in the 12th District. 7 Jun 1873. (Pp. 369-370)

J. B. Lamberson to John L. Ayers 70 acres in the 17th District. 16 Jan 1879. (Pp. 370-371)

T. J. Hass and wife, M. A., to John Blackburn 25¼ acres in the 2nd District. 31 Jan 1884. (P. 372)

R. W. Banks and wife, Samantha, to Berry Cantrell 60 acres in the 9th District. 2 Nov 1881. (P. 373)

W. B. Stokes to Thomas Bains his interest in 50 acres in the 3rd District. 12 May 1884. (P. 374)

John Harrison to James B. Harrison two lots for paying off a note held against me and Mary F. Harrison by L. J. Magness. 13 Aug 1884. (Pp. 374-375)

T. P. West to Henry Turner one acre in the 7th District. 13 Aug 1884. (P. 376)

W. A. Johnson and wife, Mary, to M. W. Driver two tracts of land in the 9th District. 30 Jul 1884. (Pp. 376-377)

J. K. Starnes to Sarah H. Starnes 35 acres in the 16th District. 21 Feb 1882. (P. 378)

Allen Trusty and wife Kisey, to John Caplinger a tract of land in the 12th District. 21 Jan 1884. (Pp. 379-380)

J. D. Tittsworth and wife, T. C., to T. J. Mangrum 50 acres in the 5th District. 29 Dec 1881. (Pp. 380-381)

C. M. Schurer and wife, Mollie A., to N. L. Corley the Hunt farm in the 12th District. 15 Aug 1884. (Pp. 381-382)

William Herron and wife, Jane, to L. J. Magness 13 acres in the 9th District. 23 Aug 1884. (P. 383)

John T. Stokes and wife, Perlina, to D. D. Driver one acre in the 15th District. 15 Dec 1879. (Pp. 384-385)

James Cantrell and wife, Sarah, to the trustees of the Methodist Episcopal Church a tract of land. 4 Feb 1884. (Pp. 385-386)

R. C. Pedigo and wife, Jane, to J. J. Pedigo 58 acres in the 9th District. 1 Mar 1883. (P. 387)

Asaph L. Sherrill and wife, Ann T., to T. M. Hooper 75 acres in the 9th District. 9 Aug 1884. (P. 388)

Bird S. Sexton to his son in law, David Rowland, 112 acres in the 16th District. 1 Jan 1874. (Pp. 389-390)

B. B. Taylor to W. E. Taylor 68 acres on Indian Creek in the 10th District. 18 Sep 1884. (Pp. 390-391)

Simeon Williams and wife, Manerva, to R. M. Webb and others a trust deed on a tract of 108 acres in the 9th District. 19 Sep 1884. (Pp. 392-393)

DEED BOOK P

Z. T. Judd and wife, Calidonia, to G. W. Null a tract of land in the 16th District. 15 Apr 1884. (Pp. 393-394)

I. N. Drake to T. W. Wade a house and lot in the town of Smithville. 30 Sep 1884. (Pp. 394-395)

Moses H. Fite, Administrator of Thomas C. Fite, to J. S. Owen a tract of land in the 13th District. 6 Oct 1884. (Pp. 395-396)

Henry George and Jane George to J. R. Byford 30 acres. 1 Aug 1878. (Pp. 396-397)

J. H. Hendrickson and wife, Sarah, to D. C. Taylor five and one half acres. 12 Feb 1884. (Pp. 397-398)

Ed Judkins and wife, Rebecca, to Isaac Denton their interest in the lands of Job Trapp deceased. 20 Sep 1884. (Pp. 398-400)

Levi Haney and wife, Elender, to Ben Lowery about 30 acres in the 9th District. 5 Nov 1883. (Pp. 400-401)

Wilson E. Taylor to James B. Cantrell 69 acres in the 9th District. 25 Nov 1884. (Pp. 402-403)

W. W. Lock and wife, M. F., to G. W. Childress a quit claim to a tract of land in the 9th District. 27 May 1884. (Pp. 403-404)

S. B. Harriman to Levi Neal 31 acres in the 19th District. 27 Aug 1884. (Pp. 404-405)

W. G. Crowley to M. H. Webb a half interest in the grist mill and saw mill known as the Daniel Smith Mill property on Fall Creek in the 9th District. 13 Oct 1884. (Pp. 405-406)

Sarah E. Adamson to A. O. Dennis six acres in the 3rd District. 10 Oct 1877. (Pp. 406-407)

J. S. Dunlap to T. W. Wade a house and lot in the town of Smithville. 11 Oct 1884. (Pp. 407-408)

John New, colored, to Van Smith about one acre in the 16th District. 7 Aug 1883. (Pp. 408-409)

M. N. Smith and wife, Sarah, to T. P. Hicks 40 acres in the 5th District. 7 Oct 1880. (P. 410)

A. J. West and wife, Adline, to T. P. West about 80 acres on the south bank of the Caney Fork in the 7th District. 25 Jan 1880. (Pp. 411-412)

James Willis and wife, Elizabeth, to J. M. Luna 100 acres in the 14th District. 3 Nov 1884. (Pp. 112-113)

Elisha Luna and wife, Hesiah, to the trustees a tract of land in the 7th District at or near Indian Mound for a Baptist Church, school house, and graveyard. The church, school, and graveyard shall be controlled by the Baptist Church. 25 Jul 1884. (Pp. 413-414)

Elisha Luna to the citizens of the Eagle Bend two acres at or near Indian Mound for the purpose of building a free school and public worship on Saturdays and Sundays and if a traveling preacher should pass and wish to address the people in way of religion, he shall have the liberty at any time so as not to interfer with the school. 11 Nov 1884. (Pp. 414-415)

T. J. Kidwell and wife, Susan, to Sol Williams a tract of land in the 6th District. (Pp. 416-417)

G. W. Hathaway and wife, S. J., to John Norton a lot in Doweltown. 1 Mar 1876. (Pp. 417-418)

John Norton to Elizabeth Moore the lot where I now live in the 2nd District. 12 Nov 1884. (P. 418)

T. J. Fisher and Prettyman Jones to John J. Presley part of the J. H. Kerr land in the 16th District. 10 Nov 1884. (Pp. 419-420)

Nancy Bond, wife of John L. Bond; and M. L. Bond, administrator of John L. Bond deceased, to T. A. Sherrill 100 acres in the 9th District. Said T. A. Sherrill is the wife of A. L. Sherrill. 11 Mar 1884. (Pp. 419-420)

Nancy Bond, wife of John L. Bond; and M. L. Bond, administrator of John L. Bond deceased, to T. A. Sherrill 100 acres in the 9th District. 17 Nov 1884. (Pp. 421-422)

T. M. Hooper and wife, M. D. to A. L. Sherrill and wife one acre in the town of Smithville. 9 Aug 1884. (Pp. 422-423)

Samuel Oakley to Charles M. Williams 100 acres in the 12th District. 2 Sep 1865. (P. 423)

F. L. Foutch and wife, America, to Isaac M. Sandlin three acres in the 1st District. 2 Aug 1884. (P. 424)

Joseph Clark to Matilda Bratten two acres in trust in the 2nd District. 15 Feb 1878. (Pp. 425-426)

Alf Neal and wife, Emily, to Mary Phillips a lot in the town of Alexandria. 2 Feb 1876. (P. 426)

Eliza Johnson to Martin Waggoner a tract of land in the 9th District. 21 Nov 1884. (P. 427)

Henderson Ross and wife, Amey C., to John Caplinger their interest in a tract of land in the 12th District. 24 Jul 1883. (Pp. 428-429)

Thomas J. Crips to Darthula Crips 60 acres in the 4th District. 9 Oct 1884. (P. 429)

John E. Herndon, William M. Herndon, Thomas G. Herndon, Albert A. Shaw, J. M. Shaw, Elizabeth A. Shaw, E. C. Murray, Annie J. Murray, P. W. Shaw, Euphine Shaw, and W. B. Shaw to Sarah Shaw a tract of land in the 14th District. 10 Oct 1884. Said Elizabeth A. Shaw and husband are residents of Alamame County, North Carolina. (Pp. 430-432)

B. F. Bell and wife, Ophelia; Carrie Baird; and Amanda R. Baird to D. W. Dinges three fourth's of an acre. 21 Nov 1884. (P. 432)

John F. Roy to R. W. and Selena Yeargin a house and lot in the town of Alexandria. 22 Nov 1884. (P. 433)

W. B. Barnes to James R. Beckwith 12 acres in the 9th District. 23 Aug 1884. (Pp. 433-434)

T. H. W. Richardson and wife, Elizabeth, to P. G. Cantrell 95 acres in the 6th District. 16 Oct 1884. (Pp. 434-435)

A. B. Hathaway and wife, Adeline, to W. J. Delay a tract of land in the 6th District. 20 Aug 1879. (Pp. 436-437)

The Executors of Andrew Allen to R. S. Duke 143 acres on Indian Creek in the 10th District, it being the tract on which said Andrew Allen once resided. 9 Dec 1884. (Pp. 437-439)

George Evans and wife, Susan, to J. A. Evans their interest in 60 acres in the 9th District, it being one sixth. 6 Sep 1884. (Pp. 439-440)

W. S. Burton and wife, R. F., to J. E. Conger 93 acres in the 16th District. 29 Sep 1884. (Pp. 440-441)

George McGee and wife, N. C., to William A. Braswell a tract of land in the 16th District. 20 Jan 1886. (Pp. 441-442)

G. W. Dildine to Thomas H. Fancher 30 acres on which I now live. 5 Jan 1885. (P. 443)

James Dildine to my grandson, George W. Dildine, 30 acres. 21 Mar 1865. (Pp. 443-444)

J. A. P. Fancher, Administrator of Thomas H. Fancher, to their heirs of William H. Clouse a tract of land. 5 Jan 1885. (Pp. 444-445)

Matilda E. Bratten to Mary A. Johnson a tract of land in the town of Liberty. 6 Dec 1884. (P. 445)

Joseph R. Sneed to D. W. Dinges a tract of land in the town of Alexandria. 24 Dec 1884. (P. 446)

Polly Johnson to D. W. Dinges a house and lot in the town of Alexandria. 1 Dec 1884. (Pp. 446-447)

P. J. Mangrum and wife, Dora, to Z. Davis 50 acres in the 5th District. 25 Aug 1884. (Pp. 447-448)

John H. Allen to William H. Allen one acre in the 2nd District. 2 Dec 1884. (P. 448)

E. T. Foster to J. B. Harrison and D. T. Harrison a tract of land. 28 Nov 1883. (P. 449)

H. H. Jones and wife, S. T., to D. A. Wiggins five acres in the 1st District. 26 Dec 1882. (P. 450)

D. A. Wiggins and wife, V. H., to D. W. Dinges five acres in the 1st District. 6 Jan 1885. (P. 451)

Samson Yeargin to E. H. Self a house and lot in Doweltown. 12 Jan 1885. (Pp. 451-452)

DEED BOOK P

M. H. Pack and wife, Martha, to J. H. Mahaffy 24½ acres in the 9th District. 11 Apr 1881. (Pp. 452-453)

J. S. Harrison to M. W. Boatwright 87 acres in the 9th District. 11 Oct 1884. (Pp. 454-455)

J. R. Lyles and wife, Mary, to Thomas Francis a tract of land in the 9th District. 22 Jan 1884. (P. 455)

Isaac Jones to P. G. Mullican 50½ acres. 2 Mar 1853. (P. 456)

T. M. Hooper and wife, M. D., to T. W. Shields a lot near the town of Smithville. 5 Sep 1884. (P. 457)

J. H. Foutch and wife, S. J., to W. S. Evans part of the old Curtis field in the 10th District. 15 Dec 1881. (Pp. 458-459)

Frederick L. Siemon and wife, Helen P., to Ella C. Ballow a tract of land. 26 Jan 1885. (Pp. 459-461)

M. T. Cooper and wife, Amandy, to J. B. Johnson 43 acres. 8 Feb 1885. (Pp. 462-463)

John Reed and wife, Sary, to W. E. Jones four acres on the waters of long branch. 5 Feb 1885. (Pp. 463-464)

William H. Jones and wife, Louisa M., to Francis Tisdale 38 acres on the Caney Fork. 2 Feb 1885. (Pp. 465-466)

W. H. Jones and wife, Louisa M., to Louisa Nixon a tract of land on the Caney Fork. 29 Jan 1885. (Pp. 466-469)

William H. Jones to W. E. Jones for love and affection 20 acres on the west side of the Caney Fork. 2 Feb 1885. (Pp. 469-470)

W. H. Jones to Caroline Martin for love and affection 20 acres on the west side of the Caney Fork. 2 Feb 1885. (Pp. 471-472)

F. A. Wright and wife, A. E., to Kinchen F. Fisher their one seventh part of the lands of George Fisher deceased. 30 Jan 1880. (Pp. 472-473)

J. T. Hollis to J. M. Fuson a town lot in the town of Smithville. 14 Nov 1881. (P. 474)

James H. Fuson and wife, Maralee, to J. M. Allen the Hollis office and lot in the town of Smithville. 7 Feb 1885. (Pp. 474-475)

Nancy Taylor to William E. Taylor, H. C. Taylor, and Horace Taylor. Ex Parte. 16 Oct 1877. (Pp. 475-477)

J. B. Walker to Mary and Nancy Walker 45 acres. Mary Walker is the wife of the said John B. Walker and Nancy is the daughter of the said John B. 16 Mar 1878. (Pp. 477-478)

M. N. Smith and wife, Sarah, to F. C. White 50 acres in the 5th District. 3 Nov 1884. (Pp. 479-480)

DEED BOOK P

People's Bank of McMinnville to W. G. Crowley a tract of land. 25 Feb 1885. (P. 480)

Abe Black & Company versus W. G. Crowley. 25 Feb 1885. P. 481)

J. R. West and wife, J. E., to J. P. Barry 40 acres in the 13th District. 30 Aug 1884. (P. 482)

James Lockheart and wife, Mary, to John Lockheart 390 acres in the 9th District. 11 Mar 1884. (Pp. 483-485)

A. S. Yeargin and wife, M. H., to W. T. Robinson a town lot in Doweltown. 21 Feb 1884. (Pp. 486-487)

Elijah Allen and wife, Caroline, to the public school directors of the 9th District one half acre in the 9th District. 30 Sep 1884. (Pp. 487-488)

A. B. Cheatham to J. E. Atnip 170 acres in the 18th District. 6 Aug 1883. (Pp. 488-490)

Angelia Settle to Byron F. Bell one acre in the 1st District. 28 Feb 1885. (P. 490)

Levi Haney and wife, Ellen, to Plummer Wade 20 acres in the 7th District. 17 Feb 1885. (Pp. 491-492)

Frederick Starnes to Samuel Stephens a tract of land in the 15th District. 23 Nov 1883. (P. 492)

H. A. Hill and wife, Martha, to Pat Garity 50 acres in the 14th District. 6 Oct 1882. (Pp. 493-494)

W. N. Wilson and wife, Frances, to T. J. Fisher a tract of land in the 9th District. 18 Nov 1884. (Pp. 494-495)

William Hunt to John Caplinger et als a tract of land containing three acres with the exception of Pisgah Church. 4 Aug 1883. (Pp. 495-496)

John Beaty died intestate seized and possessed of a tract of land and leaving Jane Payne, Grandison Beaty, Ellen Beaty, and Anderson Beaty, each of whom are of full age; and Charley Beaty of non age as his only children. Jane Payne to T. D. Oakley a mortgage. 20 Mar 1885. (Pp. 496-498)

M. L. Smith and wife, G. A., to Lafayette Burk a house and lot in the town of Alexandria. 25 Aug 1884. (Pp. 498-499)

Andrew Allen for love and affection to Artymecy Allen, Martha Emeline Allen, now Martha E. Atnip, 60 acres in the 10th District. 1 Nov 1882. (Pp. 499-500)

Horace Atnip and wife, Martha E., to Artymecy Allen 30 acres in the 10th District. 28 Oct 1882. (Pp. 500-501)

Jacob Adams, commissioner, to Wiley Estrege a tract of land in the 4th District. 8 Apr 1885. (Pp. 501-502)

John D. Bone to William P. Bone a lot in the town of Alexandria. 21 Jan 1885. (P. 502)

J. P. Tubb and wife, Roena, to Alvin Avant their interest in 150 acres which belonged to Caroline Fite and Adelia Tubb. 26 Mar 1885. (Pp. 503-504)

O. B. Staley and wife, Sopronia, to J. T. Trapp, Executor of J. J. Pedigo, one acre in the 9th District. 7 Apr 1885. (P. 504)

John D. Bone and wife, Martha P., to James Compton a one half interest in a tract of land in the 1st District. 21 Feb 1882. (P. 506)

James L. Barnes and wife, Lydia, to Richard B. Dunham 20 acres in the 9th District. 22 Sep 1870. (P. 507)

Larkin Bain, Archibald Bain, Mansfield Bain, Thomas Moore and wife Lucinda, Tennessee Hooper and wife Ann, John Pack and wife Narcissa, Moses Pack and wife Mary, Jesse Green and wife Sarah, James L. Barnes and wife Lydia to Richard Barnabas Dunham a tract of land in the 9th District. 22 Sep 1870. (P. 508)

John Lundsdon to Richard Barnabas Dunham, Fanny Bell Dunham, (Hatty) Dell Dunham about 40 acres in the 6th District. 2 Jan 1879. (P. 509)

James Redman and wife, Esther, to L. J. Magness five acres in the 9th District. 6 Feb 1885. (Pp. 510-511)

J. L. Smith and wife, S. E., to H. M. Hennessee part of the M. Ward deceased land in the 5th District. 29 May 1884. (P. 511)

James Redman to L. J. Magness five acres in the 9th District. 6 Feb 1885. (Pp. 510-511)

J. L. Smith and wife, S. E., to M. M. Hennessee 77 acres in the 5th District. 29 May 1884. (Pp. 511-512)

R. B. Floyd and wife, Ella, to Mattie N. Wood a tract of land in Alexandria. 26 Dec 1884. (Pp. 512-513)

Clerk & Master to W. H. Magness a house and lot for a lien. 27 Apr 1885. (Pp. 513-514)

W. T. Robinson and wife, Lucy J., to James Ayers three acres in the 2nd District. 18 Feb 1884. (Pp. 514-515)

John W. Cambell and wife, Alice, to James Ayers ten acres in the 2nd District. 12 Jan 1878. (Pp. 516-517)

Thomas Hass and wife, M. A., to I. H. White four acres in the 4th District. 2 Dec 1880. (Pp. 517-518)

W. T. Robinson to J. H. White a lot of land adjoining my mill lot, it being a part of the tract on which said White now lives in the 2nd District. 30 Jan 1877. (Pp. 518-519)

T. W. Eason and wife, Emma, to S. B. Franks a town lot in the town of Alexandria. 25 Apr 1885. (Pp. 519-520)

William Robinson to Thomas W. Wrenne for the benefit of Ann J. Callicott during her lifetime and then for the creditors of J. J. Callicott a tract of land in the 15th District. 12 Jan 1885. (Pp. 520-521)

J. H. Trammel and wife, Julia, to Roan Page a tract of land in the 10th District. 29 May 1885. (Pp. 521-522)

Roan Page and wife, Martha J., to J. H. Trammel 84 acres in the 10th District. 29 May 1885. (Pp. 522-524)

A. J. Fanning of Davidson County to H. C. Eastham and R. B. West his interest in the Sligo Farm Ferry Road, also ferry boat and canoe. 12 Jan 1881. (Pp. 524-525)

Tilmon Adcock to John Atnip a tract of land in the 7th District. 1 Sep 1884. (P. 525)

Silvanus Puckett and wife, Mary F., to C. N. Parker a tract of land in the 9th District. 20 Jun 1885. (P. 526)

H. C. Eastham and wife, J. J., to C. L. Frazier a one third interest in a tanyard. [illegible]4 Mar 1879. (Pp. 527-528)

P. G. Mullican to J. P. Trail 65½ acres in the 5th District. 28 Jan 1885. (Pp. 528-529)

W. H. Magness to Nancy O. Maxwell three acres in the 9th District. 1 Oct 1884. (Pp. 529-530)

John R. Lyles and wife, Mary, to T. M. Hooper a trust deed. 7 Jul 1885. (Pp. 530-531)

Agreement between A. J. Fuson and John H. Savage. 14 Apr 1885. (P. 531)

George A. Smith and wife, Mary A., to W. P. Smith a tract of land on the south side of the Lebanon & Sparta Turnpike at Liberty. 27 Jun 1885. (P. 532)

Celia A. Hale, Mary F. Reed, Allen Reed, Joseph Hale, Sarah Hale, B. F. Hale, Thomas Hale and wife, Nancy Turney and husband Joseph to A. J. Pugh 18 acres in the 3rd District. 23 Feb 1884. Pp. 533-534)

G. W. Lamberson to Elizabeth Bates and William R. Bates 65 acres known as the Elizabeth Bates dower. 6 Nov 1871. (Pp. 534-536)

A. E. Frazier and wife, N. A., to J. L. Colvert a tract of land in the 9th District. 16 Jul 1885. (Pp. 536-537)

C. S. Frazier and wife, Mary A., to J. L. Colvert a tract of land in the 9th District. 3 Jul 1885. (Pp. 537-538)

W. B. Tramel and wife, Elizabeth, to E. A. Coggin their interest in 65 acres belonging to Francis Coggin deceased. 22 Aug 1885. (Pp. 539-540)

The heirs of Thomas Moore and Lucinda Moore, to wit, Nancy E. Foster, Chesley Taylor, Mary Taylor, S. V. Moore, J. T. Moore, Mary E. Moore, M. F. Culwell, C. B. Culwell to A. Z. Moore a tract of land in the 9th District where the said A. Z. Moore now lives. 31 Jan 1885. (Pp. 540-541)

DEED BOOK P

A. W. Walker and wife, Mary, to John Bain and the other school directors in the 6th District land for the benefit of the Alexandria School near the old Bain Meeting House. When it is abandoned for the use of a school, then the same is to fall back to me. 4 Dec 1884. (Pp. 542-543)

T. J. Fisher and Prettyman Jones to Smith Brothers a tract of land at Laurel Hill in the 16th District. 5 Aug 1884. (Pp. 543-544)

E. S. Bowers to J. J. Ford 40 acres in the 1st District. 13 Jul 1885. (P. 544)

John Johnson to N. A. Johnson a tract of land in the 9th District. 14 Jul 1885. (P. 545)

John Johnson to George Johnson Lot No. 2 in the 9th District. 6 Jul 1885. (P. 546)

John Johnson to his son, J. P. Johnson, a tract of land in the 9th District. 14 Jul 1885. (Pp. 547-548)

John Johnson to Sarah E. Driver a tract of land in the 9th District. 14 Jul 1885. (Pp. 548-549)

John Johnson to Susan Allen Lot No. 5 in the 9th District. 14 Jul 1885. (Pp. 549-550)

T. W. Wade, J. S. Dunlap, and H. A. Dunlap to J. S. Gribble a lot in the town of Smithville. 17 Jun 1885. (P. 551)

Polly Wilson to A. B. Hooper five acres. 1 Aug 1884. (P. 552)

J. F. Ray and wife, Helen F., to T. H. Eason 93¼ acres in the 1st District. 21 Feb 1884. (P. 553)

W. G. Crawley to J. C. Brien and wife, Nancy A., a tract of land. 25 Aug 1885. (P. 554)

Susan Eller, Roland Terry, William S. Holliman, S. A. Terry, and Jane Holliman to W. J. Givan 11 acres in the 1st District. 19 Jun 1874. (P. 555)

W. J. Givan and wife, Tilda F., to William B. Simpson a tract of land in the town of Alexandria. 25 Jul 1885. (Pp. 555-556)

Clerk & Master to T. W. Eason about 35 acres in the 1st District. 25 Aug 1885. (Pp. 556-557)

W. C. Gilbert and wife, T. A., to J. H. Fuson a lot and stable in the town of Smithville. Bounded: the street running south from the Public Square. 18 Aug 1884. (P. 558)

R. Marler and wife, E. J., to J. L. Burch 90 acres in the 5th District. 15 Aug 1885. (Pp. 559-560)

James F. Turner and wife, Mary L., to the trustees of Earl College at Temperance Hall for love and affection a tract of land. 18 Sep 1885. (Pp. 560-561)

W. E. Bartlett to the Christian Baptist Church in the 16th

District for the purpose of building a church and school in the gap of the ridge between Maberry Smith and William (Dunnam). It is to be a free house for all Christian people to preach in and hold meeting in so that one does not interfear with another's day of meeting, but no denomination is to organse in said house but the Christian Baptist Church of Christ is to have the preference of house one week in ever summer or fall to hold protracted meetings. If the building should fail to be kept up for a church or schoolhouse, the said land is to go back to them that gave it and said house shall be sold at a publick sale and be used for the benefit of a public church or public schoolhouse. 18 Aug 1884. (P. 561)

H. M. Driver and wife, Ida, to H. K. Driver 85 acres in the 9th District. 21 Sep 1885. (P. 562)

L. G. Love and wife Nancy, N. J. Roberts, Elijah Pedigo and wife Lucy, Louisa Lafever, W. C. Love, Silvanus Puckett and wife Mary, Hesikiah Puckett and wife Mary, Joseph Bozarth and wife Martha to H. F. Love their interest in 75 acres in the 18th District. 26 Sep 1885. (P. 563)

Nancy Love to H. F. Love her interest in the Rackley land in the 18th District. 26 Sep 1885. (P. 564)

J. C. Bass to J. S. Barry one acre in the 12th District. 25 May 1885. (Pp. 564-565)

D. J. Taylor to E. N. Allen, John Mullican, and Brown Allen a tract of land on Holmes Creek. 12 Sep 1885. (Pp. 565-566)

Elizabeth Blair of Searcy County, Arkansas to Mary C. Turney her interest in the dower of Mrs. Mary Turney, widow of Joseph Turney. 6 Oct 1884. (P. 567)

Sarah Fox to Mary C. Turney her interest in the dower of Mrs. Mary Turney. The dower was assigned to the said Mary Turney about 1853. 31 Dec 1884. (P. 568)

J. S. Bates to Fox F. Bates and Charlie McHenry Bates a tract of land in the 15th District. 30 Mar 1885. (Pp. 568-569)

J. S. Bates to W. R. Bates five acres in the 15th District. 30 Mar 1885. (Pp. 569-570)

R. B. Floyd to H. L. W. Gross a town lot in the town of Alexandria. Bounded: Cumberland Presbyterian Church. 22 Feb 1884. (P. 570)

J. J. Ford to William Wood and others a promissory note. 8 May 1885. (P. 571)

Sheriff to John H. Savage a tract of land in the 2nd District belonging to J. W. Inge. 14 Jul 1882. (Pp. 572-573)

Clerk & Master to Leatha McCrea 101 acres. 10 Oct 1885. (Pp. 573-574)

J. B. Taylor and wife, Nancy, to J. C. Hale three acres in the 10th District. 16 Oct 1885. (P. 575)

W. M. Maynard to Monroe Maynard 75 acres in the 8th District. 15 Jan 1884. (P. 576)

S. E. Smith, J. M. Smith, R. A. Smith, A. L. Smith, and T. J. Smith have equal interest in a tract of land in the 13th District of Putnam County by inheritance from Jonathan Smith deceased. We have sold to John Jones, Prettyman Clemmons, John Clemmons, and George Clemmons one half interest in the said land. 26 Sep 1883. (P. 577)

W. F. Robinson, Alexander H. Robinson, Columbus C. Robinson, Joseph A. Robinson, Daniel P. Searcy and wife, Mary L., to John B. Robinson a quit claim to seven tracts of land in the 4th District, it being 186 acres that Alexander Robinson lived at the time of his death. 26 Jan 1870. (Pp. 578-579)

John B. Robinson and wife Julia M., and Josephine N. Robinson to F. Miller Schurer about 210 acres in the 4th District. 11 Sep 1885. (Pp. 580-581)

NAME INDEX

MISCELLANEOUS INDEX

www.ingramcontent.com/pod-product-compliance
Lightning Source LLC
LaVergne TN
LVHW090356210926
848480LV00002B/360